Operation Pedro Pan

To the many Cubans
Who risked their lives so we could fly;
To Monsignor Bryan O. Walsh,
Who opened the doors to this country to us;
To Nieves and Pepé del Campo,
Who opened the doors of their heart and home to me;
To all the Pedro Pans,
Brave beyond their years;
And especially to my husband, Bernabé,
Who not only believed in me,
But was there every step of the way.

Operation Pedro Pan

The Untold Exodus of 14,048 Cuban Children

Revised Edition

Yvonne M. Conde

University of Florida Press

Gainesville

Publication of this revised edition made possible by a Sustaining the Humanities through the American Rescue Plan grant from the National Endowment for the Humanities.

First edition published by Routledge, New York, NY, 1999.

28 27 26 25 24 23   6 5 4 3 2 1

A record of cataloging-in-publication data is available from the Library of Congress.
ISBN 978-1-68340-388-3

University of Florida Press
2046 NE Waldo Road
Suite 2100
Gainesville, FL 32609
http://upress.ufl.edu

UF PRESS

UNIVERSITY
OF FLORIDA

Contents

Acknowledgments

During the years of research and writing of this book, I became indebted to many people who assisted me in the research, criticism, and editing of the manuscript.

This book could not have been written without the help of hundreds of generous people, especially the children, who gave of themselves abundantly. I was a vessel into which they poured out their pain and agitated my own. Each individual story has variables that are so compelling that it deserves to be known. Deciding which accounts to use in the book was one of the hardest parts of the process for me. Out of this exodus, 14,047 more books should be written; I tried my best to select stories that would represent the whole.

The remembrances and data of Monsignor Bryan Walsh form the foundation blocks of the book. Although he was retired, the monsignor's days were always full, for he was engaged in myriad activities and was incapable of saying no to anyone. He patiently answered question after question and checked some chapters of this manuscript for accuracy. Only once did I catch him looking at his watch.

Elly VilanoChovel, who was an officer in the Operation Pedro Pan Group, helped me locate many people. She has my gratitude, as does James Baker, who had the foresight to see that some 200 children needed to leave Cuba and tried to do something about it. I'm sure he never expected the numbers to multiply as they did.

How can mere words thank those freedom-loving Cubans, many now gone, who helped get exit visas into the children's hands, risking their personal freedom in the process and sometimes losing it for many years? Among them are Nenita Carames, Sara del Toro de Odio, Margarita Esquerre, Serafina Lastra, Sergio Giquel, Esther de la Portilla,

Beatriz López Morton, Ramón "Mongo" Grau, Berta and Frank "Pancho" Finlay, Ulises de la Vega, Tony Comellas, Ignacio Martínez-Ybor, Margarita Oteisa, Albertina O'Farrill, and many others.

Gladys Ramos at the University of Miami Cuba Archives Collection at the Richter Library went out of her way to help me. I am also grateful to Esperanza de Varona and Leshia Varona. I reached out to newspapers nationwide to help me in two ways. First, I asked some newspapers in towns where large numbers of Cuban children had gone in the 1960s to look in their archives for articles about unaccompanied Cuban children dating back to 1961 or 1962. Second, I asked some to run a "Looking for Cubans" author's request. Out of this request, full articles ensued as well as subsequent responses from children. My thanks for their help in this process go to Betty Baule at the Carnegie-Stout Public Library in Dubuque, Iowa; Diane Spooner, librarian, and Linda Ann, sales, at the *Rocky Mountain News* in Denver, Colo.; Aleida Duran at *Contacto;* Judy Zipp, librarian at *San Antonio Express News*; Maya Bell at the *Orlando Sun Sentinel*; Chris Brennan at the *Pottsville Republican* in Pottsville, Pa.; Cecilia Paiz, reporter at *The Palladium-Times* in Oswego, N.Y.; H. Spitzer, librarian at the *Pueblo Chieftain*; Steve Brewer, reporter at the *Albuquerque Journal*; Gene Miller and Joan Fleischman at the *Miami Herald*; Stephen McAuliff, at the *Telegraph Herald* in Dubuque, Iowa; Mike Wright at the *Vincennes Sun-Commercial*; and staff at *La Razon,* the *San Antonio Light, Vanidades: Estado Jardin*, and *Hispanic Business*.

For their assistance and support at all stages of this project, I thank Berta Alonso, Leo Beebe and Retta Blaney; Mary Glen Crutchely at the Nuclear Regulatory Commission; Ozzie Dolan; Marjorie Donahue; Judy Epstein at the Hebrew Immigrant Aid Society; Capt. Eduardo Ferrer; Lynn and Peggy Guarch; Margo Jefferson, who planted the idea for this book in my mind; Karen Jones at the United States Census Bureau; Sister Shirley Kamentz; Nancy Kinley of Catholic Charities in Dubuque, IA; David Lawrence of the Miami Herald Publishing Group; Moises Lopez of Radio Martí; Carlos Lluch; Harold Maguire; Rick Mendosa for his fabulous COLA program; Jerald T. Milanich; Terence Morgan of the New York Public Library; Dr. Maria Prendes-Lintel and Dr. Lisa Suzuki for sharing the results of their studies; Professor

Nena Torres of De Paul University; Father Thomas Rhomberg; Rosa Villaverde, who provided invaluable original documentsl and Charles Salzburg.

I want to thank the staff at Routledge who first published this book. *¡Muchas gracias!*

This second edition carries my heartfelt gratitude to perennial Pedro Pan sleuths Manny Gutiérrez and Clemente Amezaga. They perform vital work in continuing to investigate data about our exodus. And how do I thank Oscar Pichardo, my quixotic partner in fighting for our name? *Gracias hermano.*

Very special thanks go to Stephanye Hunter, editor-in-chief, University Press of Florida, and Michele Fiyak-Burkley, associate director. When I decided to publish the second edition of this book with a new editorial house, my heart told me to offer it to the University Press of Florida since I had worked with them before and admired their work. And so it was. And so it is.

Saving the best for last, my deep thanks to my husband, Bernabé, who has always had all my love and my eternal gratitude for the myriad ways he helped me: soothing when necessary, encouraging at other times, editing when needed, but always there for me. I am truly blessed.

Preface to the Revised Edition

Over six decades.

Over one hundred and thirty-one thousand four hundred days.

This is the time that we, the children spirited out of Cuba through Operation Pedro Pan, have been out of our homeland. Our roots have grown in new soil, where they've begotten saplings, grand-saplings, and even great-grand-saplings in some cases. The generation before us, those heroes who in many cases risked freedom to give us ours, have mostly passed away, including Monsignor Bryan Walsh, the heart and motor of our exodus, in December 2001. Some Pedro Pan children, most of whom are now in their late 60s and 70s, are sadly also gone. We are the last generation who remembers the old Cuba. The free Cuba. Our Never Never Land.

A lot has transpired in the more than two decades since the original edition of this book came out in 1999. From being an "untold exodus," Operation Pedro Pan has certainly been told, although it is still unknown to many. Numerous books, museum exhibits, symposia, documentaries, a play, and a ballet have been created. Fortunately, the inescapable circle of life brings younger generations who are curious about our history and want to keep it alive. Numerous students have chosen Operation Pedro Pan as their school project. It gives me such pleasure to pass the torch and grant them interviews or help with their research.

Social media exploded in 2005, making connections and communications instantaneous and facilitating research. Pedro Pans have searched for and found each other, keeping the indestructible lifelong bonds created among the Pedro Pan children while they were alone in a school or an orphanage. We are brothers and sisters and call ourselves that. Social media has strengthened these ties. The following groups are found on Facebook: Operation Pedro Pan Group—The Untold Exodus of 14,048 Cuban Children, Pedro Pan of California, Pedro Pan CCC (Cuban Children Coalition), and Operation Pedro Pan Group Inc.

Throughout the United States, there are frequent reunions of children who were sent to different locations. Our presence is receiving historical Florida permanence. The intersection of SW 25th Street and 24th Avenue in Miami is named after The Muchachitas of Villa María, a group who went to San Antonio, Texas. A stretch of Miami's SW 80th Street between 107th and 114th Street is named Pedro Pan St. A street in Florida City is designated Pedro Pan Place, and Hialeah has its own Operation Pedro Pan Avenue. A plaque at the site of former Camp Matecumbe proclaims its history and is a historical site, as is the site of the Florida City Shelter, now a Florida Heritage Landmark. Camp Matecumbe was acquired by Dade County's Parks, Recreation and Open Spaces department with some monetary assistance from Pedro Pan children. In another gesture of gratitude, Pedro Pan Máximo Álvarez recently donated $1 million to Florida International University's Casa Cuba in honor of Monsignor Walsh.

The countless messages from Pedro Pan children I received after the first edition of this book was published validated the hours I spent poring over microfilms and microfiches and old newspapers and locating and interviewing participants. "The book opened my mind to events I never knew happened," said a reader, "My mom gave me this book to read to help me understand what happened to her as a child," wrote another. "Your book has opened so many memories that it really has had a profound impact on me," said another." Unearthing our history was my goal, and receiving messages saying I might have achieved it both melts my heart and fills me with pride. Thank you. Other Pedro Pan children reached out to share their stories after publication. This especially heartbreaking one is etched in my memory: A Pedro Pan girl was sobbing while speaking on the phone to her parents in Cuba. They tried to soothe her and explain that they couldn't leave Cuba yet because they had to care for her elderly grandfather. Unbeknown to them, he was listening on a phone extension. A few days later, he committed suicide by jumping off a rooftop.

How many were we? Not everyone agrees with the figure of 14,048 Pedro Pan children on the cover, which Monsignor Walsh, who ran the operation, gave me. Manuel A. Gutierrez, webmaster of www.Camp-MatecumbeVeterans.com since 1999, a highly recommended source of information with resources and lists of Pedro Pan names, who is also the editor of a monthly newsletter said, "I started doubting the official number of Pedro Pan kid arrivals being 14,048—which I had accepted and gladly mentioned and shared since the beginning—when I realized that the Miami Herald Pedro Pan Database (copied from George Guarch's Airport Log) had many errors, yet their number exceeded said official number by more than 80 but were missing over 900 names that I had in my website. As of November 2022, my website shows close to 15,300 Pedro Pans.

Three thousand or more Cuban children had visa waivers when the flights were stopped between Cuba and the US in 1962. Desperate parents found a way to send these children out of Cuba through Spain, where they were received by the Catholic Church. Check out La Obra del Padre Camiñas page on Facebook for further information and look for *Cuando Sali de Cuba,* a book about the topic by María Luisa and Remberto Pérez.

To the exiled Cuban community, Pedro Pan is a noun, as in "Oh, you are a Pedro Pan." We can proudly say that many success stories abound in our group. We have among us Mel Martínez, the first Cuban United States senator; the late Carlos Portes, a special U.S. ambassador for Latin American affairs (RIP); artists; concert pianists; mayors of Denver and Miami; entrepreneurs; physicians; and housewives—the list goes on.

This noun almost didn't happen. In the fall of 1999, shortly after the book came out, my editor at Routledge received a call from the president of Operation Pedro Pan Group Inc. telling him to "stop using the name Pedro Pan." The book contained PedroPanNY@aol.com, an email account that I had set up to receive emails from readers. What was the reason? She claimed that they had trademarked the name. Oscar Pichardo from the Pedro Pan of California Group and Manny Gutierrez received the same message. It wasn't so. On June 14, 2007, the board of Operation Pedro Pan Group tried to trademark the name "Pedro Pan" in order to gain sole proprietorship and control of it. Oscar Pichardo and I found out, disagreed with this action, and hired a New York copyright legal firm to argue before the United States Patent and Trademark Office in Washington that Pedro Pan was a generic and historical name that could not be trademarked. They agreed with us and issued their decision on December 15, 2009, refusing to grant the trademark to Operation Pedro Pan Group. For further reading and facts on this matter, go to uspto.gov and select Search Trademarks. The proceeding number is 91177853.

My father, Pedro Conde, who worked for Pan American World Airways in Havana, died when I was 22. We never discussed my being sent out of Cuba alone. I knew that Pan American Airways was involved in the children's departures, and when I interviewed participants, I discovered that my father and other Pan Am employees were involved in creating fake reservations on flights that would then be given to children with visa waivers. Fate intervened when Cuba unexpectedly published a book called *Operación Peter Pan: un caso de guerra psicológica contra Cuba* (a case of psychological war against Cuba) "a book about the history of 14,000 Elianes" in 2000. One of the authors works as an investigator for State Security. It claims that the Belgian embassy received envelopes for various "agents," one of whom was named Conde. It also mentions the Pan American "CIA Center." Proud of you, Papi.

Fourteen thousand Elianes. In November 1999, a five-year-old boy was found nestled in an inner tube floating at sea three miles from the coast of Fort Lauderdale. His name was Elián Gonzalez, and he unleashed a custody battle over a Cuban child's fate that played for weeks in the international press. His mother had perished in the journey to bring him to the United States, and his father, back in Cuba, wanted him back. His Miami family and the Cuban exile community vehemently opposed his return to Cuba, knowing he would be indoctrinated and used as a poster boy for the revolution. Attorney General Janet Reno ordered that Elián be returned to his father. On April 22, 2000, he was taken by force from his maternal family in Miami in a raid by BORTAC, a special Border Patrol unit that was armed and in full military gear. The photo of the frightened child clinging to his relative won the 2001 Pulitzer Prize for Breaking News. What does this have to do with Pedro Pan? The media found a parallel between both stories and I was interviewed for my opinion on several television and radio programs. Pedro Pan children were divided about the subject, as they continue to be about the unaccompanied children coming through the border today, and their opinion as people who have lived the emotional experience continues to be newsworthy.

Apology time. The first edition of this book contained many typos that were not caught by a first-time editor, about which I am extremely embarrassed. I kept a list and hoped to correct them in this edition. Unfortunately, the limited file availability from Routledge does not allow the University of Florida Press to correct the text. Thus, please be aware that Susan Garrandes should be Susana Garrandes and that Mathews's should be Mathews', by mid-August 1961 the revolution was two and a half years old, not one and a half years old. ASTA is not the American Association of Travel Agents, it is the American Society of Travel Agents. Daniel Alarcón Ramírez should be Dariel Alarcón Ramírez, Piñar del Rio should be Pinar del Rio, Bosa Masvidal should be Boza Masvidal, postestad should be potestad, Salecian is spelled Salesian and Oriente is certainly not the westernmost province of Cuba but the easternmost. These, and unfortunately others, are the kind of typos a reader will find, but not factual ones.

Due to space constraints, many stories were omitted from the book, and I have been told countless times, "You should write another book." And my reply invariably is, "Now it's up to you to tell your stories." Many have done so, in many cases brilliantly, none more so than Professor Carlos Eire, who won the 2003 National Book Award for his poignant *Waiting for Snow in Havana*, followed by *Learning to Die in Miami*.

Here is a list of other books by Pedro Pan children that deal with our exodus. Apologies if I have left anyone out.

A Boy, an Orphanage, a Cuban Refugee, by Tony Dora.
Black Pedro Pan, by Ricardo E. González Zayas
The Flight of the Mango Flowers: A Memoir of Our Flight Out of the Cold War, by Antonio María Gordon

The Unspoken Gift: How an Immigrant Cuban Child Fulfilled His American Dream, by Aldo Martinez

Cuba Adiós: A Young Man's Journey to Freedom, by Lorenzo Pablo Martínez

A Sense of Belonging: From Castro's Cuba to the U.S. Senate, One Man's Pursuit of the American Dream, by Senator Mel Martínez

Cuba Lost and Found, by Eduardo J. Neyra

Memoirs with a Cuban Taste: Seeking My Lost Cuban Roots in America, by Ernesto A. Perez

Defining Moments: A Cuban Exile's Story about Discovery and the Search for a Better Future, by José I. Ramírez

Forgotten Objects, by Carlos Rubio (a novel that deals with the Pedro Pan exodus)

A Time to Look Back: Growing Up during the Cuban Revolution, by Anthony Timiraos

The Lost Apple: Operation Pedro Pan, Cuban Children in the U.S. and the Promise of a Better Future, by María de los Angeles Torres

Crisis of Identity II, by Mary Lou Trias

Boxing for Cuba: An Immigrant's Story of Despair, Endurance, and Redemption, by Guillermo Vicente Vidal

Books by children of Pedro Panes:

The Red Umbrella, a novel by Cristina Diaz Gonzalez, the daughter of Delfin Diaz

My First Hero: A Story of Overcoming and Success, by Tony Ojeda, son of René J. Ojeda Jr.

My gratitude to Manuel "Manny" Gutierrez for his assistance in compiling this list. Pedro Pan children have written about other themes, non–Pedro Pan children have written about Pedro Pan, and the ever-changing list goes on. It's almost impossible to list them all.

Prologue

Imagine you are six, eight, or even seventeen years old and, suddenly, your parents send you away to an entirely new culture where people speak a different language. Conjure the fear and confusion that you would feel, not understanding why you are uprooted from those who you love and all that is familiar.

When nations confront nations, or ideals challenge conflicting ideals, children have often paid the greatest price for this confrontation; they have lost their innocence in a way no child ever should. The principles of their elders place them in physical and emotional jeopardy; they become pawns in a fatal game without the benefit of calling the moves.

This century has unfortunately witnessed several exoduses of children because of politics. Recall, for example, the flight of Basque refugee children from the Spanish Civil War of 1936–1939. In this war, Republicans, who were primarily anarchists, socialists, communists, and Catalan and Basque regionalists aided by the U.S.S.R. and the International Brigades, went up against the Nationalists, who were monarchists, Carlists, and conservatives aided by Fascist Italy and Nazi Germany.

In 1937, parents hastily evacuated more than 20,000 Basque children, who came to be dubbed the "Guernica Generation," after the name of a Basque town that was destroyed by bombing the same year. The children found safe haven in Mexico and several countries in Europe, including Britain, Belgium, Switzerland, Denmark, and the Soviet Union, where as many as 4,000 children are reported to have gone.[1]

Only a few years later, during World War II, the Jewish Refugee Committee set up a movement called *Kindertransport,* or

Children's Transport, which from December 1938 to August 1939[2] carried 10,000 Jewish children from the growing danger in Germany, Austria, Czechoslovakia, and Poland to sanctuary in England. Although saved from the Holocaust, tragically 9,000 of these children never saw their parents again.[3] While the Jewish children were finding safety in England, some British parents were looking even further, across the ocean, as a safer heaven for their own children. Early in World War II, 5,000 British children were evacuated to the United States in an effort organized by the Children's Overseas Reception Board.[4]

And when, during the Greek Civil War of 1944–1949, Communist forces fought Monarchist forces, more than 28,000 Greek children were forcibly taken' away from their parents to live in camps throughout the Communist bloc.[5]

In contrast to these European exoduses, the political exodus of 14,048 Cuban children to the United States in the early 1960s is the only such event in the Western Hemisphere. Not an organized mass departure and more covert than the European exoduses, the children's departures were a cautious trickling out of Cuba, on commercial airplanes, on a daily basis. The numbers speak for themselves. I was one of those children.

In 1990 I read *Miami* by Joan Didion. The words on page 122 glared back, defiant, daring me to believe them: "14,156 children, each of whom was sent alone, by parents or guardians still living in Cuba." Fourteen thousand one hundred and fifty-six.[6] How could there have such a mammoth exodus of Cuban children, and I had never heard of it?

I knew that at the age of ten, I too was sent out of Cuba alone by my parents to the United States. Did that mean that I was part of this exodus? Joan Didion's words changed my life, becoming my mind's unyielding stalker for the next several years. Now, as a grown woman, I was discovering that thousands of other children had gone through the same pain of separation, adaptation, and apprehension as I did. Yet the world didn't know! I felt a deep obligation to reveal a part of history that had never before been chronicled.

From a *Reader's Digest* article about the Cuban children's exodus, I amasssed a handful of names, among them Monsignor Bryan Walsh, the Catholic priest who welcomed the children into the United States. I dove into the search for other participants of this drama, not an easy task thirty years after the exodus. Fortunately, the names of some of the "children" who had stayed in touch with Monsignor Walsh were available from two groups, Fundación Pedro Pan and Operation Pedro Pan Group. These are charitable organizations formed by the children within the last ten years. The names helped me begin my investigation.

I quickly learned that my own search into my past was happening simultaneously to that of other Pedro Pan children. After talking with others, our consensus appeared to be that as our own children were reaching the age we ourselves were when we were separated from our parents, our children were reawakening memories of our own childhoods. Moreover, I found a group that is mature and accomplished enough in life to now have more time for introspection about our exodus.

I mailed about 800 questionnaires consisting of forty-four questions (see Appendix 1). A second mailing followed. I received 442 replies. I interviewed 173 people in all, which included children and others involved in the operation, such as parents, journalists, foster parents, psychologists, teachers, and Cuban underground fighters. In most cases, these interviews were conducted in Spanish, although sometimes during an interview we'd go back and forth between Spanish and English.

I contacted newspapers nationwide, placed ads, appeared on Spanish language radio and television, and distributed flyers at Cuban events trying to locate more children. My search yielded about 200 new names.

I placed Freedom of Information requests with the State Department, the Immigration Department, and the Central

Intelligence Agency. The CIA, while "not confirming nor denying" the existence of any related documents, denied me access based on state security. My subsequent appeal has been denied, and I was advised that legal action is the only course available. Professor María de los Angeles Torres is pursuing that option.

Arranging the information was not an easy task. For those not familiar with Cuban history, the first two chapters provide a historical background. They attempt to create a sense of the vertiginous changes occurring in Cuba prior to the children's exodus and to answer the question "Why?"

In order to help move the historical background along, subheadings were used in the early chapters, then abandoned once personal stories were told in the later chapters. Also, first-person anecdotes—my own memories of the period from the point of view of a Cuban child—have been inserted in these first chapters, then I let others tell their stories.

Writing this book not only helped me learn more about a complex period for my country, for all Cubans, for my family, and for myself but it also helped me understand it.

The more I unearthed and talked to people, the surer I became that this is a book about great personal courage.

OPERATION
PEDRO PAN

Before Columbus all human history in Cuba
is a blank, after him it is all blood and business.

—WILLIAM HENRY HURLBUT, 1854

CHAPTER 1

Adiós Cuba: 1959–1960

1959
THE YEAR OF THE REVOLUTION

José Martí airport, 16 kilometers southwest of La Habana, had become a gloomy structure by 1961. It had lost the unbridled joy of encounters. The one-story building was instead rapidly becoming a depository of farewells, sadness, and memories, a site of estrangement and endings as several thousand Cubans had been leaving the island monthly.[1] Since Americans traveling to Cuba could not be offered normal protective service, travelers required State Department permission; incoming passengers were thus reduced to mere few.

Emotional, teary good-byes were followed by separation as out-bound passengers proceeded into the immigration area where luggage was searched and luxury items such as jewelry confiscated. Strip searches were not uncommon. This immigration area was nicknamed the *pecera*, or fishbowl. It was a glass-enclosed room where passengers waited for their departure while looking at their bereaved family across the glass, the decision to leave their homeland bisecting their world. Just as mirrors are believed

I

to hold a person's soul, the uncertainty of reunification made this glass wall a silverless mirror holding both past and future.

On May 5, 1961, María Dolores and Juan Antonio Madariaga, then eight and eleven, sat alone in the *pecera,* nervously awaiting their departure. María Dolores could not contain her excitement, looking forward to the adventurous airplane ride. Juan was somber, for as he watched his parents, so near and yet so distant already, he rightly felt the weight of the world on his young shoulders. From now on he was his sister's protector.

As they walked across the hot tarmac, María Dolores looked back to the second-floor observation area where families rushed for a last look at the voyagers. Juan stoically looked straight ahead. Suddenly, as María Dolores was turning around again, she felt a pull on her ponytail. It was her brother's hand, making her face forward. He told her, "Don't look back. You are never going to see our parents again." Almost four decades later the words are still etched in María Dolores's mind. The forecasted eternal separation turned out to be four years long.

The Madariaga children did not know that their exit was making them part of history, as they were among the earliest of 14,048 children sent out of Cuba alone by their parents during a twenty-two-month period. When the Madariagas left, approximately 300 children had already departed from Cuba. Why?

Something had gone terribly wrong with the brand new Cuban revolution. It was just twenty-nine months earlier that the nation joyfully greeted its new leader. Now they were shipping their children out of the country in order to protect them. Their dreams had disintegrated into an unbearable nightmare.

"Esta Es Tu Casa Fidel"

On January 8, 1959, the pavement of the streets of Havana was torn, chewed up by the treads of the Sherman tanks that rum-

bled through the city. To the jubilant crowds, it was as if the crumbled streets symbolized the obliteration of every trace of the tyrannical Batista government. Throngs cheered until hoarse, throwing confetti and serpentine. People stood on rooftops, waving the previously prohibited red and black flags of Castro's "26 de Julio" movement, forming a bicolor canopy that welcomed the youthful bearded rebels riding atop tanks, jeeps, and military trucks. Many people had dug in their wardrobes for red and black clothing, trying to become walking banners. Hope was in the air, and the citizens of Cuba inhaled it gladly. The mantle of trust was placed on the revolutionary leaders—a new government of the people, for the people, was auspiciously starting with the new year.

Fidel, where was Fidel? With a crescendo of anticipation the crowd awaited its new leader—a handsome, charismatic, thirty-two-year-old rebel named Fidel Castro Ruz. As he reached Havana, a passion of ecstatic dimensions seized the crowd. I know it seized me, an eight-year-old participant watching from the third-story balcony of our apartment in the El Vedado section, staring at the rolling tanks less than half a block away on Linea Street. The feelings are still alive in my memory—the sheer glee, an uncontrolled nervousness that made me run around like a battery-operated toy, from the television to the balcony—all because the "bad" tyrant was out and the "good" guy had won.

I remember my surprise when I first heard my family discuss how they had been secretly involved in selling underground bonds for the revolution. After many years of secrecy, Cubans could now openly and proudly admit their clandestine cooperation with the 26th of July movement. Cuba's victory was also our victory.

A big poster, about 3 × 2¹/₂ feet, of a black-and-white photograph of Fidel, dressed in his fatigues and his cap with a white dove perched on his shoulder, graced the place of honor in the center of our living room. Many doors displayed signs reading

"Esta es tu casa Fidel," or Fidel, this is your home. The fact that the young leader had turned thirty-three that year elicited mystical comparisons to Jesus and brought out the natural reverence of the people. The long hair and rosary beads worn by the rebels were suggestive of the Apostles, an image that would further elicit reverence. And as for the dove choosing to land on Fidel's shoulder during his first major address to the people, well, that was surely an omen that he was a man of peace and good will.* Moreover, the Afro-Cuban religious figures interpreted it as a demonstration of "protection from the gods."

Fidel could do no wrong. *Bohemia*, the most important Cuban weekly magazine, swooned, calling him "the man whose very name is a banner" and "the most outstanding figure of this historic moment without precedent in the annals of the Americas!"[2] He accomplished something previously unheard of in Cuban politics—unity.

The Battle for Souls

Fidel Castro and President Fulgencio Batista locked horns when Castro, then a young lawyer and son of a Spanish landholder in the Oriente Province, led a group of 200 inexperienced students in a poorly planned attack against Batista's Moncada army barracks, in Santiago de Cuba, Oriente, on July 26, 1953. Thus, the political group acquired the name of the 26th of July movement. The attack was an effort to depose President Batista, who himself had gained his dictatorial position through a 1952 military coup. Castro was arrested and sentenced to fifteen years in prison, the longest sentence ever given to an insurrectionist in Cuba. However, he served less than two years, thanks to the implementation of a law passed by the Chamber of Representatives on May 2, 1955, which granted amnesty to all political prisoners.[3]

---

* Thirty years later, in exile, I would hear that the dove had been nothing more than a magic trick; it was filled with pellets so it couldn't fly.

Once set free, Castro left Cuba to regroup and reorganize the 26th of July movement in Mexico. Castro returned to Cuba in a purchased yacht, the *Granma,* ready for an armed struggle. He landed on the coast of Oriente Province with eight-one men on December 2, 1956. He left the ensuing attack with only eleven men, among them Ernesto "Ché" Guevara, an Argentine doctor who had made Cuba's cause his own. These men headed to the dense mountains of the Sierra Maestra, which became Castro's guerilla headquarters for the next three years.

On February 24, 1957, *New York Times* correspondent Herbert Matthews wrote the first of a series of articles about the rebels. According to the *New York Times* Havana-based correspondent, Ruby Hart Phillips, "From that time on youths flocked to join the ranks of Castro's insurgents."

Aided by the local peasants the rebels held their own and became proficient in guerilla warfare. Radio Rebelde beamed their messages from the mountains and broadcast every battle won. Helped by Matthews's reporting, the Cuban Army was demoralized, sometimes not even fighting. The United States cut off military aid to Batista in March,[4] and rebels won major battles in the Province of Las Villas. When they captured its capital, Santa Clara, on December 30, 1958, it was the decisive battle of the revolution. The improbable happened—President Batista fled for the Dominican Republic at 2:00 A.M. on January 1, 1959.

That same day, Fidel heard of President Batista's flight over the radio, yet he refused to order a cease-fire until the news was confirmed. Speaking directly to the Cuban people over the radio for the first time, Castro called for a general strike until all weapons were surrendered.

The Partido Socialista Popular (PSP) was Cuba's Communist Party at the time of Bastista's demise. Its president, Juan Marinello, proclaimed communist backing for the general strike.[5] The strike proved unnecessary, since no one stood up to

prevent Castro's total assumption of power, and it was called off three days later.

After Marinello's condoning of the strike, rumors of Fidel's link to communism surfaced immediately. The PSP, banned by Batista in 1954, resurfaced as an organized party with 17,000 members.[6] *Hoy*, the communist newspaper, was published again. The PSP took over Radio Union. After occupying small gambling locales and wrecking the slot machines and game tables, they hung signs announcing that a branch of the Communist Party was set up there.[7]

Opposition to Castro developed in waves, growing as different groups were affected by the changes brought about by the new government. The first exiles were Batistianos, the deposed president's sidekicks, government officials, and military personnel. About 400 persons fled by ship or plane to the United States and to the Dominican Republic, where Batista himself had sought refuge. Latin American embassies grew crowded with asylum seekers.

Hearing of Batista's departure on January 1, mobs immediately looted and burned some of his followers' properties. Recently installed parking meters were smashed. Casino owners saw dice, roulette tables, and slot machines at the Capri, Seville, Biltmore, St. John's, and Deauville hotels destroyed. Fidel had been broadcasting the end of casinos for months from his mountain base.

Castro believed that casinos destroyed Cuban morale and that the country could lure tourists through its natural beauty. He tried to convey this message to travel agents at the American Association of Travel Agents (ASTA) convention held in Havana that same January. Amid the wooing of the travel agents and promises of future resorts to be built, Castro was simultaneously sabotaging his public relations efforts. He stood up the agents at several activities, openly criticized the United States, and opened fire with antiaircraft shells and machine guns at an aircraft dropping antirevolution leaflets over Havana. Meanwhile, two per-

sons were killed and forty-five injured when explosions rocked Havana streets. Chanting mobs roared past the Hilton, where the ASTA convention met, demanding death to all enemies of the revolution. The schizoid convention proved to be an exercise in how to lose tourists.[8]

Student leaders and representatives of the Castro movement took over the airwaves, exhorting people to stay home and stay calm. Castro himself, speaking from Camagüey, urged the resumption of normal activities.[9]

It should be noted that 1950s Cuba had an uncharacteristically large media market. There were fifty-eight daily newspapers available in the island, placing Cuba fourth in Latin America, superceded only by Argentina, Mexico, and Brazil. In 1957, Cuba had five television channels and twenty-three television stations, more than any country in Latin America, and it ranked eighth in the world with 160 radio stations, ahead of France and the United Kingdom.[10]

Castro played his undeniable charisma over the airwaves, and the new medium of television cemented his revolution. Almost every other day during his first year in power, Castro made a public statement carried by newspapers or television. He would interrupt programming at whim.[11]

The Communist Party, legalized by General Batista in 1939 during his first presidency and banned by him in 1952 during his second, sought to ride the wave of change and seized several unions. The 26th of July militia refrained from ousting the communists from the seized locals, but did evict them from the seized *Replica* newspaper.[12]

On January 3, during his first American press interview with Jules Dubois of the *Chicago Sunday Tribune*, Castro denied any ties with communists.[13] During his university days he was involved with student organizations that harbored communists, a fact *New York Times* correspondent Herbert Matthew attributed to his having been "a wild harum-scarum . . . careless with politics."[14]

Major Ernesto (Ché) Guevara was also busy denying the same

rumors. "I have never been a Communist. Dictators always say their enemies are Communists," he said.[15] However, Soviet Premier Nikita Khrushchev cited in his memoirs that his Latin America specialists had "information gathered from various channels. We knew that Raúl Castro [Fidel's brother] was a good Communist. Ché Guevara was a Communist too, and so were some of the others."[16] Castro's new regime recognized the legality of the Communist Party. He explained that by restoring the full 1940 Constitution, ironically chartered by Batista during his first term in office, freedom was granted to all. The revolution was not afraid of any political party.

On January 8, the day he triumphantly arrived in Havana, Castro continued the process of disarming the nation, calling for all rebel fighters to lay aside their arms. "No private armies will be tolerated," he said. "There is no longer an enemy."[17] The following day on the radio and television program *Meet the Press* he announced that political parties would be organized in "eight to ten months" and that the elections, promised since the early days in the Sierra Maestra Mountains, would follow in "about eighteen months."[18]

During the first days of the new regime, approximately seventy Batista soldiers were tried and judged in a single day and shot by a firing squad.[19] The bearded rebels and citizens, in general, thus sought vengeance upon the members of the dreaded Batista military group and the police, who were well known for their atrocities and tortures. *Bohemia,* a popular weekly magazine, fueled the avenging fires by printing gruesome photographs of exhumed bodies and instruments of torture used by Batista's followers.

These shootings at the *paredón,* or the wall, sparked the first round of domestic and international criticism toward the new regime. On January 12, fourteen persons were sentenced to death, but the government denied the shooting of seventy-five others.[20] Eyewitnesses differed with the government account.[21] Three days later, Argentina urged Cuba to suspend executions.[22]

The Catholic Church, originally supportive of the revolution, because it considered many policies of the revolution Christian, asked for just and legal treatment such as clemency for the accused.[23]

In an interview for the CBS television program *Face the Nation*, Castro said that "an eighteen month period is necessary before elections can be held." In the same interview he claimed that "perhaps two or three dozen criminals" had been executed so far. Castro maintained that each had had a fair trial.[24]

However, these "revolutionary trials" had little resemblance to a court of law. They were patterned after the makeshift court Castro had set up in the Sierra Maestra Mountains during his three years of fighting against General Batista. The rebel code there provided for the death penalty for murder, treason, espionage, rape, armed assault, theft, and many major offenses against discipline.[25] It should be noted that Cuba had no death penalty law before the revolution except for members of the armed forces convicted of military crimes or traitors, per article 25 of the 1940 Constitution. The Civil Defense Code also had a death penalty provision, Article 128, allowing the death penalty for espionage.

As for the executions themselves, they were hard-hearted— the accused were lined up in front of trenches or along a wall or tied to a post and were shot with rifles and automatic weapons. The gory actions were given their full propaganda value. Cameras were allowed to capture many of the shootings, including one when a prisoner bravely faced the squad and gave the order for his own death.

Senator Wayne Morse of Oregon, a Batista critic and rebel supporter, denounced what he called "blood baths" and appealed to Cuban leaders to "withhold executions until emotions cool."[26] Castro replied with his characteristic defiance by telling newsmen that "the time for them [the United States] to have started worrying was during the Batista regime." He added, "We have given orders to shoot every last one of those murderers, and if we have

to oppose world opinion to carry out justice, we are ready to do so."[27] Most Cubans echoed the feeling and applauded this charismatic David willing to take on any Goliath who threatened his tiny country.

Another jab at the United States followed on January 15 when Castro said, "If the Americans don't like what is happening in Cuba, they can land the marines, and then there will be 200,000 gringos dead." He later apologized for this statement and assured the press that he sought favorable ties with Washington. Relations between the United States and Cuba were beginning their precipitous decline.

The revolution was fifteen days old.

On January 21, as the world watched, 18,000 Cubans congregated for a mass rally in support of the executions. Two hundred and fifty foreign reporters and two United States congressmen gathered in Cuba to attend the trial of Batista aides, held in a stadium.[28] One of the accused likened the scene to the Roman Coliseum. Chances for a fair trial in this pandemonium were nil. The U.S. press called them "blood baths." In reality, these shows served as warnings to anyone who dared commit "treason" against the new government.

Of course, treason wore many different hats.

Castro in Control

Ruby Hart Phillips, the resident *New York Times* correspondent in Havana, sounded off an early alarm in her January 27, 1959, article titled, "Reds Drive to Win Top Role in Cuba." In it she detailed examples of growing communist influence, including the fact that leftist leaders living abroad were returning to Cuba, the communist newspaper *Hoy* reemerged, and the Communist Party attempted to gain control of labor. On January 30, an inkling of totalitarian control began to show when members of Castro's own 26th of July militia were ordered to surrender their weapons

within seventy-two hours. On February 16, 1959, Castro became the island's prime minister, by his own decree.

Economic hardships rocked the island. The government faced a debt of $1.5 billion, 75 percent of the sugar crop in the eastern provinces was damaged during revolutionary guerilla fighting, and there were about six to eight hundred thousand unemployed in a population of six million. Political unrest and the closing of casinos had disrupted the lucrative income-producing tourist industry.[29]

Another economic development pointing toward total government control was established. *Intervención,* or the government's confiscation of properties and businesses, began two months into the revolution and would not stop until all private entities were abolished. The Cuban Telephone Company, a wholly owned affiliate of International Telephone and Telegraph, was put under government management on March 4, 1959.[30]

Castro had chosen Manuel Urrutia Lleó, with whom he'd worked in the Sierra Maestra camp, to be the revolutionary president of Cuba, a puppet position whose strings were pulled by then Prime Minister Castro. On February 28, President Urrutia approved a law authorizing the confiscation of property owned by Batista collaborators, including cabinet ministers, armed forces officers, senators, representatives, all those who sought office, and every provincial governor and mayor, effectively wiping out an entire political class, corrupt as much of it may have been.

During his first official visit to the United States in April 1959, Castro promised that Cuba would not confiscate foreign private industry. He again denied that his regime was communist influenced.[31] Simultaneously, Lazaro Peña, a longtime PSP member, was also traveling—to Moscow. He was under Raúl Castro's covert orders to ask for Soviet assistance to centralize control of the Cuban Army. Raúl specifically asked for men from the group of Spanish communists who were graduates from the Soviet military academy "to help the Cuban army . . . on general matters

and for the organization of intelligence work."[32] The petition was granted on April 23, and two Spanish graduates of Soviet military academies were dispatched to Cuba to be followed shortly by fifteen more.[33]

Meanwhile, back in the United States during a *Meet the Press* interview on April 19, Castro pushed the general election still further away, this time to "within four years." By May, Castro was on the verge of breaking his promise to protect private industry. On May 17, the agrarian reform became law, forbidding foreign and sugar mill ownership of land.[34] It also restricted individual land ownership to 30 *caballerias,* or 1,000 acres.[35] Seven Cuban airlines and airport companies were seized, as well as the holdings of 117 other companies, and eighteen individuals were charged with enriching themselves under the Batista regime.[36] American landholdings were "intervened"—revolutionary lingo for taken over.

Dissention in the Ranks

Pedro Luis Díaz Lanz, commander of the Revolutionary Air Force, became the first significant defector from the ranks of the 26th of July movement. Díaz Lanz escaped to the United States on July 1, 1959, after Castro forbade him from making anticommunist declarations, an order Díaz Lanz could not accept. He had become discontent after he noticed how previously unknown communists were given key positions in the rebel army. He wrote about this in a letter to President Urrutia.[37]

Once in the United States, Díaz Lanz testified before the Senate Internal Security Committee that he had left Cuba because "Castro had brought Communists to my country." He added that Castro had told him he would introduce a system like the Russian one, only better, and that he would "take land from everybody" and do away with banks.[38]

Díaz Lanz's defection cost President Urrutia his job. Going on television to criticize the defection, Urrutia was asked by the

interviewer about his views on communism. He refused to deal with "that subject" but criticized the leaders of the PSP. Castro watched the exchange in his hotel suite and exclaimed, "All this talk of communism makes me tired."[39]

The Seduction

Plotting to remove President Urrutia, the next day, June 15, 1959, Castro summoned *Revolución* editor Carlos Franqui and asked him to print a false story about Castro's resignation in large headlines. In his editorial Franqui wrote, "very . . . serious and justifiable reasons have led to this decision of one who has always been characterized by the resolution, firmness and responsibility of his action."[40] As expected, when the paper hit the street there was general outrage. Castro was not to be found anywhere. Two tension-filled days later he went on television, a medium he mastered, saying that he found it impossible to work with President Urrutia. The crowds swallowed the bait and asked for Urrutia's resignation; Urrutia quickly sought asylum in the Venezuelan embassy. Osvaldo Dorticós, a pliable lawyer who had drafted the agrarian reform legislation, was named president. Dorticós had been a member of the PSP since 1953.[41]

Major Ramiro Valdés, Castro's intelligence chief, was dispatched to Mexico in July 1959 for secret meetings with the Soviet ambassador and KGB. More than one hundred KGB advisers were sent to Cuba to guide Castro's intelligence and security systems. In an ironic twist of history, many of these agents came from the group of *los niños*, the children of Spanish communists who had been sent to Russia alone by their parents during that civil war. Because they spoke both Spanish and Russian, they were a logical choice for a Cuba–Russia link.[42]

Despite some dissension and concern, the prevailing mood was still very pro-Castro. Revolutions usually bring an affirmation of national identity, and Cubans were bursting with native pride. Consequently, the revolution had found a place in the

hearts of most Cubans. It promised the hope of new beginnings for the republic after so many corruption-laden years and after a seven-year reign the people had just lived under.

In a massive rally celebrating the anniversary of July 26, 500,000 Cubans gathered in the Plaza Civica and honored Castro with a ten-minute ovation. He claimed that it reminded him of ancient Athens, "where the people in the public plaza discussed and decided their own destiny," adding, "This is a real democracy," and that Cuba did not need formal elections.[43]

Other Cubans wanted the promised elections and a real democracy, not the totalitarian path along which Cuba was heading. There was unrest throughout the nation. Eighty "counterrevolutionary" men attacked an army post. A plot to unseat Castro's regime was crushed on August 10 and 11. By then the numbers of arrests had reached 4,500.[44]

Political Correctness Castro Style

As the regime became more established toward a military order with total control of the armed forces and repressive organisms, resignations or replacements in the government were quickly filled with Castro's sycophants. Castro's power was infiltrating all aspects of Cuban life.

In August, the Cuban Electric Company, an American & Foreign Power subsidiary, was ordered to cut its rates by 30 percent and its officers' expenses from $50,000 to $3,000 a year. In September, 330,000 tons of sugar were sold to the Soviet Union at a price slightly lower than the world price. A shift in economic partners was starting to occur, and Cuba was reaching out to the Soviet Union.

A third of Havana University's professors were deemed unreliable by the government and were removed from their posts in October. Major Rolando Cubelas, the University Student's gun-toting president who fought in the mountains with Fidel, said, "Incompetent, immoral, and counterrevolutionary professors

must go." He also asked for curricula, faculties, and examinations to be revised and foreign faculty allowed.[45] The government secured control of institutions of higher learning.*

Meanwhile, at the Ministry of the Interior, a KGB-modeled intelligence service was installed, a secret police whose mission is to protect the state from its enemies from without or within. Cuban agents were sent to Moscow for training.[46]

On October 21, 1959, Major Hubert Matos, military leader of Camagüey Province and ex-aide of Premier Fidel Castro during the days of the Sierra Maestra Mountains insurrection, was arrested on conspiracy charges after he tendered his resignation. He had made the mistake of complaining that the revolution had not fulfilled its program and charged communist penetration of the government.[47] He was to spend twenty years in a Cuban jail, courtesy of his former friend.

Land and property seizures continued. Expropriated were 50,000 acres from United Fruit Company; the 33,500-acre King cattle ranch; 10,000 acres belonging to an American, Charles Buford; the 21,000-acre El Indio ranch; and 75,000 U.S.-owned acres in Oriente Province. Even Castro's own brother, Ramón, lost all but 1,000 acres of the 21,650 he owned.[48] The U. S.-owned Havana Riviera Hotel, worth $15 million, was seized, as were fourteen tobacco farms in Piñar del Rio, Cuba's westernmost province.

In the name of the revolution, individual rights were being eroded. The right of habeas corpus† was suspended, as well as the requirement that persons be formally charged within twenty-four hours of their detention. The Supreme Court's right to decide the constitutionality of laws was eliminated, as was the powers of courts to intervene for detained persons.

Not coincidentally, military tribunals were reestablished.[49]

---

* Five years later, in 1965, Cubelas would be sentenced to twenty years in prison for plotting to kill Castro.

† The writ requiring a person to be brought before a judge or his court to investigate the lawfulness of his imprisonment.

Many Cubans simply opted to flee, and 285,967 passports were issued in 1959.[50] Castro allowed dissatisfied people to leave, because it created the effect of a valve of a pressure cooker, allowing "steam" to escape before an explosion.[51]

The year ended with Premier Castro urging workers to spy on all people opposed to the revolution.*

1960
THE YEAR OF AGRARIAN REFORM

The revolution was a year old when Cuban parents got their first direct jolt. On January 6, 1960, the education ministry announced a new military program for high school students: to support the new People's Militia. It was decreed that all Cuban students had to learn to bear arms.[51] The government recruited about 400 university students into the student militia to fight possible enemies of Cuba.[52] Parks and other open spaces in Havana and the rest of the country, once enjoyed by strolling residents, turned into training grounds for these juvenile patrols. Marching youths three or four abreast, learning to march locked step, often wearing black berets, à la Ché, and toting Belgian rifles or Czechoslovakian automatic weapons, became a common sight. On January 14, Armando Hart, minister of education, said, "The teacher has an unavoidable obligation to transmit revolutionary thinking to students."[53] Prime Minister Castro heralded on the front page of January 29's *Revolución* during the opening of a school, "We will win more battles and the children will help us."

A ten-year-old girl was quoted as saying, "Fidel is a wonder. He

---

* Castro would always continue to manipulate Cuban emigration. In 1965 he allowed U.S. relatives to pick up family members at the port of Camarioca. In 1980 he repeated the action at the port of Mariel, where 125,000 persons exited. He rid Cuban jails of many criminals. After an August 1994 disturbance at Havana's malecón, Castro allowed 33,105 rafters to leave in the next two-month period.

is the greatest thing there is." She, in fact, echoed the feelings of most Cuban children at that time, including myself. As a ten-year-old, I was enthusiastic clay in the government's hands. I knew by heart all the propagandists' slogans and songs:

> Fidel, Fidel, que tiene Fidel,
> que los americanos no pueden con el.
> (What does Fidel have that the Americans can't beat him)

> Arriba, abajo
> Los yanquis son guanajos.
> (Up, down, Americans are fools)

These are just two that come to mind.

While the children sang anti-American songs, U.S. politicians under then President Eisenhower were becoming concerned for the futures of Cubans and their country. Florida Congressman Dante B. Fascell told Congress on January 13, 1960, that Cuban land reform was not well conceived and was capable of doing harm. California Representative H. Allen Smith warned Congress the following day, "The handwriting is clear for all who are willing to observe—Cuba is well on the road toward Communist dictatorship." He warned about the Soviets setting up a political base in Cuba, just 90 miles from the United States, at the height of the cold war.

Anastas Mikoyan, first prime minister of the Council of Ministers of the U.S.S.R., arrived in Havana on February 4, 1960. He and his entourage of seventy-five Soviet delegates inaugurated a Soviet exposition of industry and commerce, giving Cubans a new choice of commercial suppliers.

Anticommunist demonstrations greeted his arrival, with police firing into the air to quell demonstrations. Mikoyan placed a wreath with a sickle and hammer, a symbol of communism, in front of a statue of Cuban patriot José Martí. University students drove by, removed it, and replaced it with one bearing the colors of the Cuban flag.[54] Andrew St. George and Jay Mallin, American reporters present at the event, were thrown in jail and their film confiscated.[55] After demonstrating against Mikoyan's visit, the 1,000-member Catholic Action Group of students was forced out of the university, denounced as counterrevolutionaries. When group members attempted to distribute literature, they were beaten and their pamphlets burned.[56]

After Cuba secured a commercial and political agreement with the U.S.S.R., the *New York Times* reported that communist influence was growing in Havana.[57] Pennsylvania Congressman Flood reported to Congress on the threatening significance of Mikoyan's visit to American properties and interests. He believed that Mikoyan "used Cuba as a rostrum to proclaim openly that in Russia private property was confiscated by Soviet power without compensation to the owners." A Soviet trade commission with one hundred members established itself in Cuba.

In its March 21, 1960, issue, *U.S. News and World Report* showed a pictorial spread of Cuban children in their daily drills, marching three abreast, reporting that "boys join a Juvenile Patrol as revolutionaries at the age of seven." The pictorial follows a typical revolutionary ten-year-old boy at home, in school, marching, directing traffic. His mother is shown in her militia drills. The article mentions that there were 100,000 juvenile patrol members but that the goal was 500,000.

Castro truly believed in helping and educating peasants, because he himself had come from the countryside and it was there where he had been the happiest in his youth. Constantly helping peasants was crucial during his Sierra Maestra insurrection days. On May 13, 1960, *Revolución* published photos of the first group of volunteer young women headed for the mountains in a mission to teach peasants how to read and write. Although undeniably this was a worthy cause, it clashed with Cuban social standards and distressed many parents. Cuban women led sheltered lives, chaperoned until their wedding day. The thought of young women living alone, unsupervised among strangers was

not culturally acceptable. Banners stating "Every Student a Teacher"[58] frightened the parents of teenage girls.

Revolutionary teachings were to be woven through daily routines. Armando Hart, minister of education, announced on television, "We are using [in elementary schools] a new type of pedagogy that takes from life itself ... so that no course is isolated. Every lesson is a motive for explanations of a series of knowledge tied to another."[59]

During this political honeymoon, some dissenting voices rose, voices that did not equate being anticommunist with being anti-Castro and counterrevolutionary. Those who did not agree with every facet of the new regime, or with the slogan *Patría o Muerte*, or Fatherland or Death, were called *gusanos*, or worms, and disdained.

The easiest way to squelch dissenting voices was to assume control of opposition press by taking over radio, television, and newspapers. *Time* magazine's June 20, 1960, issue mentioned that the Cuban government ran 4 of Havana's television stations and 128 radio stations. Titled "Cuba—the Marxist Neighbor," the article also referred to the "sometimes subtle, oftener crude" brainwashing occurring throughout the island.

On the same date, *U.S. News and World Report* ran an article with the headline "Communists Take Over 90 miles from U.S." It said, "Children in the Juvenile Patrols—which the government organized to replace Boy and Girl Scouts—are instructed to inform on their parents and neighbors." This article also contained a warning to parents, quoted from the *New York Times*:

> The Castro regime is bending every effort to capture the minds of youth. The pattern of training is similar to that used by many totalitarian governments. It included indoctrination in schools, on radio and television and in the press, military training starting at seven years of age, a hate campaign, this time directed against the United States; the organization of work brigades of boys from fourteen to eighteen, and the meetings and fiestas, all with a political purpose.

> The government feels that, once the youth of Cuba is indoc-
> trinated with hatred towards the United States, the relations
> between the two countries will be permanently damaged.

No More Yanqui Dollars

Nurturing the seed of *Yanqui* hate to germinate among the island's youngsters was not the only way to damage U.S.–Cuba relations. By mid-1960, more than 300 million dollars in American property had been seized under the banner of "nationalism." Cuba also blamed the United States for sinking the French ship *La Coubre*, which exploded as its cargo of ammunitions and weapons was being unloaded at Havana harbor, an incident that was most likely an accident.

On June 23, 1960, Castro threatened to seize all U.S. investments in Cuba,[60] valued at approximately $1 billion. Not only was Soviet propaganda infiltrating every sphere of the island but also the presence of 1,000 communist Chinese "technicians" was being felt. According to New York Senator Kenneth B. Keating, these technicians were in Cuba "to lure Cuba's 30,000 Chinese into the Communist Camp."[61] One hundred to one hundred and fifty million dollars was invested in new weapons,[62] even though the government had captured large reserves of weapons from the toppled Batista government. Cuba's military was expanding rapidly. When Batista had left Cuba the armed forces numbered 29,270 and military expenditure was 2.2 percent of the GNP. By the early 1960s the armed forces swelled to 300,000 and military expenditure ranged from 4.4 to 8.0 percent of the GNP.[63]

The ideas of the revolution were being exported to Latin America and the Caribbean. *Prensa Latina*, a Cuban news service, was distributed free to Latin American newspapers. Powerful radio stations beamed (and still do) their message from "Cuba—Free territory of the Americas."

By July 5, the threat to the gringos came true. All U.S.-owned businesses were ordered appropriated, and by October, $1 billion in U.S. business assets had been seized.[64] The United States retal-

iated by canceling Cuba's sugar quota.[65] Cuban economy, dependent on sugar, lost its principal customer.

The Federation of University Students (FEU) was at the forefront of the attacks on the United States; as *The Reporter's* August 4, 1960, issue described, "The closer you get to the university [of Havana], the more prolific the propaganda becomes. Shop fronts proclaim 'Cuba si, Yanquis No' and a huge banner just beneath the long steps of the university announces a series of lectures on the duties and functions of the 'revolutionary family.'"

The FEU was also active among student groups in many Latin American countries. The Youth Congress, held that summer in Havana, welcomed more than 1,500 delegates, among them the Chilean Socialist Youth, the Chilean Communist Youth, National Federation of Chinese Youth, Committee of Organizations of Soviet Youth, Polish Socialist Youth, Czechoslovakian Union of Communist Youths, Popular Youths of Yugoslavia, Italian Communist Youths, and the Left Wing Socialist Youth of Italy.

"Castro: Once a Hero to Latin Americans, Now an Enemy" was the headline of a *U.S. News & World Report* August 29, 1960, article, which reported on the feelings of the hemisphere toward Cuba. It ended by stating that "Latin [American] diplomats all agree that Castro came to power on New Year's Day, 1959 with all the support he needed to give Cuba a new deal after the Batista dictatorship. He was a hero to Cuba and the rest of Latin America. Almost all Latin Americans here feel he betrayed the trust of the people of the Hemisphere. To them, Castro has now become a recognized enemy."

Hunting Down Enemies

Enemies of the revolution seemed to lurk everywhere. On September 2, Cuba broke relations with Nationalist China and established diplomatic relations with Red China.[66] This was a matter of supply and demand. China could supply assistance. Latin America could not, although Castro would provide his neighboring countries with much Cuban ideology throughout the years.

Cuba needed a strategy to sort their friends from their enemies, both foreign and domestic. The Ministry of the Interior
created on September 28, 1960, a vehicle for locating domestic
enemies, the Committees for the Defense of the Revolution
(CDR). The *comités* were the brainchild of Enrique Lister Farján,
a Spanish Republican veteran.[67] This was a web of neighborhood
watchdogs, usually one per block, whose sole function was to spy
on and denounce their neighbors. They were allowed to enter
Cuban homes suspected of counterrevolutionary activities,
backed by the militias. It was an effective government response to
the growing opposition, terrorism, and sabotage.

Fear and paranoia hung over Cuba and no one felt safe. In
1960 my family had moved to a residential neighborhood, a
street of similar two-story houses. Our *comité* was in a mirror-
image house directly across the street. It was always full of
olive-green-garbed militiamen and women. By then, my family
had also gradually turned against the government. The poster of
Fidel that used to grace our living room was never unpacked.
Our next-door neighbor, a doctor, was planning to leave the
country. So were the people across from them and the family on
the corner. Another neighbor, who had several children around
my age, had left already. Within a half block area the lives of five
families had been fractured. We started associating more with
similar-thinking Cubans, diplomatically avoiding our Fidelista
friends. My mother had a political disagreement with her lifelong best friend at work, a fanatic revolutionary, and their friendship terminated. It would resume many years later in exile.

I remember much pretense in our lives then. We were sitting
on our balcony more than ever to show that our conversations
were open and could be listened to and that we had nothing to
hide. At the same time, many whispered conversations went on
behind closed doors and among the neighbors. We tried to be
very friendly to the *comité* people, sharing with them a plate of
sweets or freshly brewed dark and sweet *café*, trying to gain their
trust. Although relations were cordial, they knew we did not

belong to the militia, we did not participate in military drills against a possible *Yanqui* invasion, nor did we display 26th of July movement flags on our home.

To leave Cuba, Cubans needed an exit permit. They also needed a U.S. visa or visa waiver and a ticket, bought with American dollars. Neither money nor valuables could be taken out of the country.[68] To be granted a permit, an inventory of all household goods would be taken by the military. All those items had to be accounted for the day of departure or exit would be denied. My uncle was planning to leave, so he left certain valuables with us before the inventory. Photographs, documents, and tall Chinese vases were brought in through our house's garage to avoid the CDR's scrutiny. The whole neighborhood felt the *comité's* presence and lived under its watchful eye.

The Uprising

In mid-1960, some 8,000 guerrillas took to the mountains trying to stir a revolution. Although fragmented, these groups were successful in evading Castro's troops until January 1961, when Soviet Spanish-speaking antiguerrilla units commanded by Red Army Lieutenant Commander Anastas Grigirich crushed the insurgency.[69]* Small pockets of opposition resurfaced through the mid-70s.

The United States called for the now-renowned Cuban embargo on October 19, 1960, which banned exports to Cuba of most products other than food and medicines. On October 15, the regime seized 380 Cuban enterprises, including private dwellings that were rented, the rent to be paid thereafter to the government.[70]

---

* In his book *Memories of a Cuban Soldier*, Daniel Alarcón Ramirez says that Cuban counterrevolutionary uprisings were much larger than what is generally known. About 10,000 men were in the Escambray Mountains, and about 300 were in Piñar del Rio and about 1,000 in the Sierra Maestra Mountains. Even in a few sites in Matanzas, there were groups of 20 to 30 men.

Dr. Nieves Valmaña, president of the National Private School Federation, issued a statement on November 1, in which she denied rumors that private schools would be taken over by the government. She added that the schools would support the efforts of eradicating illiteracy and that "every [private] school would be a fortress at the disposal of the cultural army."[71]

Castro showed up at the editorial offices of *Hoy*, the PSP newspaper, after attending a reception at the Soviet embassy on November 8. He gathered with an admiring crowd of journalists and editors for five hours and admitted that he had been a Marxist since his student days and that he had even introduced his brother Raúl to communist theory. This was his first admission to being a communist, although a semi-private one.[72]

A pamphlet, published by the Ministry of Education, for school children from the fourth grade up, opened with a poem. The last stanza read:

> I swear to you, Uncle Sam
> That one day in Algiers or Siam
> As is done with the dead,
> We will bury close together
> The dollar and the Ku Klux Klan.

The illustrations were just as anti-American. One showed a group of children carrying a sign in English: "Gringos. Go Home."[73]

Havana's Catholic university, Villanueva, took the bold step of expelling those students it considered troublesome, which the government viewed as a counterrevolutionary measure. It accused the school of sending "students and professors abroad" and of plotting to eventually close the university, a plan denied by the dean, Monsignor Eduardo Bosa Masvidal. Rolando Cubelas warned Cubans to keep an eye out for "those that from its privileged University try to attack the Revolution following the orders of its imperialists masters."[74]

Revolution Is Impossible as Long as the Family Exists

A week later, the Friendship of the People University opened in Moscow. Khrushchev invited the youth of Asia, Africa, and Latin America to study and "receive a superior education that they could later give back to their homelands."[75] The Soviet Union offered more than 400 scholarships, and other Communist nations initiated cultural and educational exchange agreements with Cuba.[76]

Headlines from the December 13 issue of Costa Rica's *La República* newspaper heralded, "The State in Cuba Will Assume Guardianship Shortly." The article said that children were being currently trained to inform on their family if they were not in agreement with the measures of the government. It also added that children were being taught to read with "F is for Fidel," "R is for Revolution," and so forth.

Declassified State Department papers dated December 19, 1960, from the American embassy in San José, Costa Rica, show that on December 13, members of the Frente Revolucionario Democrático (FRD), an exiled Cuban political group returning from a tour of Bogotá, Quito, Guayaquil, and Panamá, met with the Costa Rican press. The women in the organization "stated that their mission was to awaken the conscience of mothers all over America to the threat that Castro-Communism is to them and their children," according the letter from H. Franklin Irwin Jr., second secretary of the embassy.

Lenin once stated, "Revolution is impossible as long as the family exists." When Cuban parents who sent their children alone out of Cuba are asked today why they took such a drastic step, they cite many reasons, but two are usually mentioned—fear of communist indoctrination and fear of *la patría potestad*. *Patría postestad* comes from *patría potestas*, a concept codified in ancient Roman law referring to the power, *potestas*, exercised by a father, *pater familias*, over his children.[77] The two dreaded words conjured a rumor that the government was going to take over the legal guardianship of children from Cuban parents. It presupposed that the state would become the children's legal guardian and guide their education, provide their living accommodations, and possess the power to send them abroad to study behind the Iron Curtain.

A great number of Cubans had in their family a relative who had lived through the Spanish Civil War of 1936–1939 and remembered the hordes of Basque children being sent to other countries, including to the Soviet Union. The notion of children being sent to a communist country was very real to these people.

The government even acknowledged the rumors of *patría potestad* through its official mouthpiece, *Revolución* newspaper. On its December 26, 1960, cover it announced the establishment of a *Ficha Escolar Acumulativa,* or Accumulative Student Index. This index was created to collect family data so educators could "understand the child's problems and difficulties as well as learn of its interests and aptitudes, by observing and registering all activities inside and outside school." Each child, whether in public or private school, would have such a dossier. *Revolución* added that this file had "nothing to do with the false versions about the state being wardens of the children, although it looks like certain religious schools are twisting the facts and openly engaging in counterrevolutionary activities and they have connected one thing with the other."

Frightened Cuban parents saw the index as another government maneuver to reach its tentacles into the family unit and as an effort to register and keep track of all Cuban children. Some saw it as a way to sort out the smartest children, the children with the highest IQs, and send them to Russia. *Revolución* praised the measure as "something to be grateful to the Ministry of Education for improving all Cubans culturally, vocationally, civically, morally and intellectually." Another article on the same front page welcomed the first batch of Soviet tourists to Cuba.

The revolution ... is a dictatorship
of the exploited against the exploiters.

—FIDEL CASTRO

Adiós Cuba: 1961–1962

1961
THE YEAR OF EDUCATION

The third year of the revolution, 1961, began with Castro's demand, on January 2, that the U.S. embassy whittle its staff from eighty-seven to a mere eleven persons, within forty-eight hours. The embassy was accused of being the center of counterrevolutionary activities against the new regime. "We are going to eliminate all terrorists and counterrevolutionists in Cuba and all support of these criminals," Castro said in front of a crowd of more than 100,000 celebrating the second anniversary of the revolution's triumph.

A military parade, showing off weapons purchased from the Soviet Union and other Communist-bloc nations, included about 1,000 youth work brigades, "not more than 17 years old."[1] While Castro spoke, a bomb set by the opposition went off in the vicinity. At the same time, hundreds of thousands of militias were on alert throughout Cuba, expecting an imminent American invasion. According to *New York Times* correspondent Ruby Hart Phillips, the island became "an armed camp." Guns were distributed throughout the city and machine guns placed on the roofs

27

of buildings. Militiawomen took over the Church of San Francisco in Havana. Catholic Youth headquarters in Havana were also seized. The printing shops for *La Quincena,* a Catholic magazine, were also occupied and publication suspended.[2] The popular slogan *Patría o Muerte,* "Fatherland or Death," made its debut.[3]

On January 3, the U.S. government responded by breaking relations with Cuba. As U.S. aides started leaving the island, federal agencies studied the problem of providing Cubans wanting to leave the island with permits; the two U.S. consulates in Cuba had been issuing about 1,000 visas a week. Crowds of distressed, even hysterical, Cubans gathered in front of the embassy, waving passports, pushing doors, and begging for exit visas. None were to be had. Local photographers documented those "traitors" trying to leave the country, who were denounced as such by the media.

The Swiss embassy took over U.S. matters and was looked upon as a visa-issuing alternative. This, however, was soon found to be illegal.[4] Cubans without U.S. visas had to leave through a third country such as Mexico or Spain and get a U.S. visa issued there. Meanwhile, some Cubans unable to obtain visas found that like the Hungarian refugees of 1956, all Cubans entering the United States in small boats without visas[5] were admitted under the "parolee" provisions of the immigration law set up at the end of World War II, which allowed entry on an individual-case basis.

Back in Cuba, on January 4, the Council of Ministers approved several laws, among them Law 924, by which "any Counterrevolutionary activity will be cause for dismissal from the workplace, apart from the accompanying criminal charges."[6] Any Cuban suspected of not being a good revolutionary could lose his or her job. Life became a constant charade, a game of hypocrisy for Cubans who did not agree with the turns the revolution was taking.

At a meeting for thousands of public high school teachers called to Havana the following day, President Dorticos denounced Catholic schools. "Teachers today must occupy the trenches and positions of combat in education to defend the revolution and its culture against those who have selected the schools for their criminal work against the revolution," said the Cuban president. He also warned teachers to decide whether they would comply with their duty or "betray it." He claimed that Catholic schools were teaching that the revolution was communist. "This is a crime against our country," he warned.[7]

On January 7, Raúl Castro held a rally for students. Rain-soaked, they chanted:

> Raúl, Raúl the priests should cut cane,
> And if they don't want to cut cane,
> Let them go back to Spain.

Raúl agreed, saying, "Priests are trying to poison the minds of our children against the revolution."[8]

On January 8, the militia closed the printing press for *La Quincena,* a Catholic magazine.[9] The tirade against religion was gaining speed. This would prove to be one of Castro's most disputed moves in a country that was predominately Catholic. Meanwhile, in the United States, on January 20, the first Catholic president, as well as the youngest American president ever, was inaugurated—forty-three-year-old John Fitzgerald Kennedy.

Parent Fears Become Reality

On January 21, parent fears became reality when Castro announced the departure of the first batch of 1,000 Cuban students for the Soviet Union. Minister of Education Armando Hart said on January 29 that no divergence from the revolutionary doctrine of education would be tolerated.[10]

"Education plans stir Cuban fears," heralded a *New York Times* article on February 19, 1961. It quoted from leaflets, signed by Catholic student associations and private schools, that had circulated in Havana The pamphlets called the government's cam-

paign to end illiteracy "a plan of totalitarian indoctrination." Cuban fears were exacerbated when, on February 17, the government seized La Luz, a private school in El Vedado.[11] On February 23 it confiscated La Salle, one of Cuba's most prestigious private schools.[12]

Militia guards were placed around La Salle's school in Santiago de Cuba after a group of "counter-revolutionary students marched to the cathedral shouting 'Down with Fidel and down with Communism.'" Four youths were shot down by firing squads for terrorist acts.[13]

Parents also saw that a revolutionary army major could be someone as young as seventeen. One such juvenile major, Joel Iglesias, arrived in Moscow on February 27, heading a delegation of the Revolutionary Youth Movement.[14]

During a three-hour speech on March 27, Castro addressed the first national meeting of student members of the Rebel Youth Association, a new government-formed group. He said, "It is possible that many youths coming from well-to-do families could be saved for the Revolution and the fatherland, above the class resentment from which they come from, if it wasn't for that plague of reactionary professors and hired ruffians with cassocks that hate the revolution." He added that the Catholic Church was carrying out the orders of "Yankee imperialism," inducing young people to put bombs in schools, carry out sabotage, and fight against his revolution. Sarcastically he said, "If this is communism, we are in favor of communism."[15]

On April 1 the literacy campaign began in earnest. It was set up in six-month stages. Student *brigadistas,* or members of a brigade, arrived in Varadero Beach for literacy training sessions.

In early 1961, Castro announced the establishment in Cuba of "farms of the people," where children age ten and older would be taught agricultural methods. On April 1, 1961, *America,* a U.S. magazine, reported, "Some months ago 88 children from orphanages were shipped off from Havana to the Soviet Union in

the name of cultural exchange."

On April 4, the Union of Rebel Pioneers was created. Modeled after the Soviet Union's, the Pioneers' membership was made up of seven- to thirteen-year-old children who wore red scarves to proclaim their membership. Its goal was to train future members of the Association of Rebel Youths, the organization for youths ages fourteen to twenty-five, and "to report 'sabotage and counterrevolutionary attitudes' in elementary schools," according to the *New York Times*.[16]

Army of Education

Another development occurred fifteen days later and hit Cuban parents like a two-by-four. On April 15, 1961, Castro ordered schools closed, from the sixth grade through high school, for eight and a half months so that an "Army of Education" of 100,000 uniformed youngsters could be organized to go into the island to teach illiterate people to read and write. These crusaders would actually move in with peasant families while instructing them. Their teaching manual, titled *We Will Win*, instructed that "A is for Agrarian reform," "F is for Fidel," and so on and condemned "Yanqui Imperialism."

New York Times correspondent Ruby Hart Phillips called the plan, "a wonderful scheme. The children were first indoctrinated with the 'ideals' of the revolution, which were Communist doctrine; then the peasants were to learn Communist doctrine with their letters."[17] The Year of Education was in full swing.

Mirta Almeyda remembers that at fourteen she was an above-average student enrolled in the third year of a Havana public high school. The private school she previously attended had been taken over by the government. She recalls that one day the school director, a "rabid" communist, approached the students and said, "All students with good grades are going to the Minas del Frio [literally the cold mines, a region in the mountains of

Oriente, the westernmost province of Cuba] to eradicate illiteracy for the rest of the semester. When you come back, as a reward, you'll be graduated in three years instead of four." When she got home and gave the news to her father, his reply was, "You are not going to school tomorrow." She never went back to school in Cuba; instead, her parents sent her out of Cuba to the United States alone on February 13, 1962.

Since the closing of the schools also applied to the island's 1,245 private schools, *Newsweek* was correct when it announced on April 3, "In one stroke, he [Castro] will have imposed his will on the whole education system."[18] Meanwhile, all Cuban teachers were required to take a summer course for military training. Failure to do so meant job dismissal.[19]

Zenaida Bustillo was a teacher who had chosen to send her children out of Cuba, while she stayed behind undergoing hardships until they could be reunited.

> When they closed the school [where she worked] they sent me out to the country to the town of Guasimal to teach first to sixth grade. The idea was that I had to teach reading and writing, but it was a subterfuge to spread their ideals. Every day I had to take a train to Guasimal, a small town, and then ride a horse for an hour.
>
> There was another sixth-grade teacher who was a communist, so I would give her all the government material to teach. I never taught any of it myself. I'll never forget that teacher. Once she told the little children to ask God for an ice cream and of course, there would be no ice cream. Then she told them to ask Castro for the ice cream and some would be brought to them. I witnessed this with my own eyes and I'll never forget it, because I am a devout Catholic. I got away with not participating because they needed me. Once a government inspector came out and she said that just making the daily journey proved that I was a good revolutionary!

The story of the ice cream with variables such as candy or toys

was repeated throughout the island. Up to this point, contrary to mounting evidence, Castro still maintained that his revolution was neither socialist nor communist in nature, holding on to the purposely vague word "revolutionary."

However, on the same day that Castro had ordered the schools closed, an unrelated event occurred. Cuban exiles bombed air force bases. The detonations seemed to blow off Castro's desire to remain undercover, and on April 16, 1961, he declared that his revolution was a "Socialist revolution." Before the year was over he would change his tune to that of Marxist-Leninist, as he eventually defined himself.

Bay of Pigs Invasion

The aerial bombings of April 16 were a prelude to the April 17 Bay of Pigs invasion. The U.S.-backed and trained 2506 Brigade, made up of more than 1,400 Cuban exiles ready to fight for their homeland, had trained in Guatemala for the attack. Their eagerness could not compensate for the fact that only 135 of these men, whose ages ranged from sixteen to sixty-one, with the average age of twenty-nine, had ever been in the military.[20]

For the exiled invaders to have a successful operation, three elements were necessary: an amphibious/airborne assault at Trinidad; tactical air support; and seizure of a beachhead with access to an airfield. These were to be followed by the constitution of a Cuban government-in-arms in free territory.[21]

President Kennedy changed the plans at the last minute and instead of Trinidad, the area of Bay of Pigs in the Zapata swamp was chosen for landings at Playa Larga and Playa Girón. This decision had been made without first surveying the terrain. The plans also included and counted on an uprising by people in Cuba against the Castro government to swell the brigade's ranks, but the new chosen site was as desolate as it was difficult.

As the brigade attempted to land on Cuban soil, a sentinel sounded the alarm warning Castro. Antiquated amphibian boats

were ripped by coral reefs. For Cuban exile pilots, the 520 nauti-cal-mile flight aboard an obsolete World War II B-26 took three hours and twenty minutes flight time. Aerial support by the Cuban exile pilots flying was short because orders were received from U.S. organizers to cancel the air raid against Cuban bases. "The B-26's were now limited to air cover for the Brigade," said Captain Edward B. Ferrer.[22] Promised American air support was denied. A jet fighter squadron, VA-34, ordered to fly recon-naissance over the invasion, was now forbidden to engage in combat, its pilots were "moved to tears" at their inability to help the brigade.[23]

The brigade faced a Cuban army composed of 32,000 men and 200,000 militia units. Castro himself, who was very familiar with the terrain at the Bay of Pigs, as it was his favorite fishing spot, led the Cuban troops while he directed Cuban defenses. Doomed from the beginning, the brigade faced a magnificently equipped and mobilized Cuban army. After courageous fighting, within seventy-three hours, 1,200 invaders were captured and the Cuban exile invasion was declared a failure. American prestige suffered a massive blow. "We felt betrayed," says Captain Ferrer, echoing the sentiment felt by the entire Cuban exile community toward the United States, specifically toward President Kennedy.

After the Failed Invasion

It was also the end for any serious hope of toppling Castro. Within forty-eight hours, more than 200,000 persons in Cuba were arrested, including priests and clergy. The repressive appa-ratus went into overdrive. Stadiums, ministries, and schools served as temporary jails to house anyone who was not a bona fide revolutionary.

Throughout Cuba, boys and girls, some only thirteen years old, were armed for police and sentry work. All Catholic schools and churches were closed and guarded.[24]

The *New York Times* reported on April 20 that bands of youths roamed the streets of most major Cuban cities, intimidating the people and aiding the secret police in roundups of suspicious persons. Julio Nuñez, then a fourteen-year-old student at the Instituto de Matanzas, was a victim of such a mob. He was walking down the street when he heard, "Let's get whitey," only to look around and realize in horror that the mob was referring to him as they started throwing rocks and stones. After the incident he changed his style of clothing to the most nondescript so as not to stand out, but he was still beaten up on other occasions. He started procedures to leave Cuba on his own and then informed his parents, who agreed and sent him out.

Private Schools Nationalized

During the May 1 parade celebrating International Labor Day, revolutionary pride was bursting. The Lilliputian nation had foiled a U.S.-backed invasion! Half a million Cubans participated in the usual forces and weapons display where many banners were paraded. One read, "If Fidel's doings are those of a Communist, put me on the list, because I agree with him." Another said, "We won't take a single step backward."

During this speech Castro announced that permits held by foreign priests to remain in Cuba would be voided. He also announced that the government would immediately nationalize all private schools, invalidating the statement issued by the president of the National Federation of Private Schools six months earlier assuring that private schools would not be affected. When Castro asked the crowd, "Do we need elections?" they roared back, "NO!"[25]

Elsa Cortina and her husband had bought the Record School in 1954. He worked as a lawyer, and she ran her beloved school. She remembers that a group of worried nonreligious school principals met with Armando Hart some time in February or March,

1961, and he assured them that their schools would not be con-fiscated. The Monday after Castro announced that all schools would be confiscated, Mrs. Cortina showed up at school to find two men in militia garb bearing guns at the school gate. She introduced herself, opened the door, and they told her, "You know that from now on nothing here is yours; it is confiscated, but you have to continue coming to school for a month to sort things out." One of the men was the new administrator, Amaro García. "He would mock me, telling me, 'You see this, it is no longer yours,' or 'too bad this doesn't belong to you anymore.' I wasn't allowed to sit at my desk anymore and I had to take my orders from the former cleaning lady. I earned heaven during that month," Elsa recalls.

On June 7, the Council of Ministers formally approved the na-tionalization of private education, and the previously announced batch of 1,000 U.S.S.R.-bound students left Cuba on June 11 to live on collective farms and study cultivation methods.[26]

Living in Fear

As these students were leaving Cuba for the Soviet Union, Orlando Conde was preparing to go to Miami. The thirteen-year-old belonged to the Catholic Youths and admits to having partic-ipated in trivial antigovernment action such as distributing flyers and pasting paper fish logos, a sign of Christianity, on walls. The fish symbol, also known as ichtus, was used as a secret sign of Christianity as early as the second century.

The militia knew that his family and those of some of his friends did not agree with the regime, so militiamen would rou-tinely harass them. They would be picked up and taken for rides while they were questioned. Then, one night, it was different. "It was around 10:00 P.M. I was alone, waiting for my friends at the park in Artemisa. Four or five militiamen showed up and told me to get into their jeep. We rode around and suddenly we were at the cemetery. And they ordered me to kneel down in front of a

grave and put a rifle to my head while they questioned me. I was scared. And I had my ticket to leave for the United States, which I did."

Life magazine's July 18, 1960, issue reported on an agreement between Cuba and Czechoslovakia to train Cuban students in Czech technical schools. In a speech on July 26, Castro stated, "The revolution has organized the country." He added, "Two years and seven months into the revolution, the country is organized through its labor syndicates, committees of the Defense of the Revolution, militia battalions, youth associations, women's federations. Even the children are organized in the Rebel Pioneers Associations."[27]

By the summer of 1961, a Cuban child faced the following prospective: if he or she was age seven to thirteen, he or she would have to join the Union of Rebel Pioneers. Those twelve years of age or older had to go the mountains to alphabetize the peasants and, upon turning thirteen, they had to join the Association of Rebel Youths. Refusal to participate equaled isolation, labeling oneself as an outcast and therefore a counterrevolutionary. There were no gray areas in Cuba at the time.

Fourteen-year-old Silvia Alfonso left Cuba on August 26. Her mother had refused to send her to teach illiterate peasants as required, after the seventeen-year-old girl next door came back pregnant from her alphabetizing journey into the Cuban countryside. The child's father was the soldier in charge of student-teachers' care.

All the airports and ports of Cuba were closed on August 6, while every Cuban was forced to exchange their pesos for newly printed currency. Two days were allowed for this process, and hundreds stood on endless lines. Heads of families were allowed to exchange two hundred pesos. Anything over that would be placed in special accounts.[28] Cubans found themselves with very limited cash resources. By August 1961, Cubans could leave the country with only one suitcase. Armylike duffel bags with a tubular shape, known as *gusanos,* could hold the most items and

became the luggage of choice of fleeing Cubans who were also called, like the bags, "worms." By late 1961, exiting Cubans could take only three changes of clothing out of the country. The government had nationalized the entire contents of Cuban households.

"I have recurrent dreams of going into my house and finding everything just as we left it," remembers one exile who left almost thirty-five years ago. "We were told we had to leave right away. We left clothes hanging out to dry and food on the stove. But sometimes my dreams turn into nightmares. In them I see people rummaging through my underwear drawer and my personal papers."

Lines formed in front of the offices of Pan American Airways in Cuba as early as the evening before the offices opened, as desperate visa-holding Cubans clamored for tickets to get out. While waiting, they endured jeers and shouts of "Traitors" and "Gusanos!" An estimated 20,000 Cubans waited for an airline seat, a wait of several months, since Cubana Airlines had stopped its Miami–Havana service back on February 9.[29] Pan Am had only fourteen flights a week.[30] KLM ran two flights a week to Jamaica; Delta, a weekly one to New Orleans; and Cubana flew once a week to New York.

In order to leave the country, an exit permit from the Foreign Ministry was required. Those trying to leave the country bore a label and brought about harassment from every revolutionary source, starting with the neighborhood committee of defense and even members of the family. By mid-August of 1961, when the revolution was a year and a half old, 939 priests and nuns had been expelled from Cuba to Spain.[31] Also by then, the only Jewish congregation in Cuba, with two thousand members, had been disbanded under government pressure.[32]

Reporter Tad Szulc described a propaganda poster depicting a small boy and a caption asking, "Will He Be a Patriot or a Traitor? It Is Up To You ... Give Him Revolutionary Instruc-

tion."[33] My mother decided that I should be a traitor. I would be sent to Miami and the rest of the family would follow shortly. By then the Castro poster was long gone from the living room and the political honeymoon was over. It seemed like all of our friends were leaving. After my school, the American Dominican Academy, was intervened many of my friends left. Cuban parents needed to sign an individual authorization allowing their child to leave. My mother, divorced from my father, asked for his approval, which he denied, because he didn't agree with the idea.

I remember shopping for clothes with my mother, preparing for the journey. There weren't many items to be found, since the country's economic crunch showed in the empty window cases of glum Havana stores. Afraid of what the future would hold, people were buying goods and squirreling them away. A pair of hideous brown and white shoes that were too big was a precious find at the almost empty Buster Brown store. We bought them, despite my protests. My towels and clothes were all embroidered with my initials, and some thick burgundy wool material my grandmother had hoarded for many years was turned into a coat that was not very practical for Miami and about two sizes too big. Looking back I see that my family really didn't know how long we were going to be separated or what would be my final destination.

My father relented and signed my exit authorization, and, because he worked for Pan American Airways as a ticket agent, any wait for an airline seat was circumvented. I left Cuba on August 11, 1961. At that point two hundred unaccompanied Cuban children were arriving in Miami every week.

On September 14, Cuba voided all air tickets to the United States and changed exit rules. Permits to leave would be good for only seven days.[34] The following day the government changed its mind and announced that tickets already sold would not be canceled.

Patría Potestad—True or False?

By then rumors of the impending *patría potestad* doom were everywhere. Some people swore they had seen the printed document, circulated by the underground. School principal María Josefa Gasset-Torrado was one of them: "Someone brought me the patría potestad document to school, sometime around early 1961. Every Cuban mother I spoke to was willing to take to the streets if the measure went through. It was vox populi in Havana—mothers were just not going to let their children be taken from them. That is why the government backed down."

María E. Rodríguez was shown the *patría potestad* by a neighbor who was an officer in the Ministry of the Navy. From her apartment, María had seen her neighbor's sister-in-law, a member of the committee of defense, going through their closet and had warned them. He returned the favor by showing her the *patría potestad*. "It was an official document with the government's seal and the signatures of three ministers," she says. "One was Fidel's and the other two I don't remember, but I saw it with my own eyes."

Finally, in a September 16 speech Castro addressed the issue publicly by blaming the counterrevolutionaries for printing and distributing a fake *patría potestad* document, with the intent of fueling unrest among Cuban parents. He announced that fourteen persons had been jailed on charges of circulating this false document.

The document stated that all children would remain with their parents until they were three years old, after which they must be given over for physical and mental education to the Organización de Circulos Infantiles, a network of state nurseries. Children from three years of age through their teens would live in government dormitories and would be permitted to visit their families "no less than two days per month." Those ten and older would "be assigned . . . to the most appropriate place."[35] Carlos Franqui, director of *Revolución* newspaper and one of Castro's

closest coworkers in those early days, says now that he believes Castro's speech was a deception and that the plans for implementing the *patría potestad* law really did exist.

According to passengers arriving in Miami that same day in September, a near riot ensued at José Martí Airport when authorities refused to allow a group of children to fly to the United States without their parents.[36]

The fact that Fidel himself had sent his own ten-year-old son, Fidelito, to the U.S.S.R for schooling did not appease rumors. *Time* magazine reported, "Stories about trucks picking up unaccompanied children on the streets have swept Cuba." The government admitted having placed 700 youngsters in state homes, "at their request." An article entitled "And Now the Children?" mentioned that in the town of Bayamo, fifty mothers had signed a pact to kill their children rather than hand them over to Castro.

Meanwhile, on September 17, 1961, 131 priests and male members of religious orders, both Cuban and foreign, were deported on the Spanish passenger ship *Covadonga*. This reduced Catholic clergy in the island to 223. Public religious events were banned, thus limiting religious practices to churches.[37]

"Hundreds of Cuban families are frantically trying to get their children out of the country," reported *Time* magazine on October 6, 1961. "At Havana's José Martí Airport last week, adults with airplane tickets were implored to give their seats to children. Some Pan American flights arriving in Miami have as many as 60 children on board."

Castro announced on October 23, 1961, that to be a young Cuban was a privilege, but "Being young and not to understand the revolution is a crime." He also said that those who left for the United States needed a special permit to return to Cuba.[38] Five hundred more Cuban students left for the Soviet Union and Czechoslovakia with scholarships.

The most startling announcement of the year came on December 1, when Castro proclaimed that he was not just

a socialist as he had claimed in April but indeed a communist and a follower of Marxism. Castro confessed on December 22 that he had been a communist believer since his guerilla warfare days and had hidden the fact because otherwise he would not have been able to press his revolution to a successful conclusion.[39]

In the town of Caibarién, the La Guardia family grappled with the decision of whether to comply with the wishes of thirteen-year-old Louis or not. The boy pleaded to be sent to the United States, but his parents found it painful to separate from their only child. "It is difficult," says Fé, Louis's mother. "But then I would say to myself, 'And if I oppose myself to his leaving and he gets drafted into the army and gets killed?'" Louis left on December 15.

Fé was assured that she had made the right decision when tragedy hit her family. Her cousin's fifteen-year-old daughter had been sent to Russia:

> She was very intelligent and she didn't want to go. After a year they let her come back to Cuba and she would cry bitterly, because she didn't want to go back, but she had to. One day there was a knock on their door and her sister answered. Two army members told her that the body of her sister had arrived the previous night from Russia and that it would be transferred to the funeral parlor the next day. They said she had killed herself, but the family never believed it. Several officers and a doctor brought the body back to Caibarién in a huge box. They agreed to exchange boxes, but would not let her family or her doctor look at her. They sealed the box.

The Year of Education ended. Just like it promised, it focused intensely on education and accomplished the funneling of all learning through the hands of government.

1962
THE YEAR OF PLANNING

By the time 1962 arrived, Cuban parents were feeling that 1962 couldn't be worse than turmoil-ridden 1961. Castro had already closed all Catholic schools, declared his government socialist, and then communist. A totalitarian government was firmly entrenched, controlling all social institutions except for the church, which managed some vestiges of independence, although these were slim indeed. The number of Catholic clergy had been reduced from around 1,000 in 1960 to 223.[40] By 1962, the world was ready to react to these changes too. On January 25, the Organization of American States expelled Cuba.[41]* Also by the beginning of 1962, thirteen Latin American countries had broken relations with Cuba.[42]

President Kennedy ordered a total embargo on Cuban imports on February 3, which went into effect at 12:01 A.M. on February 7, depriving the Cuban government of approximately $25 million of annual income and cutting off Cuba, except for pharmaceutical trade. The president said that the ban would reduce the capacity of Cubans to engage in acts of aggression and subversion in the Americas.[43]

Cuban Children Make U.S. Headlines

On February 22, 1962, the *Cleveland Plain Dealer* newspaper wrote a piece on the unaccompanied Cuban children, citing from an intelligence report that between 1,000 and 2,000 Cuban children had been sent to Russia and Eastern European countries in 1961. An avalanche of other stories followed.

---

* With thirty-two member countries, the Organization of American States was formed in 1948 to settle disputes peacefully, create a collective security system, and coordinate the work of other intra-American bodies.

In February 1962, William L. Mitchell, director of the Cuban Relief Program, gave a speech at New York's Waldorf Astoria Hotel to the Women's Division of the United Jewish Appeal, revealing that there were "thousands of unaccompanied Cuban children"[44] in the United States and 73,000 Cubans ready and waiting to leave the island.

The following month, Secretary of Welfare Abraham A. Ribicoff appealed to American families to help care for the approximately 300 Cuban children arriving unaccompanied each month.[45] On March 9, the *Miami Herald* ran a front-page story on the juvenile exodus. Other publications followed. At the same time back in Cuba, Castro was urging the nation's youth to develop a more intense "Marxist spirit, a more Communist spirit."[46]

The *New York Times* wrote a full-length article on May 27 on the unaccompanied Cuban children program, a program set up to place the Cuban children in the United States and subsidized by federal funds, calling it "the largest peacetime program for homeless children in this country." The article said that there were 10,000 unaccompanied Cuban children in the United States, with about 500 arriving each month.

Rita Martínez, a teacher who arrived in Miami in early 1962, recounted to *New York Times* reporter Hart Phillips about her duties as a teacher in Cuba, "We were obliged not only to indoctrinate the illiterates according to the primer, but also to explain to them the *Fundamentals of Socialism* written by Blas Roca [a long-time Cuban communist leader]."[47]

Testimonies

Meanwhile, in Cuba, others were deciding their fate. Thirteen-year-old Rafael Carvajal was one of the children who had volunteered to go into the countryside. "My parents had bought me a horse and would give the peasants money so they would feed me, so I was a spoiled alphabetizer." His parents had been early supporters of the revolution and had hidden guns in

their home. In fact, he was among the youngest to go to the west-ernmost area of Cuba for a year. "When I returned to Havana the revolution had totally changed, and so had my family and I." Rafael then got involved in counterrevolutionary work; on August 18, 1962, he left Cuba, alone, for the United States.

Another child of the exodus explains her decision to leave her country: "I felt like a pariah at the Institute in Matanzas," says Beatriz Infiesta, then fourteen, of the time before her departure. "Sometimes you were in class and they would ask for a minute of silence for Patrice Lumumba [the slain Congolese Premier], or they asked why you had not gone to alphabetize peasants. I didn't like what was happening."

Josefina Santiago* remembers that her family was very politi-cal in Cuba:

> We had a false [floor in the] courtyard. Underneath there was actually a cache of ammunition. My father worked for the revolution but he turned around shortly thereafter. He would listen to Radio Swann, which wasn't allowed at the time, and turn it up as high as he could; my father made sure that the *comité* heard it, and I was petrified. He started helping the *gusanos*. At the time there were simultaneously little insurrections in our town, Cienfuegos. Once I was with him and he pushed me to the ground and when I got up I saw a bullet right where my nose was. It shook me up! And I also saw things happen in my house. Once the militia came in and my father was on top of a ladder and they grabbed his heels and yanked him down. One time they were interrogat-ing him and shoving my mother aside and one of the militia put a rifle to my face and told me to stay back. And I was eight years old! And it started all over again with the ammu-nitions, and the rifles, and the guns—everything under the courtyard over again. This time I was shaking in my boots

---

* a pseudonym

thinking, "Daddy please stop this I want to have a father, I don't want you in prison." But he never stopped.

Josefina left Cuba in May 1962. "I know why I came to the United States. It was because my father wanted me to be better off. He'd rather lose me to a Democratic country than to a Communist country."

Those who left Cuba in 1962 didn't realize at the time how fortunate they had been to leave when they did. The world held its collective breath during the October missile crisis, when nuclear war over Russian missiles positioned in Cuba seemed certain. On October 23, 1962, 150,000 Cubans who were ready to leave the island were deprived of their dreams of freedom when all scheduled flights between both countries stopped. Flights would not resume for three long years.

To be a small but vital part in the drama
of taking from the grasp of communism but one
little child is a stirring accomplishment.

—WENDELL N. ROLLASON
DIRECTOR, INTER-AMERICAN AFFAIRS COMMISSION
BEFORE THE COMMITTEE OF THE JUDICIARY,
UNITED STATES SENATE, DECEMBER 1961

Cuban Children's Program, Miami: 1960–1961

Mounting worries about the future of Cuban children triggered the formation of a clandestine operation set up specifically to get children out of Cuba. In a March 9, 1962, article, Gene Miller, then a reporter for the *Miami Herald*, would call it Operation Pedro Pan, a Hispanic version of the James M. Barrie novel about a boy who could fly.[1]

In the fall of 1960, James Baker, director of the Ruston Academy, an American school in Havana, received the first of many frenzied requests from Cuban students' parents. Could Mr. Baker manage to get a United States scholarship for his two sons, a fifth grader and a high school senior, one parent asked. Normally, Baker could intercede in getting such a scholarship if notified during the spring semester, but the new school year had already started. "I knew that this parent was very much involved in the opposition to Castro." Baker says. "He told me, 'The trouble is, those of us who are fighting Castro are willing to give our lives for our country, but we are concerned because we are afraid that if

we are sent to prison our children will be sent to Russia. That's why I want to get them out. Could you do anything?'" remembers the octogenarian Mr. Baker, a still-dashing presence with white hair and mustache and a perennial twinkle in his eye. Sitting at his dining-room table at his home in Daytona Beach, Florida, Baker remembers how the exodus began. "As the school year had already started, I said no, but at that time, you see, no one expected this [Castro's government] to last."

U.S. News & World Report echoed those feelings and questioned the transitory nature of the new regime in an October 31, 1960, article titled, "Castro's Days Now Numbered?" Even owning 90 percent of all Cuban property and $1 billion stolen from Americans, Castro's piggybank was down to its last $100 million, and running out fast. The government had been unable to break even financially. A large American community was sitting in Miami, just waiting for Castro's demise so they could return to Cuba and claim their confiscated industries.

As relations between the United States and Cuba were deteriorating rapidly, Baker knew it wouldn't be too long before he himself left Cuba with his family. His plan was to stay in Cuba as long as the U. S. embassy was open.

Armed with the names of fifteen or twenty children that he knew needed to leave the country, Baker planned a Miami trip to talk to a group of American businessmen about the children's problem and to seek their financial assistance to set up a school in Miami. Before he left Cuba, Baker told a teacher at his school, Mrs. Rosa Guas Inclan, that he was going to Miami to try to secure student visas; he asked if she was interested in some for her own children. "I knew her husband was involved in counter-revolutionary activities. I think I knew more than she did because she said, 'Thank you Jim, but no.' The next morning, at 7:30, she was waiting for me at my office and said 'Oh, Jim, I was wrong. Yes, we do want to get our daughters out.'"

Baker flew to Miami in mid-December and had a meeting with eight or ten heads of American companies, leaders of the

American Chamber of Commerce in Cuba, whose children had attended Ruston Academy. "I talked to them and explained the problem. They said they could get financial help for the project if I found a place."

Baker began searching for a location for his school. He wanted to set up a temporary school in Miami for those students in greatest need, children whose parents were fighting Castro in the underground and Catholics who had a very strong opposition to the new government. Someone told Baker, a Protestant, to talk to Father Bryan O. Walsh, who ran the Catholic Welfare Bureau (CWB). Father Walsh, a priest who was also concerned about Cuban children, might know of a site for the proposed school. Baker and Walsh met on December 12, 1960.

Father Walsh was already involved in the care of unaccompanied Cuban children. Around mid-November, as executive director of the CWB, he had received Pedro, a fifteen-year-old Cuban boy who had been passed around from family to family to friends, all of them unable to care for him. The CWB, which at the time was a small, licensed, child-care and adoption agency attending to about eighty children,[2] gave Pedro shelter. Father Walsh made additional inquiries and found out that a small number of unaccompanied minors were in Miami.

One of these was Jorge Carballeira, sixteen, who had left Cuba on November 1 with his eighteen-year-old brother. They didn't know anyone in Miami other than a business friend of their father's whom they could ask for money if they found themselves in a bind. After a month in Miami with scant employment opportunities, the older Caballeira brother headed for New York to send for Jorge later, and the sixteen-year-old found himself alone in the city, in a rented room, enduring financial difficulties and working at odd jobs. Told about a priest that helped youths like him, he approached Father Walsh and was taken in: "Without their help I couldn't have done what I did; at least they got me started, they got me going and it was easier for me after that. For somebody without family, for me, it was the

only way to finish school. You couldn't if you had to work until your parents arrived."

Also in November, a Cuban mother had taken her two children by boat to Key West and asked the judge of juvenile court to find homes for them. The judge assumed jurisdiction and placed the children in foster care. The mother returned to Cuba to be with her husband and to continue her work in the counterrevolutionary movement.[3]

Father Walsh realized that as the political situation deteriorated in Cuba, the number of truly dependent children in Miami would increase.

Many children who were already in Miami were undetected by authorities because they had been entrusted to friends or family: they were not a public burden. Ruby Hart Phillips, the *New York Times* correspondent in Cuba, told her own story:

> About December 15, I went over to Miami with my sister, Irma, who, having closed her dance studio in my house, was leaving the island for good. Irma had assumed the guardianship of a six-year-old Cuban girl, whose name was Amalín, and I had obtained a U.S. immigration visa for the child. Hundreds of children were being sent out of Cuba and the authorities were not pleased to see an American taking one. At the airport, the young officials examined the document carefully, one declaring it not valid. However, another youth convinced him that it was, and we were allowed to take the child.[4]

Father Walsh and James Baker were working hard to ensure that Cuban children could be admitted into the United States. Together, they worked out a plan to get youngsters out of Cuba—they would get them student visas. To receive a U.S. student visa, proof that the child had been admitted to a school in the states was needed. Baker went to see Mrs. Agnes Ewald at Coral Gables High School, and they set up a plan by which he would get names to her, and she would get the proper papers in return. With these, the United States embassy in Havana could provide the children with student visas. The embassy's diplomatic pouches would transport the papers safely. The basic plot to get unaccompanied children out of Cuba was in place. Baker went back to Cuba and started working. "Everything looked very good," he says.

On December 15, Mr. Kenneth Campbell, Mr. Bob O'Farrell of Esso Standard Oil, and Mr. Richard Colligan of Freeport Sulphur Company, all members of the American Chamber of Commerce, went to see Walsh,[5] bringing to him the first list of 125 names.

After sending the student visas to Cuba, Father Walsh went to the airport to meet every arriving flight. On December 26, 1960, the clandestine operation yielded its first fruit. Vivian and Sixto Aquino, the first children, stepped off at Miami International Airport along with three others. "Penny Powers had been our teacher in Cuba," says Sixto. "She had approached our parents about our leaving Cuba as she knew that Vivian and I did not hide our opposition to the government." That same day, the first group of Soviet tourists arrived in Havana. No children arrived on December 27, two arrived on December 28, none the next day, and six on December 30.

However, also on December 30, there was an unexpected and risky phone call from James Baker in Havana to Father Walsh. Walsh and Baker had decided not to communicate over the phone, since international calls were monitored. Baker explained that the U.S. embassy was holding up the issuance of student visas. Father Walsh called Frank Auerbach of the visa section in the State Department in Washington. He discovered that the U.S. government was willing to issue 200 visas requested by Mr. Baker, on one condition: "A recognized and established organization in the United States would have to assume ultimate responsibility for the children. The Catholic Welfare Bureau, a licensed child welfare agency, would be most acceptable to the State Department."[6]

Rumors abounded in Cuba and Miami that no children would

be allowed to leave the island after January 1, 1961. "When push came to shove, the ambassador didn't want to issue the visas," says Walsh. Father Walsh had to make a quick decision involving a huge responsibility—the care of 200 children. In a bold move, the daring thirty-year-old Irish priest signed the required statement on his own authority, not knowing the impact that this action would have on his future.

Twelve children arrived on December 31. On January 3, 1961, the United States broke diplomatic relations with Cuba and the American embassy in Havana closed. James Baker and his family left Cuba, their home for twenty-two years, on January 5, with just five suitcases. As he explains, "We were refugees just as the Cubans were." Upon his arrival in Miami, he told Father Walsh that there had been difficulties in getting the children's visas. In the chaos that existed as the embassy was shut down and the staff burned papers, he was allowed to stamp twenty-five passports himself.[7] When diplomatic relations were broken, the number of children in Havana for whom Mr. Baker and his staff were seeking care from the CWB had grown to 510.[8] As of January 6, 1961, the Cuban government suspended the issuance of exit permits to Cubans and foreign residents except Americans.[9] This blocked the exit of Cubans except those already holding permits.

From January 1 to 3, no more children arrived in Miami, leaving those waiting in Miami to wonder if indeed no more children would be allowed to exit. But on January 4, four more children arrived.

Mr. Baker designed a plan where some children exited through Jamaica, with a British visa, on the twice-weekly KLM flights. Once there, they were issued a U.S. visa. Father Walsh traveled to Jamaica to set up a program for the children's transit in that island. He received the full cooperation of the Bishop of Kingston, Bishop McEleney.

Now together in Miami, Mr. Baker and Father Walsh began direct discussions with the United States Department of State and the Immigration and Naturalization Service about the possibility of bringing in other Cuban children without visas.

On January 9, in an unprecedented move, the State Department granted Father Walsh the authority to grant a visa waiver to any child between the ages of six and sixteen who wished to enter the United States under the guardianship of the Catholic Diocese of Miami.[10] Those sixteen to eighteen needed their names to be cleared by the U.S. government beforehand. A visa waiver meant that the bearer did not have to have a visa to enter the United States. Airlines could then accept the person as a passenger without being fined.

By February 1, 1961, 174 children had come to the United States. Friends and family housed 53, the CWB 119, and the Jewish Family and Children's Service was caring for 2.[11] That same day, Father Walsh met with the secretary of the U.S. Department of Health, Education, and Welfare to brief him on the plight of the unaccompanied children.[12]

Father Walsh was justifiably anxious about undertaking such an enterprise. His first concern was that the program for the care of unaccompanied children should be handled by child welfare agencies. His second concern was that the religious heritage of the child be safeguarded. This was one of the chief reasons why parents were sending their children into exile. His third concern was money—how would a foster care program be funded?[13]

Three agencies agreed to care for the children within their religious heritage: the Catholic Welfare Bureau; the Children's Service Bureau for Protestant Children; and the Jewish Family and Children Service.[14] This was on a local level. Federal funds were needed for the onslaught of children.

"We always distinguished between two different operations," says Father Walsh. "One was Operation Pedro Pan, which was a semiclandestine operation in Cuba in helping them to get here. The other, the Cuban Children's Program, was the care of the children who were in the United States without the care or protection of their parents. So they are really two different things. And although they were both activated roughly at the same time, that was coincidental. It was not planned that way, it just happened."

President Eisenhower had named Mr. Tracy Voorhees to look

into the Cuban refugee situation in Florida. Mr. Voorhees had previously headed the Hungarian Refugee Program from 1956 to 1957, resettling many unaccompanied Hungarian teenagers. At the time, Mr. Voorhees returned to President Eisenhower with the recommendation that, "If it should prove necessary, beyond what private charity can do, such Mutual Security Funds [$1 million allocated by President Eisenhower on December 2, 1960] will also be utilized for assistance to Cuban refugee children in extreme need."[15] In his last official act as President Eisenhower's representative, on January 31 he released $100,000 to aid 900 Cuban students in universities throughout the United States.[16]

Ray McCraw, a social worker with Catholic Charities, explains:

> Father Walsh asked me if I would work with the Cuban program, because the children were coming in by the hundreds and we didn't have any social workers. I knew differentent schools in the United States where I'd sent people, and I made personal contacts with these schools. Father Walsh and Bishop Coleman Carroll called on dioceses in the U.S. The directors of Catholic Charities came from ninety-seven dioceses and they all met in the Columbus Hotel in downtown Miami, in a great big ballroom. They outlined what they wanted to see done. Every diocese should take some responsibility in providing foster homes, foster care, and education for these Cuban children. Their response was magnificent. We had priests flying in from all over the country. Then after they went back, they were to reassess their foster home situation, then contact us, so Father Walsh could get the children transported.

McCraw recalls, "It was an extremely difficult thing to do, to see those little ones getting on airplanes and just going off into a whole new world. They were the bravest kids I'd ever seen. First of all, very few tears, and just walk in [with] perfect strangers."

On January 20, 1961, the nation inaugurated its thirty-fifth president, John F. Kennedy. The new president was facing a crisis in Florida with he onslaught of Cuban refugees. He sent Abraham A. Ribicoff, secretary of health, education, and welfare, to Florida to study the situation. Ribicoff extended his stay an extra day, because of the "deep and complicated nature" of the situation in the area. The "complicated" situation was potentially explosive, with 50,000 to 60,000 refugees in South Florida and 500 additional refugees arriving each week. Upon his return to Washington, D.C., Ribicoff described the refugees as "proud and resourceful people," but he also reported that many of them were in serious need. He described voluntary agencies as overextended financially. Finally, he named Dillon S. Meyer as director of the emergency Cuban relief program.[17]

On February 3, President Kennedy ordered aid for Cuban refugees as part of a nine-point program that provided $4 million in assistance to relief agencies, help from government and private agencies for jobs, essential health services, and aid to help people in need in Miami meet basic financial requirements. During a speech outlining his program, President Kennedy asserted his conviction to "provide financial aid for the care and protection of unaccompanied children—the most defenseless and troubled group among the refugee population."[18]

This brief mention of the refugee children by the *New York Times* in February 1961 would be the first news of their fate in the United States by the American press. Father Walsh had asked the press not to report on the unaccompanied Cuban children, as it might endanger their exit from Cuba, and they complied until the following year.

In light of the fact that the children's bureau was part of the Social Security Department, the secretary of the Department of Health, Education, and Welfare delegated responsibility for the program to the commissioner of social security.[19]

The Federal Children's Bureau negotiated a contract with the state of Florida's Department of Public Welfare and on March 1,

1961, signed an agreement to provide temporary aid for Cuban refugees, including care and protection of unaccompanied children. This agreement provided for federal funds to carry out the plan. At that time reimbursement rates were $5.50 a day in individual homes or $6.50 a day in group settings. (Five dollars and fifty cents in 1961 equals $29.72 a day, or $891.60 a month in 1997. Six dollars and fifty cents equals $35.13, or $1,054.50 a month.) This reimbursement was allotted for food, shelter, and clothing.

The children's bureau recognized the uniqueness of this situation. They appointed a special staff consultant to work directly with the agencies involved in the program throughout the country. The children's bureau implemented a new method of cost analysis to operate the unaccompanied Cuban children program.[20]

The voluntary agencies were also reimbursed for actual transportation costs and expenditures incidental to travel. These costs were incurred as a result of relocating the children outside the Miami area; costs of special services, such as psychiatric treatment or serious illness requiring extensive treatment, were also provided. [21]

Never before had the U.S. government funded foster care of refugee children in the United States.[22] With the immediate financing problem solved, the exodus could continue.

Katherine Brownell Oettinger, chief of the children's bureau, summed up the program's goals:

> When the program will end, no one can predict at present. It will continue as long as there is a need for it. Its impact will be felt long after its termination. In the long run, the peace of the world and the preservation of free societies depend on the development of the individual capacities of children and of a vast "common market" of ideas, knowledge, cultural interchange, and good will. The program for the displaced children of Cuba represents a long-term investment on this side of the ledger.[23]

No one can fly
Unless the fairy dust
Has been blown on him.

—J. M. BARRIE, *PETER PAN*

CHAPTER 4

Operation Pedro Pan, Cuba: 1960–1962

As the male figure exited the elegant house of former Cuban president Ramón Grau San Martín and started his car, a beaming searchlight pierced the black midnight, creating a tunnel of light. Carlos Stincer knew what was to follow: it happened every time he visited the home of the former head of state. The light picked him up at Fifth Avenue, and then at Seventh Avenue, a blue Mercedes Benz, driven by a mulatto with a Trotsky-like beard, took over from the light, following Stincer the rest of the way home. The message was chilling in its simplicity—we are watching you.

Mr. Stincer, a lawyer and a friend of the Graus, still shudders when he remembers the visa waiver papers he would usually carry under his shirt on those hot Havana nights. Sometimes it was Mr. Stincer's wife, Ofelia, who hid them beneath her ruffled skirt. "It was suddenly like daylight," he says of the blinding light. He still marvels at their good luck, since they were never detained. "We knew they were on to us. If we hadn't left Cuba in 1962, we would have been arrested."

Not only visas but also guns, rifles, machine guns, money, and passports found their way into and out of the Miramar estate.

Directly across Fifth Avenue, on Fourteenth Street, a colonial mansion that belonged to writer Jorge Mañach until he fled Cuba now housed the source of the searchlight—the feared state security, or G2, as it was commonly known.

Ramón Grau San Martín was a university professor and had been president of Cuba from 1933–1934 when he was first placed in power and then deposed by Sergeant Fulgencio Batista. He was elected president again in 1944 and served until 1948.

Eleven years later, in June 1959, Castro expelled former president Grau from his post at the university and confiscated all his properties. Then on May 4, 1961, Castro had a change of heart, perhaps because he respected Grau for his wisdom, his age (80), and because he had not left Cuba as all the others had. Castro announced that he was returning Grau to his university post; and Grau declined. Castro's mother, an admirer of the former president might have intervened on his behalf.[1]

During this time, Grau shared his home with his brother's widow, Paulina, and her two grown children, Ramón, known as Mongo, and Pola, or Polita. Mongo was always involved in his uncle's affairs and for many years served as his personal aide. He continued in this capacity when the former president became elderly. The old gentleman depended on him for most everything.

When Grau's house was built, Mongo had bought the lot behind it and built his own home; their quarters were separate, but linked. A porch, the *salón verde*, or green room, connected the two houses. According to Mongo, it was the ideal place for underground work. It was almost as if he had built it with a premonition of his future counterrevolutionary ways in mind. "I could receive someone on Twelfth Street and send them off through the Fourteenth Street or Fifth Avenue exits. I had built two garden walls. The first was the house's natural wall full of tall plants. Some five feet behind it, there was a second wall. This self-contained corridor went from Twelfth to Fourteenth Streets. I could meet people there and they would not even have to step into the house."

Mongo, a jovial, *simpático* character, truly enjoyed the social whirl his privileged position provided him. Taking full advantage of his status, he entertained often. His gregarious personality and facility with multiple languages made him popular with the ambassadorial crowd, cementing friendships that would prove to be very useful as the Castro regime tightened the watch on his home.

After the U.S. embassy closed in early 1961, Penny Powers, a British teacher at Ruston Academy who worked under James Baker, visited Mongo, accompanied by several women involved with the Catholic Church. Since Mr. Baker had left Cuba to settle in Miami, she was looking for someone to take over his work with her. She asked him if he wanted to participate in helping get visa waivers to help Cuban children exit the country. He immediately said "yes" and added, "We are going to operate out of here!"—referring to the Miramar estate.

An alarmed woman replied, "Across from the G2?" He in turn asked them, "Which one of you knows someone in this house?" Because society circles in Cuba were clannish, it happened that they all did. One knew the uncle's former minister, another his mother, another was a niece of a cousin, and so on. Encouraged, he replied, "You see, we have the perfect alibi to operate out of this house."

At that point, one of the women produced a box full of passports. Mongo was shocked. "You are never to run around with passports," he said, for he knew that being found in Cuba with identity papers that were not yours was grounds for arrest. This became the group's first rule. They were to bring the names of those requesting visas written on pieces of paper or in books—anywhere—but *no* passports. Second rule: alternate your visits to the house. If you come a Tuesday this week, come on a Monday next week. Do not come the same day of the week. Avoid routine movements. The newly founded operation was created.

Trusted Cubans traveling from the United States were recruited to bring visa waivers into Cuba. Sara del Toro de Odio

was one of these people. She had taken her five eldest children to Miami at the end of 1960. There, she met with her good friend Maurice Ferré, who took her to meet Father Walsh. On her return trip, she brought back one of the first batches of visa waivers to distribute to Cuban children.

Cubans returning to Cuba were becoming such an oddity that Mrs. de Odio's reappearance generated interrogation by airport authorities. Officials quizzed her as to why she had sent her five children away. She replied that since their school had been closed, she wanted them to continue learning English but offered as unquestionable proof that she was still a *Fidelista* the fact that she had kept in Cuba her smallest children. They were waiting for her at the airport with her husband, which handily verified her claim.

Meanwhile, her husband, Amado, was worried. He had run into the son of an old acquaintance who was now working for the immigration department at the airport and told him, "They've detained Sara!" to which the son of the friend replied, "Don't worry, nothing will happen to her." He proceeded to talk to Mrs. de Odio. She felt as if he was scrutinizing her as he spoke to her. The authorities released her, without searching the checked suitcase with the blank visa waivers. However, Mrs. de Odio claims that from then on, her family was under surveillance.

Meanwhile, Mongo was thinking of ways to bring more needed visas into Cuba. He had to find someone who had unlimited entry and exit in and out of Cuba. He needed to find someone who could not be searched by the Cuban authorities. Who could he find?

The answers were easily within his reach: diplomats. But how would he find the appropriate one? His first contact was Marie Boissevant, the wife of the Dutch ambassador in Cuba. He thought that she would be sympathetic to their cause because of a direct anticommunist connection, an elderly aunt who lived with the ambassador's family. The aunt, whom they called "the princess," belonged to the Russian nobility and had fled Saint Petersburg during the revolution. Mongo approached Polita

with the idea, "Who better than a white Russian to understand our plight and help us?" She agreed with the idea.

Mongo went to visit Mrs. Boissevant and asked for her assistance. He explained to her that her contribution would involve going to Miami occasionally and bringing over some things. "Just exactly what things, may I ask? Not arms?" she inquired. "Papers," he replied, "to see if we can get children out of Cuba to save them from communism." As soon as she heard that request, she replied immediately, without any trace of hesitation. "You can count on me for whatever you want. You tell me when I have to go. KLM, Royal Dutch Airlines belongs to the government, so as the ambassador's wife, I don't pay for a ticket and I can travel anytime." Thus, Mrs. Boissevant started her life as a very successful visa smuggler, bringing in as many as five hundred or more per trip.

Obtaining these visas was not an illegal activity per se. Anyone with family or friends in the United States could request one to be mailed to Cuba. But the postal service could not be trusted as letters were intercepted or censored. Also many people did not have acquaintances in the United States, or they needed a visa quickly.

One day Mongo saw his fourteen-year-old son asking the cook to save him potato skins and fruit rinds. Mongo asked him if he wanted these leftovers for the animals, and the boy replied, "No, a group of us are going to get together and throw them at the Russian embassy." Images of arrested youths flash through Mongo's mind and he decided that if he stayed to fight Castro, he too, would have to place his children in a safe environment.

He discussed this with Polita, who also decided to send out not only her children but also her squirmish husband, Pepé, who could be potentially dangerous to their underground activities. A recent episode was very troubling to Mongo and Polita. Pepé had seen a group of persons sitting in the *salón verde*. He had suddenly burst forward uncontrollably, screaming at them, "Go on conspiring, you are all going to end up in jail!"

Polita and Mongo thought they had perfect alibis for staying— he had to care for his uncle, who was an octogenarian and refused

to leave his country. Polita, for her part, also had to attend to her ailing mother. The mantle of the former president emboldened not only his niece and nephew but also the many people who thought his political aura would shield them from punishment for the antigovernment activities being carried out from his house.

Flights out of Cuba were booked months in advance, so airline contacts were needed to procure seats for the children once the visas started coming in. Early in the program, the Harry Smith Travel Agency in Havana received a few visas from Miami. Teté Cuervo worked there during that period and remembers that Gilbert Smith, the agency founder's son, would book five seats a day with dummy passenger names to give to unaccompanied children.

Francisco "Pancho" Finlay was the head of KLM Airlines in Cuba. He and his wife Berta were very active antigovernment conspirators. They had sent their own children out already and had received visas directly from Miami for distribution. Pancho and Berta agreed, through James Baker, to work with Serafina Lastra and Sergio Giquel on other children's behalf.

Some personnel at Pan American Airways became involved as well. One of them was station director Ignacio Martínez-Ibor. Leopoldo Arista, a lawyer for the company, remembers that a decision was made at the local level to block seats for children on every flight. Penny Powers had already paid them a visit in 1960, requesting help with seats. "Airlines could not sell a ticket without a visa, they were liable. This is why visa waivers were used."

Tony Comellas also worked at Pan Am's Havana office. "We would always give unaccompanied children seating priority, about ten or twenty per flight. I took a flight to Miami sitting on a toilet so a child could have my seat." Comellas had sent his family ahead and would commute on weekends to Miami until he left for good. One of his most memorable flights was one in which he recalls arriving at Miami covered in vomit after offering to carry a little girl who got airsick on his lap.

Demand for children's visas in late 1960 and early 1961 was small but steady. However, once the American embassy was

closed, an increase in demand was triggered immediately. Parents would usually seek help in obtaining exit visas from a trusted source: the church. They asked their parish priest, a trusted teacher, or a nun at their children's school.

Ester de la Portilla was a teacher at the American Dominican Academy when the principal's secretary called her in. She said, "Ester, I know your sister Berta Finlay is involved in getting the children out, so you should know that I am the liaison for this school." She explained how her husband, who was studying medicine, was being sent to the Sierra Maestra Mountains. She confessed, "I am afraid that he can get in trouble if I am discovered. Would you take over the school?" Since her children were already out of Cuba, she empathized and agreed. In her new role, she explains, "If a parent wanted to get a child out, he would contact one of us."

The Bay of Pigs fiasco made matters worse for counterrevolutionaries in Cuba. The invasion proved to be a turning point for many involved in underground work. Virtually no suspected opponents of the government escaped the brief but massive arrests, rumored to have included 250,000 people in Havana alone.

Among those picked up for questioning were Teté Cuervo, Pancho and Berta Finlay, Ester de la Portilla, and Mongo Grau, who was held across from his home. He says, "When I was released, after ten horrible days, since they had no evidence against me, I crossed the street to find my mother drinking coffee with four *milicianos* [militiamen]. Taped, under the table where they were sitting, were two machine guns."

After her release, Teté fled the country. Pancho and Berta refused to have any more incriminating papers at home, but they continued to receive them directly at KLM. Berta would use KLM as her new "office," giving parents appointments to see her there.

Treachery within one's own home is frightening and painful as well as difficult to accept. Ester was betrayed by her maid. She had instructed parents to call her house only after 2:00 P.M. when she would be there to answer the phone, but unfortunately, they would call at all times and talk to the maid or, worse yet, just show

up at her door and leave names and passports with her. One day, Ester noticed a man walking up and down her street, dressed in cowboy boots and hat. She went out, came back, and the tropical cowboy was still be there. This went on for several disconcerting days. Finally, a neighbor's cook befriended the cowboy and learned that he was, indeed, surveilling Ester's home.

In a panic, Ester removed the concealed passports and papers she kept behind a set of encyclopedias in the library. She took them out and put them in a can of crackers, then she put on her bathing suit and made a big to-do about going on a picnic to Tarará, a beach resort. She packed the can of crackers and other food items. Once away from the watchful eyes that had been surrounding her, she handed the cracker container to her sister, Berta, who then took them to the Dutch embassy for safekeeping.

At the time of her arrest, seventeen *milicianos* broke into her home. During her interrogation Ester discovered that the maid had stolen a list of names and turned it in. This list had a space next to each name for passport, visa, and ticket information. She recalls, "A lieutenant would question me once, sometimes twice a day, and always asked about the list. 'Is it yours?' he asked. I said it was. 'So what are you doing with this?' I would reply over and over that they were scholarships given by the school. He asked how many scholarships I had given. Fortunately, as a teacher, I remembered that a page had twenty lines and replied that about nineteen or twenty. This seemed to satisfy him. Little did he know that I had really given visas to about 250!"

Margarita Esquirre de Valdés Cartaya distributed visas in Matanzas Province. She remembers being very impressed with how smooth the operation was. She would go to the Grau residence, give them children's names, and would get the visa waivers without a hitch. Once the first obstacle, visa waivers, was cleared, parents faced a second one: airline tickets had to be purchased with dollars or U.S.-drawn money orders. Some people showed up at the airline ticket office with pennies, dimes, and quarters to reach the amount.

After the Bay of Pigs, most Cubans were disheartened about any possibility of toppling the Castro regime. The invasion gave the government the needed excuse to install drastic repressive measures. The futility of fighting became apparent to most of those who disagreed with the government. Many of these people decided to go into exile. Of those who decided to stay, however, many chose to send their children out. Demand for children's visas skyrocketed overnight.

As the demand for exits increased, so did the difficulty of getting a passport or a visa. Counterfeit documents were the only means of exit for some Cubans, especially for those involved in the underground movement. The Grau household became a forging factory.

Alicia Thomas became their master forger. She had studied art in Cuba and was quite skillful with a pen. Alicia was taken to the home of the person who altered passports, who was leaving the country, and she was taught the basics. They altered passports, then resewed them. They would get passports that had expired, or even from dead people, and then they would remake them so they would fit the description of the person leaving. Alicia recounted, "We removed numbers with a Gillette blade. It had to be Gillette; no other brand would do. Then with sharpened orange sticks, the kind used for manicures, and black ink, we had several shades of ink, that, combined with a little resourcing, and we would alter numbers and names." Sometimes passport pages would be set out in the sun to change the shading of the paper. Lolita Formosa, a friend of Polita's, was responsible for carefully resewing the passports.

Sometimes, in spite of all their hard work, they could not succeed. Mongo remembers a particular passport that just could not be altered. Dates could not be made to match. So he told the woman, "The only solution here is a *café con leche* [coffee with milk]." They plotted for the woman to go early to the airport on her scheduled departure day, sit at the coffee shop counter, and order a coffee with milk. Then she was to have her passport and

tickets on the counter, examining them while the waiter was watching so she could have a witness to her dilemma. She was to spill her coffee all over the documents. It worked.

They worked daily and fast. Alicia also remembers helping men and women escape the country by passing them off as minors. "There was a skinny guy, very fair, no beard. He was married with children. But we put a school uniform on him, white shirt, navy pants, and sent him off with a minor's visa waiver. Mongo said that I shaved fifteen years off off him."

Aiding those in political hot water was a crucial part of the group's activities. "One day I had to go to a very well-known optical store in Cuba," remembers Alicia. "They were hiding a wanted man there. A female cousin and myself were to pick him up. We got him out and he stayed with us the whole day. When we delivered him to the agreed drop-off place, it didn't feel right, so we didn't leave him there and took him somewhere else, an attic in the Vedado section."

"When I got to Mongo's house, one of the servants told me, 'You know they have been taking car loads of light blond women to the G2 all day.'" Alicia is a very attractive green-eyed blonde. So was her cousin. "Right across the street! It was nerve-wracking. Needless to say, I was a brunette the next day."

Beatriz López is a distant relative of the Graus. She worked mornings at the National Museum. Afterward, Emilio, Mongo's chauffeur, would pick her up and take her to the Grau residence where she would type children's names in the visa waivers. "We had folders filed alphabetically and I would type and type, 100, 200, or 300 names. It was like a chain. Friends would tell friends who would tell friends."

Members of the Catholic Church played a very important role in the children's exodus, albeit not purposely arranged by the church as an organization, but spontaneously. As most of the children attended Catholic schools, nuns and priests were trusted persons sought out by frantic parents. Brother Tomás Ciuro,* a

---

* a pseudonym

Jesuit, recalls that after schools were closed, he was reassigned to a church on Reina Street. One day, one of the brothers approached him and proposed getting involved in helping children leave. He agreed. One brother would receive the names mostly from young men from *Acción Catolica* who would hang around the church. Brother Ciuro would fill out the visa waivers and another brother would take them out to the Panamanian embassy. "Once we were told that the G2 was on to us, so we held back our work for a while, but nothing happened."

When his own sister needed assistance to leave the island, Ciuro asked for assistance from one of the Catholic young men, who instructed him to get his sister to move into a certain police precinct temporarily and file her departure papers there with a certain official. Fortunately, she had a friend in that locality and was able to do so. It turned out that the government official had sent his child out of Cuba with a visa obtained through the church in Reina Street, and he was grateful.

Mongo recalls that Ofelia and Carlos Stincer would get names from a Marist priest and from a priest from La Salle school and then bring him the names. "These priests would go to her house at all hours, as early 7:00 A.M. People would bring us lists of names and we'd get visas from the embassies—Argentina, Switzerland." In order to protect their identities, they all had given themselves code names. Beatriz was Soledad, one of her middle names. Mongo chose Pimpi, as in *The Scarlet Pimpernel.* "But visas were only part of what we did; we hid people, we would get them asylum in embassies." The operation worked Monday through Thursday. Mongo had decreed that Friday through Sunday would be for resting.

Wanda Forcinni, from the Italian embassy, would get Mongo movies not available in Cuba and they would be shown in the Fifth Avenue house on Sunday evenings, the garden overflowing with diplomatic cars. "Once I counted and we had 200 persons," he remembers. These reunions provided the ideal backdrop for counterrevolutionary activities.

Elvira Zayas was a Panamanian in charge of business relations

for the Panamanian embassy. When she discovered that passports were being falsified and altered at the Grau home, she offered that the group use the Panamanian embassy as a safe haven for their work. As Polita recalls, "'Borico' Padilla, Julio Bravo, and I would then go to the embassy once a week. They even had a room for us with a huge fan, a maid for us. We would joke that we were in the big leagues now. We had an office!" The group worked there for about a year until that embassy was closed as well.

Padilla used to say, "This whole thing of the passports is real bullshit. My wife, my children, my whole family is now in Miami. I am the only asshole here, because one day they are going to send me to jail. And I know it. And it means more to me to be making these passports than to be there with them."[2]

Padilla could fake perfectly the signature of Philip Bonsal, the last U.S. consul in Cuba. This signature would go on passports. Polita would sign as Walter O. Fung, an embassy functionary. Mongo had Father Walsh's signature down pat for the visa waivers. And it was a good thing he did, because when visas had not come in or more were needed than were available, the group would make them in a Thermofax copying machine. "We would make a slot and inset a typed name in it, and make a copy," says Mongo. His statement is confirmed by his chauffeur and collaborator, Emilio Molina, who would help in the copying and often drive wanted persons to rendezvous.

After the U.S. embassy closed its doors, an official had given someone the embassy's visa stamp. Somehow, Mongo and his group acquired it, and with predated relevant information, passports were stamped with genuine exit visas and "signed" by the consul.

Embassies, especially Latin American ones, played a very important role in the Cuban underground movement by sheltering activities under their diplomatic shield. Panama, Uruguay, Britain,* and Holland were some of those that helped. "They helped a lot, but they also got paid in many instances. It was not

---

* Phillip Brice, who worked at the British embassy in Cuba, initially agreed to discuss his embassy's involvement, then refused an interview.

all charity work," says Alicia Thomas. Indeed, among the exile community there are countless tales of people who had jewelry, papers, heirlooms, or art taken out of the country by friendly embassy personnel. Payment was sometimes required. There are many sad tales of objects never again seen by their owners after being entrusted to embassy personnel.

In contrast, the underground group never accepted money for their work. Alicia Thomas remembers receiving in her home a woman sent by America Nuñez Portuondo. After the woman, who was requesting two visas, left, Alicia realized she had left behind an envelope. Alicia ran after her, catching up to her as she was getting into her car. "You've left an envelope behind," she told the woman, who replied, "No, that is for you." When Alicia peeked inside the envelope, she saw that there was money; she told the woman, "We don't do this for money. I can't take this."

Polita last saw Penny Powers, the link to the original operation, one day when Penny drove up, presented her with a then scarce hen, and told her, "Here is a hen for Mongo. I am afraid."

An insider had turned them in. "We knew that this would explode somehow. We knew we were followed, but what were we to do?" says Alicia Thomas. "But since they were trying to round up everyone involved, they gave us plenty of rope, and we kept doing our work."

Alicia's husband Manolo was imprisoned first. When Alicia went to tell Mongo that her husband had been taken prisoner, he said, "Well, what is to be done? Go home and be quiet." They arrested Mongo on January 21, 1965. He was released on September 15, 1986.

Alicia Thomas was arrested on January 2, 1965. She was released and picked up a week later. Alicia was charged with Delito 100, or Crime 100, against the integrity and stability of a nation. She was case number 538; more than 500 persons had been picked up since January 1. Alicia was released in 1970. She left Cuba in 1980. She did not see her daughter Alicita, who was in the United States, for nineteen years.

Polita was arrested soon afterward. She was in jail for fourteen

years. Sara del Toro de Odio was arrested in October 1961 and released in 1967.

Beatriz López Morton worked for a CIA operative and was on the CIA payroll. After being detained for three days, she became a double agent working for both the CIA and the G2, but she gave the G2 innocuous information. Finally, in 1963, she was spirited out of Cuba in a clandestine operation involving hiding in mangroves on the coast of Cuba for three days until she was picked up by an American mother ship. She was taken to a safe house in Miami where she was debriefed. Unbeknownst to her, a bank account awaited her as payment for her CIA work.

Emilio Molina, Mongo's chauffeur, was also arrested in 1965 and spent seven years in jail out of the fifteen he had been sentenced to for "conspiring against the powers of the state." He left Cuba in 1974. Ironically, he had sent his eight-year-old son out of Cuba alone. He saw him again when the boy was twenty years old. "I recognized him only because he had sent me photographs of himself." Emilio cries remembering the moment they embraced again.

Penny Powers died in Cuba, a frail old woman. Before her death she had received a much-needed wheelchair from the Operation Pedro Pan Group, whose members are the same children she had aided more than thirty years earlier.

Sitting in her low-income apartment for the elderly in Miami, Polita recounts a recent incident. "I was walking in downtown Miami when this woman approaches me and says, 'Aren't you Polita Grau?' And she points to her son, a grown man accompanying her and says, 'Look, you helped me bring my boy out.' This is such a wonderful feeling for me. The same thing happened in a restaurant. This time it was a very emotional woman, and she brought me her two daughters. I would do everything all over again," says Polita, adding with a smile, "But perhaps I would be a bit more discreet."

CHAPTER 5

The Temporary Shelters
in Miami

The volunteer approached the little girl at Miami International Airport and noticed a sign pinned to her dress. It read, "My name is Carmen Gomez.* I am five years old. Please be good to me." Taking the little girl's hand, Mrs. Margarita Oteisa tried to imagine the pain and fear her parents must have felt when they put their little girl on that Miami-bound airplane. Mrs. Oteisa had been a teacher in Cuba and had worked for James Baker at the Ruston Academy in Havana, where she had also distributed visas. Once in Miami, James Baker knew he could count on her love of children and recruited her as a volunteer to pick up youngsters at the airport.

Miami International Airport was a frightening place for the recently separated children. "We arrived at Miami airport and I started crying because there was nobody there to meet us!" says

---

* a pseudonym

Iraida Iturralde. She and her sister Virginia, aged seven and twelve respectively, started asking for the next plane to return to Cuba.

"This man approached us and started asking, 'Do you want chewing gum? Do you want chewing gum?' And I thought, 'Is this guy nuts?' As if chewing gum was going to replace ...'" Iraida's voice trails off as if remembering the loss of a family and homeland that befell her in one fell swoop. Many children share the memory of being offered gum, an item no longer available in Cuba, by airport officials upon their arrival. "We were at the airport for what seems hours and were taken to Florida City."

Arriving unaccompanied, refugee children faced two destinies: either they were claimed by family or friends, as half of them were, or they went to temporary shelters until permanent homes were found for them.

"When I got into the airplane and everybody said good-bye to me, all of a sudden I felt there was an emptiness in me," says then eleven-year-old Marlene Fiero,* remembering that somber January 6, 1962. For years, Marlene couldn't talk about her departure from Cuba without crying. She claims that over the years talking about that dark period has helped. However, a tear sliding down her cheek betrays her denial. As an only child, she had grown up very sheltered and protected by her family in Cuba.

"I felt that I was alone in the plane and I was really afraid of where I was going. I didn't know anything about the United States," she says. "So, when I got to the airport in Miami I realized that there were a lot of kids like me. There were about fourteen or fifteen of us, and they herded us together and put us in these little vans and took us away and all of a sudden I felt like I was lost, and I thought, 'Oh my Lord I don't have anybody here.'"

But there was someone there for the children whose full-time job was picking up the youths arriving on any of the Havana–Miami flights and delivering them to the camps—George

---

* a pseudonym

Guarch, who was once described by the *New York Times* as tall, dour, and not beyond smashing a photographer's camera.[1] The story, however, didn't mention the expanse of his endless compassion.

The children, although alone, did have their instructions. Many were told by their parents before getting on the plane that when they landed, they should "ask for George." One child recalls that he thought they were talking about George Washington, the only George he knew. But this George, who was really named "Jorge," was Cuban. He had lived in the United States since 1947. He had met Louise Cooper, a social worker he knew from Miami's Catholic Welfare, at the airport and volunteered to help her take some children in his station wagon. Soon, his job as a volunteer became a full-time, paid job. "He worked the whole day up until the night, midnight every day, in and out, in and out," says Peggy Guarch, George's widow. "I never knew when he would be home."

George had clearance to meet the children before the airport's immigration area. The Guarch family conveniently lived five minutes from the airport. Sometimes when the flights would back up, George would take the children home to Peggy while he picked up the next group. Other times, the Guarchs provided them shelter: "Sometimes there was just no room for the children and he would bring them here. I would put two couches together, we would put our children's mattresses on the floor, and our children would sleep in the box springs."

George's commitment to his role was never-ending, whether he was finding children shelter or offering them advice. His daughter Lynn remembered, "He had a little talk that he would give the kids when he got them into the van. He would tell them they were safe now, but that their parents had sent them here and that they had to make their parents proud."

Rafael Yaniz, then sixteen, fondly remembers asking George for a cigarette and getting some solid economic advice instead: "Don't give away the liquor or the cigars you brought with you.

Sell them because you are going to need the money." Many of the children exited Cuba with the allotted three bottles of liquor and two boxes of cigars.

One day after George delivered the children, a boy could not be located among the different camps. Peggy remembers that after locating him, George, in order to prevent another such incident, started a log with the arrival date, name of child, birth date, visa type, and where he or she went. This log grew into a huge loose-leaf binder book, where the children today eagerly look themselves up.

While George managed airport arrivals, there remained the unending problem of finding lodging for all the children. Father Walsh had been dealing with a housing shortage from the first day the children started arriving on December 26, 1960. At that moment he had nine beds available for six- to twelve-year-olds at a home run by the Sisters of St. Joseph. Assumption Academy also had space for 200 children during the holidays, until January 6. As he scurried around Miami trying to find permanent beds for the arrivals, Father Walsh located an empty governmental facility, at Kendall, which was no longer used as a home for dependent black children. The government rented it for $1 a year.

The Ferré Home

Father Walsh approached Maurice Ferré, who later became mayor of Miami from 1973–1985 but in 1961 was an enthusiastic twenty-six year old. His father owned several properties around Biscayne Bay, and young Maurice intervened on Father Walsh's behalf asking for the use of one. Maurice explains, "I said to him, 'Dad, for the $200 or $300 rent we can get for those houses, why don't we help these poor people?' and he immediately acceded." The house was located at 175 SE 15th Road, one-half block from Biscayne Bay, and which is now the swank Costa Bella Condominium.

Father Walsh decided to use the Ferré home, as it was first called, to house teenage boys. Governmental clearances from the zoning, health, fire, and building departments had to be secured for these two locations.[2] "As I drove home, the enormity of the task ahead slowly dawned on me. What would we do if all 200 arrived within the next couple of days? There would not be time to gear up the program, open up the buildings at Kendall, hire the necessary staff," recalled Father Walsh in his article on Cuban refugee children.[3]

On December 26, the first children arrived, and they went to St. Joseph's. On December 29, the first boys moved into the Ferré home, now stocked with borrowed bunk beds, chairs, and tables.[4]

"My wife and I actually cleaned the first house, Cuban Boys Home [as the Ferré house was officially named, although it would also be known as Casa Carrión after houseparents Ángel and Nina Carrión], a couple of days before the boys were expected in," remembers Ray McCraw, a social worker who worked with Father Walsh at Catholic Charities:

> We got beds out of what became Camp Matecumbe, but it was then a day camp for Catholic boys from all over the archdiocese. My brother and I went and got the beds and we rented a truck, took the cots and took them to this first house, and put them up. Then my wife and I cleaned it, and then we went to the Red Cross where we got bars of soap, towels, wash towels, and toothbrushes and put one on each bunk for each one of the youngsters coming in. So when they'd come in that night, everything was pretty well ready for them.
>
> There was a girls' high school down the street, I guess it was the Dominicans, a very private, a very wealthy school. They agreed that our boys could go down there and eat. So they would walk down and they'd have breakfast there, until they got into a routine.

Temporary aid for Cuban refugees, including the care and protection of the Cuban unaccompanied children, became reality when the Florida State Department of Public Welfare signed an agreement on February 21, 1961. The agreement provided for the use of federal funds to carry out the plan.[5] By February 1, 174 children had arrived.[6] The government made money for the program available by the middle of February, by which time Monsignor Walsh says they were $100,000 in debt, which is equivalent to $536,607.12 in 1997 dollars.

On March 1, contracts were signed between the Florida Department of Public Welfare as agent for the U.S. Department of Health, Education, and Welfare and Florida child welfare agencies. These agencies were the Catholic Welfare Bureau, the Children's Service Bureau of Dade County, the Jewish Family and Children's Service, and the United Hebrew Immigrant Aid Society (HIAS).[7] The Jewish Family and Children's Service placed Cuban Jewish children in Miami, while the United HIAS Service took over the placement of Cuban Jewish children outside Miami. The 391 unaccompanied Jewish children who arrived under the program were resettled in forty communities in twenty-three states, Puerto Rico, and the District of Columbia.[8] The Catholic Welfare Bureau and the Children's Service Bureau of Dade County placed children both in and outside Miami.

During the next few years, as housing needs for the children changed, different shelters would open and close. By March 1962 the Miami Unaccompanied Children's Program under the Catholic Welfare Bureau had expanded to employ 300 persons, including 21 priests, social workers, doctors, office personnel, cooks, social workers, drivers, and others.[9]

CAMP MATECUMBE

Matecumbe was a Native American chief of a tribe that inhabited the Florida Keys and for whom the upper and lower Matecumbe Keys were named. Camp Matecumbe, a temporary shelter for teenage Cuban boys, was a true wilderness paradise to some and a "green hell" to others. When the first group of teenage boys arrived, they were greeted by an Olympic-size swimming pool, more than 150 acres of slash pine trees, and four wood cabins housing twenty bunk beds each. World War II tents were added to provide additional sleeping quarters. Because there were no lockers for some of the tents, those occupants had to keep their clothes in their suitcases. For the lucky few who did have lockers had to share.

There was nothing in the vicinity of 13700 SW 120th Street except miles and miles of tomato fields. Orlando recalls his amazement. "I had a very big surprise. It was a very hard day for me when I saw what Matecumbe really was. I thought it was a school, I thought it was something different." Orlando had friends from his hometown of Artemisa already at Matecumbe, and they had never told anyone of the bleak reality of the place. This was a common trait among most children, who proved to be mature beyond their years because they tried to spare their parents additional anguish.

Upon arrival, Rafael Carvajal was separated from his younger brother, who was sent to Florida City. Driving to Matecumbe, he remembers seeing cars that looked like futuristic rocket ships, actually late-model cars that he had not seen in Cuba. The gloomy surrounding that enveloped his new home made a bleak impression on him. "It was like the end of the world to me. Pitch black." Upon arrival he was ushered into one of the tents, which in the early days were lit by kerosene lamps.

The group of new boys arrived with suitcases under their arms and fear written on their faces. They were greeted by one of the boys who drew a line on the floor and said, "Only those who are real men will dare cross this line." They all looked at each other wondering, "Do we or don't we?" And Rafael thought to himself, "Hell, I've already been through a lot in Cuba. I don't care if they kill me in a beating." So he crossed the line only to be

hugged by the adversary and congratulated. "You are a real man," he told him. But he remembers one boy that didn't cross the line. He would get slapped around daily.

An initiation ritual many newcomers experienced was a dunking in the pool—fully clothed. Rafael again lucked out. "Before I was thrown in, George came and took me to his home where I had dinner, and then he took me to my godmother's house who was a friend of his."

Father Francisco Palá was the first administrator of Camp Matecumbe when the camp opened in July 1961. He remembers the camp as about 50 acres of woods and weeds. "We had fifteen to eighteen year olds, the most troublesome. The camp's capacity was for about 100 and we had about 500 there. We used tents, and when it rained, everything flooded. We had a couple of showers, and that was it. We built a new building, but that took some time."

Orlando Conde experienced a different kind of shower firsthand. The night of his arrival, it rained and leaked right through his tent and over his bed. His sadness and silent crying coupled with the water dripping on him kept him awake his entire first night in America.

On future nights, other things would keep him awake: "There were wildcats, snakes. The wildcats would come into the tent and if we were sleeping it was fine, but if someone woke up and the screaming started then the cat would get confused and couldn't find his way out and attack."

Screaming and chaos reigned other nights when the boys would play "Playa Girón," a game named for the Bay of Pigs invasion. If someone yelled "Playa Girón," shoes, replacing artillery, would start flying all over the place.

One boy remembers another type of midnight assault: occasional unwanted midnight sexual predators in your bed. "There were some cases of boys with homosexual problems," said José Prince, then a live-in twenty-one-year-old counselor. "We had to stop not only the behavior, but also the scandal that the others made out of it. We tried talking to them, but if that didn't work, they were handed over to the counselors." Carvajal remembers one such case in which the boy was taken out of Matecumbe, but not before being beaten up by the other boys. He remembers the boy, nicknamed *conejito*, or little rabbit, saying, "I don't know why you are beating me up when some of you have been intimate with me."

Each boy had to adapt to many new situations. Some had it easier than others. Rafael Yaniz remembers a boy arriving who had silk pajamas and robe and who was given a cot to sleep on since all bunk beds were occupied. The boy said that in Cuba even his dogs had beds, and that he wasn't sleeping in a cot. "He slept in a chair for three or four nights with an incredible air of dignity about him until a bunk bed was available," remembers Rafael.

Food became an issue for many of the boys. For a Cuban teenager, breakfast would typically consist of *café con leche* (expresso coffee with a lot of hot milk) and toasted Cuban bread that is somewhat like French bread. Eating cold milk with cereal was not something they were used to, and they had to adjust. Cubans are not known for eating vegetables. In fact, a typical Cuban dinner consists of meat and two starches such as rice and potatoes. Onions, garlic, and spices such as cumin and oregano are used liberally in Cuban kitchens. American meals of bland meat and potatoes and vegetables were not appealing or satisfying. Sometimes the boys went hungry, and they tended to raid the pantry at night. "We locked up the refrigerators but on several occasions they forced them open," said José Prince. "We found out about a specific boy and held an informal hearing about the matter. The teenager explained that he was hungry and there was no other place to go and get food. There were small incidents, small thefts, some fights, but nothing major."

Harold "Mac" Maguire worked for Crotty Brothers Florida,

Inc., the company that supplied food to the shelters. He started work in July 1961 and worked with the program until 1967. He explained how he would go to the various shelters every day. "At the beginning we had 125 children, but a couple of months later the population increased; sometimes 125 arrived in one night, so we had quite a struggle feeding them," he says. Luckily, the purveyor was responsive. Mac would call, report the shortages, and they would go right out with more food. At the beginning the food was American, but when it didn't seem to satisfy the boys, they changed it to Cuban fare. "I set up the menu but we worked with dieticians. I had eighty-two Cuban cooks and handymen working for me. We were allowed $1.37 a day to feed them. Remember, at that time chickens were twelve cents a pound. The most expensive thing we were serving was Uncle Ben's rice at eighteen cents a pound, because they wouldn't eat government rice. Brussels sprouts had to be taken off the menu. They drank a lot of Tang because it had Vitamin C."

Quantities of food used by the program in the first two years:*

	1961	1962
Total Meats	41,724 lbs.	271,565
Fish	3,099 lbs.	36,902
Milk	78,168 qts.	466,929
Bread	25,457 loaves	154,200
Pastry	18,329 dozen	87,226
Eggs	3,944 dozen	17,025
Cheese	1,597 lbs.	12,069
Butter	2,702 lbs.	25,507
Ice Cream	1,886 gal.	6,143
Fruits & Veg.	41,212 lbs.	165,073
Coffee	1,558 lbs.	2,710
Rice	4,600 lbs.	48,580
Sugar	4,800 lbs.	36,380

---

* Crotty Brothers Florida, Inc., 1961, 1962

	1961	**1962**
Juice	116,974 qts.	119,417
Prepared Cereal		287,300 1oz. pks.
Salt		1,874 lbs.
Jelly		2,340 #10 cans
Oil		1,000 gal.
Shortening		2,507 lbs.
Beans		23,315 lbs.
Condiments (pickles, mustard, etc.)		1,353 gal.

As is fairly typical of teenage boys, the boys at Camp Matecumbe were easily bored. To kill time they would swim or play basketball, but their options were limited. Some chose to explore the woods. Rafael Carvajal, who now views himself as having been a nonconformist at the time, explains that he had built a little shack in the woods, as had three or four other boys. To kill time and avoid classes they would visit each other's shacks. "After breakfast, I would run off into the woods. We would get $1.50 a week, but if you missed classes, you'd be fined. I never got the entire $1.50."

Ray McCraw, the social worker who had been transferred to Matecumbe, explains: "I used to worry about them and say, 'Hey, come on, guys, don't go running through the woods with bare feet . . . you know, a hundred of those little things are out there, like scorpions.' Coming from Cuba they didn't realize about rattlesnakes, and all the funny little things we have in our forests around here. They used to call it 'infierno verde,' or green hell, because of the green pine trees all around." It wasn't unusual to run off to the hospital or the Serpentarium for an antidote for a snakebite.

Education was important for the children on many levels. First, they needed to become more familiar with American culture. Second, it was an opportunity to socialize in a more structured environment with adult supervision. Third, for those who wanted to learn, it alleviated boredom that comes from unstructured

time. As administrator, Father Palá talked to Father Walsh about opening a school. English classes were agreed upon, knowing they would be very useful to the children outside the camp.

Margarita Oteisa started working in Matecumbe, teaching English, in September 1961. Although she didn't even have a room in which to teach, she compensated with a lot of enthusiasm. She nailed a sign that read "Mrs. Oteisa" on a pine tree, and outdoor classes commenced. Her pupils attentively sat on old bleachers, not just because they wanted to learn their new country's language but also because Mrs. Oteisa, a strikingly beautiful brunette widow, was the main attraction. Sometimes she would see, among her pupils, boys that belonged in another teacher's class. "They must have thought I was scatterbrained and didn't notice, but I'd rather have them in my class than running around," she explained. After some time, Mrs. Oteisa finally managed to get a blackboard, which she kept in the trunk of her car, together with the few books she could get her hands on.

She also recalls:

> I would drive into the camp's dirt road in the mornings and you would hear a bellow, "Mrs. Oteisa's safari," and they would come out of the woods like ants. They would then go to my car, take out the blackboard and books and we'd settle on the bleachers for our lessons. If it rained, we sat inside the bus.
>
> One day they put a snake inside my car, but since I knew who had placed it there, I knew it could not be poisonous. So I grabbed it and handed it to the boy standing next to me as I told him, "I think you forgot this." Needless to say, they never bothered me with a snake again.

To get to Camp Matecumbe, Mrs. Oteisa would drive down South Dixie Highway entering from 17th Avenue. Every Monday, she would pick up boys who had spent the weekend with relatives and had "missed" the bus Sunday night. She knew that they knew she would give them a ride Monday morning, and she didn't have a problem allowing them to enjoy a few extra hours of freedom.

Upon arrival at Camp Matecumbe, the teenagers were given a list with eleven rules. The first rule reminded them that they were in a temporary situation and would be relocated somewhere else in the United States. The second stated that while in camp they were subject to all the disciplinary norms of the camp. Other rules concerned: the weekend outing schedule (Fridays 4:00 to 8:00 P.M., Saturdays 9:00 A.M. to midnight, and Sundays 9:00 A.M. to 8:00 P.M.), mandatory class attendance, mandatory daily shower, mandatory Sunday Mass, and no phone calls to Cuba from camp phones. The last rule expressed confidence that the boys would follow the rules. However, if they were broken, the penalties were that the weekly allowance could be debited or even eliminated, or the weekend pass suspended.

On weekends, the boys were taken on an hour-long bus ride to downtown Miami, where they had a day of leisure. Rafael Carvajal remembers, "I would get my weekend passes suspended regularly, so I would sneak into the bus with a fictitious name, Ángel Ramos or whatever. They didn't notice." The ride from Matecumbe to downtown took more than an hour back then. They would leave around 8:00 A.M. to be picked up at 5:00 P.M.

One profitable, if illegal, pastime was grinding down pennies on the rough cement until the size of dimes, and then using them in the soda machines or pay phones. Carvajal remembers a very tall guy, nicknamed Horqueta, or Beanpole, had the procedure down pat. He had a clamp and a metal file and would do it very quickly. "He would do five pennies and keep one as payment."

Carvajal remembers another teenage prank with amusement: "Remember those Coca Cola machines with the doors?"

he inquired. "We would take a bottle opener and pry them open, pour what flowed out into a glass and then sip the rest with a straw, right from the machine."

Orlando Conde recalled how he used to escape and go join the Mexican migrant laborers in the nearby tomato fields in order to make some money, even though this was forbidden. "I picked up a lot of tomatoes. I paid for my parents' visas by picking tomatoes. We weren't supposed to do it, but we would sneak away. We would show up at the plantations where we would be welcomed and get paid fifteen cents per basket."

Despite the occasional boredom, the isolation, and the less than ideal conditions, staying in Matecumbe was important to the boys. They wanted to stay in the Miami area because it was close to Cuba and their families. Also, they preferred the known hardships to the unfamiliar. Letters that came into camp from those who had left often told nightmarish tales from orphanages, frigid temperatures, and loneliness.

While Matecumbe wasn't perfect by any means, it was preferable to the alternative. "They would write to me," says Margarita Oteisa. "Sometimes they were beautiful letters about the kindness of a foster family. Or 'I have a bad scholarship,'* please Mrs. Oteisa, try to get me out of here.' I would immediately take such a letter to the social worker, but frankly, once they were gone . . . Bad scholarships were horrifying."

Everyone knew that the camp offered temporary housing until more permanent accommodations could be found for each child. Once you were assigned a departure date and destination, it was set in stone. Room had to be made for the constant flow of new arrivals. A group of enterprising young men decided there was no way that they would leave. Orlando was among them. He arrived in June 1961 as a bewildered thirteen year old and managed to stay until almost the last days of Camp Matecumbe in 1964. By then, he was a savvy seventeen year old.

---

* Relocations were known as *becas,* or scholarships.

He tells how he managed to stay: "What I would do is I would run away a day before or two days before I was to leave, I would escape. Let them look for me and find me if they could! I had friends in Miami and I would stay with them. Monday mornings, or when the danger was over, I would show up at the barber's home or the chauffeur's and they would drive me back. So what could they do, punish me, or withhold the weekly allowance? That was okay with me if I avoided the trip."

Orlando's motivation to stay was that he wanted to get his parents out of Cuba and he thought Miami provided more opportunities; it provided more tomato picking and funds. "I applied [for his parents exit permits] through various places, I wrote to Mrs. Jackie Kennedy several times telling her that I was alone and wanted to have my parents with me."

Although he did not get a reply from Mrs. Kennedy, Orlando's persistence paid off. He explains, "When they were trading medicine for people my parents came, in the last boat. I always, always, always kept my hopes up that they were coming, escaping in a boat or however. I never gave up. And the social workers finally gave up on trying to relocate me out of Matecumbe."

Camp Matecumbe underwent some changes in the years it was open. A lake was dredged, and a huge gymnasium was built and the bunk beds placed within. The brothers from La Salle, a school in Cuba, took over the camp and improved the schooling by adding courses. The tents became classrooms. There was even an accredited graduating class of Matecumbe High. "The La Salle brothers were wonderful," remembers Ray McCraw. "How they got those kids into tents in the middle of the summer, when the heat was coming off those tents, and keep coming in there and teach them. It was amazing! I would go and sit in the back of a tent just to get the experience and the feeling. To see those kids concentrate in the heat! And when it got so hot that they couldn't bear it, then they had the swimming pool."

Matecumbe left indelible memories on all the teenagers who transited through its doors. It also left most of them with

nicknames that they still use when referring to each other. Carvajal's was The Camel, given to him by Father Maximiliano because he walked with slouched shoulders or a hump. Mosquito, Snake, the Seal, and Cut-Face are others.

"There have been two types of reaction to Matecumbe," says Margarita Oteisa. "There was the reaction that Matecumbe bonded them and they even have reunions; perhaps these were the most sensible ones. For others, it was so horrible, the separation from their parents, that they have wanted to erase all memory of Matecumbe. It was too painful."

SAINT RAPHAEL HALL

The Cuban Home for Boys on SW 15th Road operated until September 1961, when Father Walsh and the boys moved to Saint Raphael's, and Jesuit Brothers took over the Cuban Home for Boys. It then became known as the Jesuits' Boys' Home, or Whitehall, and housed twenty boys. Father Jesus Nuevo ran the home. Both St. Raphael's and the Jesuits' Boys' Home were different from the other shelters in that they were not run as transient shelters; those that got a place in either stayed there until parental arrival.

The newly opened Saint Raphael's was the Ritz Hotel of the shelters in Miami. Places there were very coveted and a source of much jealousy among the boys. This was an apartment building with an ideal location in an urban setting on 325 NE 21st Street, by Biscayne Boulevard, and close enough to downtown Miami that the boys could walk there. Other features that made it attractive was that there were only eighty boys, divided into groups of twenty under the supervision of eight sets of married Cuban foster parents.

According to Jorge Finlay, who resided there from the time it opened until the facility closed, "Saint Raphael's was so nice. It had no gates or fences. You could stroll around, as long as you

were back for dinner." The boys would play basketball or football in the parking lot, which was empty most of the time.

Monsignor Walsh recruited Ray McCraw to work at Saint Raphael's. "I was totally impressed with the boys' study habits. My goodness, they would sit for literally hours studying, and I mean studying—no horsing around or anything. They wouldn't stop until they finished what they set out to do. I was amazed, but evidently their parents had instilled this in them in Cuba, and then when they came here they promised their parents that they would get an education, and boy, they did." The boys were distributed among Archbishop Curly, La Salle, and Belén high schools.

Since Monsignor Walsh lived at St. Raphael's, he also brought along Alicia Honen, then fifty, to be his housekeeper and assistant. She was nicknamed *Abuela,* or grandmother, by the boys and was in charge of buying their clothes and taking them shopping. She says St. Raphael became her life. "They were extremely loving toward me. They suffered, and we did along with them; but we also had good times. Monsignor didn't want them to feel they were in a school ambiance. They were a family. Monsignor would eat with them, Cuban food, everything there was Cuban."

As in all families, there were disciplinary problems for which Monsignor had a fail-safe method: the paddle. "There was the famous paddle," says Willy Chirino. "It was an act of discipline, but it was also like a joke to get the paddle from the priest. The others would wonder, 'Wow, what must he have done?' But it was always deserved. Children sometimes test adults to see how far they can go. And that was the case with Father Walsh. *El cura* [or the priest], as all the boys called him, was an extraordinary man. I hardly ever saw him angry and when I did, it was because of a disciplinary problem. He was always in a good mood, cracking a joke, or offering a kind word." Rafael Yaniz never got the paddle. He said that Father Walsh always offered choices and Rafael seemed to have made the right decision. He explains, "You chose your punishment. You could choose not to go out on

the weekend, or forfeit your weekly allowance. Monsignor never hit a child needlessly. As a matter of fact, we would gang up on him on the beach and tumble with him, and he was the one who would get beaten up."

Yaniz chose to have his money taken away instead of the paddle because he had a side business washing cars, as many as fourteen or fifteen a week. "Hey mister, I wash you car," he would tell those parking in the medical office building next door. When Walsh found out why he didn't care about having his allowance forfeited, his punishments changed to no car washing for a week when applicable.

Father Walsh made it a practice of walking through the whole house whenever he would come in. "Monsignor could walk into a room and we'd pretend to be asleep. He'd know you weren't. When asked how he knew we weren't asleep he'd say, 'You sleep on your side or you put your feet like this.' He was amazing. He knew how we all slept!" remembers Finlay. Father Walsh made it his business to know each and every child at Saint Raphael until he could read their expressions and would eventually even learn to speak Spanish. Father Walsh recalls that he would tell them they had *una cara culpable,* or a guilty face. To this day they approach him and tell him, "Remember cara culpable."

On weekends he would take some boys out on his sailboat. "He had a group of favorites, those who had earned his trust," remembers Chirino. "I was lucky to have been one of them on certain occasions." Word of these outings got to the boys of Matecumbe who resented *el cura* and St. Raphael even more.

Rafael Yaniz's love for Walsh is apparent. He calls him the "second St. Patrick." The relationship was cemented when Yaniz was chosen to go to St. Raphael's and he refused, saying that he would not go without his brother. Walsh promised him that if Yaniz proved himself to be well behaved, he would bring in his brother as soon as there was an opening. And he kept that promise.

"To me, he was a second father. He is a saint. But more than a priest, I like the fact he is an executive," Yaniz explains. "A child never went without food or clothing. He never asked anyone if you had received communion or had attended Mass. On Sundays some kids would taunt him by saying, 'I don't feel like going to Mass.' He would reply, 'That is between you and God. However, you are not having breakfast until we all come back from church.'"

Yaniz tells of how when they returned from Mass and everyone would sit for breakfast, Father Walsh would tell the strayed sheep to remember that there was a later Mass at Gesu Church downtown. "It wasn't the mentality of a priest who would call you a sinner and scold you. He was more effective this way. Usually the boy would get on the bus and go to the later Mass."

Abuela Alicia Honan remembers a day when they received the news of the death of a boy's father. Monsignor arrived at lunchtime and, upon hearing the news, went upstairs to talk to the boy. An hour later, he came down and told me, "Alicia, let him cry, let him cry." She went upstairs and gave him a small towel for his tears. "It was a very sad day," she says.

On a Cuban April Fool's Day, or All Innocent's Day, December 28, the boys pulled the fire alarm at 6:00 A.M. The fireman arrived and a big commotion ensued. Yaniz remembers that the following Friday, when it was time for the allowance, the boys noticed that there were coins inside the envelope that usually contained two $1 bills. They were delighted thinking they had a raise, until they opened it and realized there was $1.75. "April fools," said Walsh. "The fire department's fine for the false alarm cost me $200 which will be deducted from your paycheck until you pay for it." He always had a way of making everyone accountable for their actions and the punishment always fit the crime.

KENDALL CHILDREN'S HOME

On January 1961, as the Cuban children started to arrive, Father Walsh had rented the institutional grounds of the Dade County

Welfare Department, which had room for 140 children. But who was going to run Kendall, as the facility had been named after the neighborhood where it was located at SW 76th Street and 107th Avenue? Providence intervened during one of his runs collecting children at the airport. Father Walsh saw a Piarist priest disembark and approached him. Walsh asked him what his plans in the United States were. The priest replied that he had not left Cuba willingly and if he could help Cubans in any way he would. The next day he was working at Kendall. This priest sent other Piarist priests in Cuba the necessary dollars for their airline tickets, and they too went to work at Kendall upon their arrival. Among them was Father Francisco Palá, who would head the soon-to-be opened and much larger Camp Matecumbe.

"I was terrified of that place. They were old barracks. We lived in bunk beds," says Ana Gema Lopo, then thirteen, who arrived in Kendall with her sister Lourdes, then eleven. "I remember it was Mother's Day, and we all went to bed and someone started crying and I started crying, since it was the first Mother's Day away from our mothers. Before you knew it, the whole entire floor was crying. Oh, it was so awful! Some little girls came over and held other little girls, it was the saddest thing."

Not everyone was as lucky as Ana, who had her sister with her and a bed in which to sleep. Roberto Zaldivar remembers being separated from his brother, due to their age difference, and asked whether he wanted to sleep in the laundry or the social worker's office. Since another boy had requested the laundry, Zaldivar headed off to the social worker's office. "Not finding any beds, I inquired where we were going to sleep. 'In cots,' I was told. We had to prepare them ourselves. I had never set up a cot, but that night I learned. We had to put a small mattress with sheets on top and a pillow. Our *gusanos* had to be left on the hallway and we had to keep and eye on them, so others would not open them." Sleeping arrangements were by seniority with the new arrivals being closest to the door and getting walked over as others entered or exited the room. "You prayed for seniority so you could have the back of the room," he says.

Another boy remembers the lack of privacy being the most difficult circumstance for him. "To take a shower you had to get in line, nude, and do it fast. Therefore, I did not shower until I went out on weekends. The same thing happened with the toilets. There was no privacy, so I did not defecate until I went out on weekends. I would hold it in."

On January 25, 1963, *The Voice*, a Catholic newspaper reported that 134 young men who were living in Kendall had moved to the Naval Air Base of Opa-locka. For many months the teenage boys had been living and attending classes in overcrowded quarters in Kendall where two main buildings and a small classroom building were loaned to the Catholic Welfare Bureau by the Dade County Welfare Department. Facilities of the Kendall Children's Home were formally returned to Dade County Welfare Director Joseph R. Ems by Walsh.

FLORIDA CITY

Florida City, opened in October 1961, was the largest shelter, one that would house girls of all ages and boys under twelve. Of all the shelters, it was the farthest from downtown Miami, about 35 miles south, and was run by the Sisters of St. Phillip Neri from Spain and administered by Father Salvador De Cistierna.

The compound of two-story buildings, which was licensed to accommodate 700 children, was surrounded by chain-link fence so the children could play safely in the streets. A nylon tent was set up for celebrating Mass. It was also used for playing or dancing and provided the children shelter from the Florida sun. The quaint town of Homestead, located in an agricultural area, was nearby, as was Homestead Air Force Base. A small nearby park provided the children with some diversion. An innovative setup was created in this shelter, allowing the children to live in apartments under the supervision of Cuban couples, which created a more homelike atmosphere.

Isabel and Raúl Rodríguez-Wallings, who had both been lawyers in Cuba, became foster parents at Florida City. They remember a time when there were as many as forty-two sets of foster parents. The Rodríguez-Wallingses took care of girls, starting out with eight in a three-bedroom cottage: two rooms for the girls and one for them. "Some nights we had as many as twenty, and then we would put out folding cots," remembers Isabel.

Arrivals in Florida City were more welcomed and accepted than were arrivals at Matecumbe. "The girls really helped each other out and were very kind to the new arrivals, sometimes giving up their own beds," says Isabel. The new refugee children were first taken to an administrative office, where their papers and health certificates were examined. When necessary, immunizations were given. Once the paperwork and other adminstrative tasks were complete, the children would be assigned to a foster family.

Foster parenting was a twenty-four-hour-a-day, six-day-a-week job, with one day off when other substituting foster parents would take over. The Rodríguez-Wallingses recall getting paid $150 a month each; however, the Pérez Planas remember being paid $225 for both of them, certainly not a lot of money for such long hours. But it was a job that fulfilled a newly arrived refugee couple's basic needs: housing, food, and an income.

Children were required to eat with their foster parents in the overflowing cafeteria that sometimes had three seatings for breakfast, three for lunch, and three for dinner. One Christmas Eve, however, they had a celebration during which everyone sat together and tables were put out on the street in order to accommodate everyone. Suddenly, the temperature dropped to 30 degrees, and although the roast pork and black beans grew cold, they were nevertheless gladly eaten.

Foster parents undertook many responsibilities beyond those of caretakers. They tried to provide a loving family atmosphere while helping the children to be responsible. Isabel Rodríguez-Wallings undertook the task of teaching them to save money. "The children would get two dollars a week and some girls would save it all for their parents' arrival. I opened bank accounts for them at the town of Homestead. When they had eight or ten dollars, we'd put it in the bank. I remember a fifteen year old who saved $60 this way. I remember another who would spend it all on stamps. She wrote letters to every family member and friend she had in Cuba."

Administrative orders were given for the girls to clean their sleeping areas, bathroom, and living room. Some houseparents, who used to spoil the girls and do the work for them, were scolded by the administrator, who believed the girls had to learn. "We got a black girl and I told her, 'Tomorrow is your turn to clean,'" says Isabel. "She said, 'I'm not the maid,' so I explained that I wasn't either, that there were no maids here and we all had to do it or no one would do it for us." However, that wasn't entirely true. There were others who, for a small fee, would do chores. Mrs. Pérez Plana remembers one such enterprising girl who would charge two cents for doing household chores others didn't want to do.

Two Cuban psychologists, José Ignacio Lasaga and his wife, Ageda Demestre, were assigned to the children. Ageda went every Wednesday to Florida City. "One day I was called in by Mrs. Jones, the director, and she told me, 'Some of these girls have arrived at a very difficult age. Perhaps their mothers haven't talked to them, so I want you to give them some sex education classes.' I thought that they were going to make fun of the issue, but they accepted it very well."

Mrs. Demestre says adaptation problems in Florida City were easier than in other locations. She attributed the foster-parent concept as being the key to the success of the place. "Evidently, the main conflict was the family separation, but it never presented deep conflicts," she recalls.

Eight-year-old María Dolores Madariaga took adversity into her own hands. Separated from her brother, who was sent to Matecumbe, she cried for a week. She recalls that one day she got up, looked at herself in the mirror, and said, "I'm not going to cry anymore. And that was it." She asked repeatedly to be united with her brother but was only granted visits once a week. Finding this less than satisfactory, María took action. She had been told that a priest who worked in Florida City administration was the person who could help her. She tried to see him several times but was refused admittance, so she decided she'd do something else. During one of her attempts to see the priest, María Dolores was able to glance into his office, where she noticed that his window faced an area under construction. So she went into the construction site, piled up some bricks, climbed in through his window, sat down, and waited.

When the priest walked into his office, he found the feisty little girl sitting there, waiting. When he asked why she was there, she responded that she wanted her thirteen-year-old brother with her. She added, "Either the priest who got us the visa in Cuba lied to our parents or somebody did, because we were told we would be together and if you can't do that, I want to be sent back to Cuba." The priest smiled and told her that because of the courage she had shown by coming in through his window, something would be done. And it was. An exception to the twelve-year-old limit was made, and thirteen-year-old Juan Antonio Madariaga was allowed into Florida City.

Leopoldo Arista, a lawyer in Cuba, was debating whether to leave Miami for South America when he was tricked into going to Florida City by Mother María Paz, a friend of his, who told him she needed to talk to him. As he waited in an improvised classroom, children started arriving, asking if he was the new teacher. He said no but with a little prompting from the children, he started working with them anyway, doing math problems on the blackboard. Mother María Paz watched him interact with the students. When she offered him a teaching job he replied, "I'm not a teacher, I'm a lawyer." But she assured him that he was actually both. She said she'd been observing him and he would do fine.

He promised to think about it, and as he was leaving, he heard someone cry out, "Teacher, teacher!" It was one of the children who begged him, "Please do not betray us!" He asked the child why he said such a thing, and the boy answered, "We have been abandoned; please do not abandon us now." Tears flow as he remembers the encounter. He returned the next day and stayed on as a teacher until Florida City closed.

Arista says that he has never held a job that paid less financially but rewarded more emotionally than his years as a Florida City teacher. "We once had 1,122 children in Florida City. Imagine the situation that we had, sometimes two children per chair. I couldn't stand to see the bare walls, so I bought a picture of Saint John the Baptist and hung it up. Later I added a Cuban flag. The classes were very informal, as you didn't know how long you would have a child in them. We taught them a small English vocabulary, tried to explain the differences between American and Cuban cultures, things to help them assimilate."

One Christmas Arista told the children that they would make cards in class; his gift to them was that he would mail all their cards to their parents in Cuba, an idea they loved. He recalls that Christmas for another reason as well. "As they lived in such a bizarre world they decided that they wanted a banana tree for a Christmas tree and they built it out of newspapers. I don't know where they found the pole, and hangers to make the frame for the leaves. It turned out to be beautiful."

Arista paid for many of the school supplies out of his own meager salary. He would also take home children for the weekend. His wife would cook for them, and his whole family would include them in weekend activities such as Mass and a trip to the beach. His involvement was such that his own children became jealous. He recalls how once, when he went to take a nap, one of the Florida City children said, "Can I lay down next to you and take a nap also?" When his own son came into the room and also laid down, the Florida City boy told him, "Please don't be jealous. Let him pretend he is my father for a while."

Monsignor Walsh tells two stories that relate some of the unusual situations they dealt with:

Once in Florida City we had a girl twelve or thirteen, and the day came time for her to leave to go to Buffalo, or somewhere else, her *beca* had arrived. She had been there a couple of months. When the social worker went to the apartment where the houseparents were helping her pack, the girl started crying and she threw a terrific tantrum, I mean really refused to go, crying and hanging on to the foster mother. They almost lost the plane.

They calmed her down and got the girl in the car and they are driving down through Homestead, US1, to go to the airport and the little girl is sitting there perfectly calm, laughing and talking. Suddenly the social worker said to her, "Are you happy about going?" And she said, "I'm delighted. I can't wait to get to Buffalo," or wherever she was going. So the social worker said, "But you were so upset back there." And the little girl said, "I was afraid that if she [housemother] knew I wanted to leave, that she wouldn't like it." Kids' minds can work in strange ways.

The other story was about an aunt and uncle who were in Miami and had been visiting a couple of children. When they found out the children were being transferred somewhere else, they came down and they complained that they didn't want the children transferred. We had been through this before and we said, "You have a choice. You either take the children or we have to move them because we have more children coming in tomorrow. It's one or the other."

The children got to the airport and the aunt and uncle showed up at the airport and they created such a fuss that the police were called. The policeman is trying to solve this problem and he doesn't have the foggiest notion of what's going on. The whole lot ends up downtown at the Catholic Welfare Bureau. And the policeman decides that we should resolve this. I explain to the police what the problem was; we really have to move the children on. There is no choice. Suddenly there is a dead silence and I say, "This is the way it has to be." And the aunt says, "Look, they are our children." They were the mother and father.

The parents had been here for a couple of months and had visited the children and told them to keep it secret saying they were an uncle and aunt. They were trying to get established and wanted the children taken care of. These are some of the incidents that we can now tell that made it very difficult to know what was happening. If the children were confused, we sometimes were confused as well.

Many of the houseparents became very involved with these children and wanted to find ways to have fun. They brought the idea of a weekly dance to Father Walsh, and he thought it was a wonderful idea. The dance was rotated among the different shelters, Florida City, Camp Matecumbe, or Saint Raphael's, and quickly became the most popular activity. Brothers and sisters had an opportunity to see each other and romances bloomed.

Ray McCraw is still amazed that a conservative Irish priest was liberal enough to allow the boys and girls to mix. "It was great!" says McCraw, who also remembers the children responding as if they knew the dances were a privilege and acted accordingly. "The houseparents were present, but they weren't there like police or patrol people. They mingled right in with the kids, and it was just like a big family."

Mirta Almeyda remembers her first dance, a St. Valentine's dance on February 14, as something fantastic. She had been allowed to bring 44 pounds of clothes out of Cuba and among them she brought three long-playing records that she still treasures: Cuban instrumental music, Blanca Rosa Gil, and Benny More. She searched for her nicest dress and off to Matecumbe she went with the rest of the girls. She recalls there being pretzels, potato chips, and punch at the dance. "And we all knew how to dance!" These were among the happier memories of that time in her life.

OPA-LOCKA

When the flights between Cuba and the United States stopped during the missile crisis of October 1962, so did the direct exodus of children. The only means of exiting Cuba was through third countries, usually Spain or Mexico. More children would be sent alone to Spain where the Catholic Church cared for them. This made sending a child alone a much more difficult proposition. Some children trickled into the United States; others were turned in to the Catholic Service Bureau by relatives who couldn't care for them anymore. However, mass arrivals stopped abruptly on October 23, 1962, and the number of children in the camps started shrinking. Some of the children turned nineteen and had to leave the program. Some parents arrived through third countries. Once it seemed certain that flights would not be resumed, a new direction for the temporary shelters had to be taken.

Monsignor Walsh knew that the program had achieved the best results under the foster-parent system in St. Raphael's and Florida City. He wanted to close Matecumbe and distribute the children to a couple of small homes like St. Raphael's. However, Walsh's superior, Archbishop Coleman Carrol, and his advisers thought differently: they deemed that consolidation of all the shelters into one was the proper solution. Father Walsh was ordered to do so and Opa-locka was opened. The facility had been a marine base and naval air station with barracks where beds lined up one next to the other in a cavernous hall. The six buildings could accommodate 500. The facilities included dining rooms, recreational areas, a chapel, twelve classrooms, and administrative offices. Six Marist brothers and more than thirty lay persons taught the youths.[10]

Saint Raphael's was closed, and with great resistance, all the boys were moved. "We were furious," remembers Jorge Finlay. "Opa-locka was barracks. You couldn't escape because if you did, you had no place to go. As we were driving up we saw the Ali-Baba Hotel and one of the boys sarcastically said, 'Look, the Fountainebleau Hotel of Opa-locka,'" refering to the most luxurious hotel in Miami Beach at the time. Developed as an architecturally themed community in 1926, all of Opa-locka's main streets were named for the characters in the book *The One Thousand and One Tales from the Arabian Nights*. That didn't seduce the boys. "We were going back to open showers, to hearing the guy all the way at the end of the dormitory snore. It was a step back for us."

By then Father Walsh had become a monsignor, promoted in September 1962; he was the youngest monsignor in the United States. He thought this consolidation was the wrong decision to make. He also moved to Opa-locka and described living there as the worst period of his life.

A loud bell would to wake up occupants at Opa-locka. While no one really liked the bell, one day one of the boys had a more extreme reaction. He awoke one morning, dug a hole in the backyard, pulled off the bell, and buried it there. The next day a bigger bell was in its place, where it remained, according to Jorge Finlay.

Opa-locka closed in June 1966, when the unit was down to only twenty-five boys, who were then moved to a boy's home at 83 SE Eighth Street, the site of the former Sweet Dreams Motel. Here, the program received some of the boys who had exited Cuba through Spain, according to Gerardo Girado,* who, with his brother, were possibly the children longest in the program. The program stayed in this new location for four years. Later the group would move again, to the Bimini Motel in 1970.

The program was shut down for good in 1981. "At that time we didn't have any of the original boys. We were getting boys who had arrived on boats or who swam to Guantanamo," says

---

* a pseudonym

Monsignor Walsh. One of these boys was a tall black boy nick-named Watusi. Gerardo remembers that Watusi had left Cuba on a boat with other youngsters and that two in the group had been shot while escaping. Watusi had been one of the lucky survivors.

Kites rise highest against the wind
Not with it.

—WINSTON CHURCHILL

CHAPTER 6

Assimilation and Adaptation: When Pedro Became Peter

In lieu of personal contact, letters were the most common and often the only means of bridging the gap between the children and their parents in Cuba. Telephone service between both countries was sporadic at best, with operator-assisted long-distance calls sometimes taking more than twenty-four hours to connect. Both parties would have to stand by the phone the entire time because it was never known when the call would go through.

Letters indelibly capture the feelings of their writers at the moment. Abraham Lincoln once told his secretary of war, Edwin Stanton, to write a letter replying to an offense. When Stanton showed the finished letter to the president, Lincoln applauded its powerful language and asked what Stanton was going to do with it. Surprised, he answered, "Send it," to which Lincoln replied, "You don't want to send that letter; put it in the stove. That is what I do when I've written a letter while I am angry."[1]

Children, in their innocence, write simple but honest letters. The Cuban children wrote of their assimilation problems and their eventual solutions, of new friends and surroundings, of their loneliness and their longing for their family and their

homeland. Some children, however, prematurely crossed the threshold into adulthood by writing letters that did not convey their true feelings; instead they pretended that all was fine to spare their parents additional heartache.

The following letters, now crumpled and aged, bear testimony to the writers' adaptation and assimilation to the United States more than thirty years ago.

The Pichardo siblings, ages twelve, eleven, nine, and eight, each wrote pieces of the following cheerful letter to their parents from Miami. The letter is dated January 1, 1961:

Dear parents,

We have arrived well and without any problems. We are very happy and we play a lot. Yoyi and Batty play with us.

It is raining a bit today and we can't go out to play because the field is wet. We are very happy and we go out almost every night.

Dear Parents we arrived well and happy. Do not worry about us, we are fine.

Mom and dad, I am very happy, we are having fun with Yoyi and Batty and I hope you are also happy.

Gabriel, Eugenio, Adolfo and Josefina

While the attempt to be cheerful may have succeeded in the first letter, the hardships endured by these children made it difficult to maintain a brave front. The January 1 letter was followed by this downhearted letter dated February 2, 1961:

Dear parents,

We want you to come soon, because they are going to send us to Philadelphia and we don't want to go. We cry every night because we miss you very much. We are living in a hospital in the beds of the sick and also with their bed linen.

Come anyway that you can, we are doing very badly here. The food

is very bad and we don't want to be here anymore. We are asking you
to please come. We are waiting for you.

> Your four children who love you,
> Gabriel, Eugenio, Josefina and Adolfo
> P.S. The address here is: Box 1017-Cot 6
> South Miami FL

Once in Philadelphia, Adolfo wrote on April 15, 1961:

Dear Dad and Mom,

How are Chico and Norita? When I go back to Cuba I want to see
them fatter, I want them to eat their food or I won't bring with me any
of the things they are always asking for, candy and chocolates.

How are you? I am very happy because the nun hugged me today
because I did very well in my schoolwork. Now school is over and they
have given me homework. I am doing the homework with this letter as
my brother told me to.

I am playing a lot with my two brothers and many more friends
that I have here. I am very sure that I am going to behave well in
school.

Lots of hugs and kisses from your son who loves you,

Adolfo

Ana María Carnesoltas, now a Miami judge, had been a lonely
fourteen-year-old girl in Villa María, a home for teenage girls in
San Antonio, Texas. She poured her soul onto paper in June
1962 (published by the *Miami Herald* on October 18, 1987):

This is the first time since I've arrived in the United States that I've
expressed my thoughts in a diary. I won't write more than a few lines:
the complaints and all the rest I'll save forever.

I am in San Antonio. Where? In an old house with a mysterious
aspect that would make even the most valiant person tremble.

What is in the interior? Some old furniture, some women, mostly single and old on the second floor and on the first floor, nuns, sometimes caring, sometimes aloof. In whom can I trust? In God and this piece of paper that I fill with irregular and ugly lines. There isn't even a priest to whom I can confess my poor sins. Writing is not easy, the way I'm feeling today. A few moments ago, I thought I didn't care.

It is about 8:00 p.m. There is still some daylight left. They have not turned on the lights in Villa María, not even the Virgin's statue. I am writing sitting by a window. I can't see, because there is so little light.... (I miss my mother more than ever)

They just turned on the lights to the Virgin ... today I cried in chapel and after praying the Rosary.... I've asked God to help me survive....

From here I can see a small store, and it reminds me of my aunt's house in Santa Clara. I think I'll never see my homeland again, the country that witnessed my birth....

July 4, 1962

Today is July 4th, 1962. It is the day that celebrates this country's independence. When will I be able to hear rockets and fireworks celebrating Cuba's independence?[2]

Sara Yaballi was a nurse at Camp Matecumbe. She became a surrogate mother to many of the teenage boys who continued to correspond with her after they left Matecumbe, telling her their adaptation stories and asking her for advice and even for money on some occasions.[3]

From Silvio, Portland, Oregon,

2328 N.W. Everett St., Portland, Oregon
May 9, 1962

I got your letter which made me very happy and you know we are where the devil screamed thrice and no one heard him.... [Cuban

expression meaning this place is in the middle of nowhere.] This is stranger by the day. At 9:00 p.m. it is daylight, it rains night and day and the cold is bitter.

November 4, 1962

Sara please forgive the handwriting, but my throat hurts a lot today and I am pretty fed up with this and this garbage of a country. I think that there is nothing like Cuba in the whole world. We are all well here, we lack for nothing we live well and we study and we might even get some work next week and we still complain, but one never gets used to it. If Fidel doesn't fall or leave soon, the day least expected I am arriving in Cuba.

From Portland, Oregon, Julio wrote:

2328 N.W Everett St., Portland, Oregon

Here in Portland, the six of us are living in a very large house, it is three stories high, downstairs the living room, dining room, kitchen with pantry and two huge hallways. There are two bedrooms and a bath and the third floor had 2 bedroom and a sitting area.

Porfilio and I have a room in the second floor. It is very homelike, the beds are comfortable, 2 drawers and two night tables and two closets. It has curtains and carpets and it is very pretty. Guillermo and Carlos share another room and the couple who look after us the third. They are a Cuban couple and treat us very well.

The city is very pretty. It looks like it is in a valley as you see mountains all around.... We live like royalty ... people are very polite, they speak very softly and slowly and pronounce words very well.

From José, Reno, Nevada:

101 Boynton Lane

We have been given things, but they keep rubbing it in our face all day long. And on some occasions some have been hit. Well, they say things will improve but they have been saying that since we got here.

From Raúl, Helena, Montana:

203 N. Ewing Street, Helena, Montana
January 10, 1962

I am well, but very cold, it is now 30 degrees below zero. As we were going to school today, the wind would hit our face and make us cry and the tears would freeze. On New Year's Eve I went to the home of an American friend and I had a good time although I could not help remembering my family.

But I have faith in God and know that he will grant the miracle that we can return to our beloved and far away homeland.

May 24, 1962

On June 15 we are moving to the house Monsignor bought for us. It is magnificent. I wish you could come and live with us. That way we could have someone to take care of us and guide us.

I think they are going to send for some more boys. We want you to send us a list of 10 boys so we can give it to Monsignor. Before they send anybody, we can choose better boys who will give a good example.

June 18, 1962

On my birthday I had lunch with Monsignor and then we went for a ride. His secretary gave me a beautiful cake, in all, I had a really nice time.

August 13, 1962

What have you heard about Cuba? We don't get a lot of news here, except that things there are going from bad to worse. I was granted the exit visas for my parents and grandmother and I am very happy.

Two months later, flights between Cuba and the United States stopped, crushing Raúl's hopes.

June 6, 1963

Graduation day. At the end all the graduates get on line and people come to greet them. It was one of the hardest moments for me, as all those parents went to hug their children and all we could do was watch and think of ours. We have faith in God that we will soon be together and hope that although they were not with us physically, they were thinking of us.

From Pablo, Helena, Montana:

Helena, Montana
4/14/62

About the town, I'll tell you that it is small and you can get quickly from one place to the next. I still don't know if I like it or not. The food is great, yesterday afternoon we got steak and French fries, sweets, juice, milk, salad etc. . . . The food here is delicious.

4/30/62

I am trying to adapt, and I am having a good time even though their customs are so different from ours and the morale of most of us is very low. Deep down inside they are not bad even though they believe us to be uncivilized, we who have enough to teach them! But I'll tell you that here they are all good, it was worse in Miami.

From Enrique, Helena, Montana:

Helena, Montana
September 16, 1962

My first letter to you was returned unclaimed. I don't understand why. Several of us are working at the college. We wash dishes, clean floors, freezers, whatever it takes.

I have earned some money, which will never be enough as I have to buy clothes and school supplies, but I'll be reimbursing you for at least one money order as soon as I get paid.

October 6, 1962

First of all, please forgive me for not writing, I haven't forgotten you for I love you like a mother. The problem is that I have no time, Sarita. I knew that this was going to be hard and I was willing to sacrifice, but it is really hard. In many classes I have no problem with English, but in others I don't understand anything. The earliest I go to bed is 1:00a.m. because they give us a lot of homework. I hadn't even written to my parents in 10 days.

I am sending you the amount for the money order. My mother wrote that she got it with no problems. We got paid yesterday and we hardly have any money as we had to buy winter clothes.

I'd like to talk to you sincerely, as I always have: I have the money to give back to you for the other money order. If you need it let me know, and I'll send it to you immediately. Now, if you don't need it right now, I rather owe you because I really need the money. You know I keep my word, and as soon as I can repay you I will. I will pay you even if I have to work in the cemetery. Tell me and please be sincere with me.

November 10, 1962

About my schooling I will tell you that the results have been a disaster. I passed three courses and failed two. Now the second set of tests is coming up and we'll see if I can pass all. One really has to buckle down to study and English really complicates things.

December 29, 1962

I haven't written to you, and only to my mother because she get very nervous and worried, but the truth is these days I don't feel like living. Monsignor didn't even give us a penny for Christmas and only today do I have money for stamps. I couldn't even send cards. I got yours today. It is beautiful, thank you.

I don't know if I told you that we have to pay $255.00 this semester as the so-called scholarship is not one. Monsignor paid part and we have to pay the above-mentioned amount. It is really cold, the temperature is 25 degrees below zero. The facial pain was unbearable.

April 19, 1963,

I went to California with some of the boys and we really liked it and had a good time. The temperature is wonderful, like in Cuba. I finished my exams and I have a 2.7 average, which is pretty good.

June 9, 1963

Tomorrow I am moving to California. Monsignor gave us $184.00 and I think we'll be well as far as money is concerned.... I will sign off as I am packing my bags.

From Jorge, Albuquerque, New Mexico:

Route 1 Box 1486 Albuquerque, New Mexico

Of all my Christmas cards none was as sweet as yours, when I read, "Loves you, mami Sara" I almost cried, one feels so unloved here. They tell us we are men, but when I go to bed most days I feel like crying like a baby and I ask myself, "How much longer dear God?" ... there are forty of us here and we don't understand each other, what can we expect of a nation!

January 21, 1963

I know that my actual duty is to shape myself emotionally, physically, intellectually and morally for the church and for Cuba and also for my parents who have sacrificed everything for me.

From Fernando, Albuquerque, New Mexico:

Albuquerque, New Mexico
August 27, 1962

I am painting the neighbor's house, yesterday I made $5.00. Today he is going to call for me again, we can usually find work around here.

From Jesús, Austin, Texas:

St. Edwards High School Room 309 Austin, Texas
May 2, 1962

When we arrived at the Austin airport they were waiting for us with a sign that welcomed us, there were also two photographers and we were on television.

From Fernando (nicknamed Sex Appeal), York, Nebraska:

February 21, 1962
Dear "Aunt" Sara,

Last Friday, Valentine's day there was a dance and your new American niece thought I was an orange, as she squeezed me all over, could I be so sweet? This Friday I am going to another dance with yet another American girl who also wants to be your niece. Should I comply?

February 8, 1962

I have a cold and the lady of the house has seen me feeling down and bored and she gave me some red wine to drink (we drink a lot of it since the priest comes over to drink and they make themselves martinis). I have said that I don't like them and then they give me wine. In other words, wine has turned into "my daily bread." She played some Pérez Prado records for me.

From Pedro, Wilmington, Delaware:

De Sales Home, 1300 North Broom Street, Wilmington, Delaware
August 15, 1962

How wise your advice is! Even more now that we feel lonelier than ever. Yes, this is an emotion I have never felt. In Miami we were only missing our parents, and you were their representatives. The homeland was very near that is why we didn't miss it so much. Now I have only one good friend in which to trust: God. But the homeland is farther away than ever and I don't even have my parents. And you are

always battling for the good of those boys that one day took the same route through that green hell.

From José, Marquette, Michigan:

Marquette, Michigan
July 8, 1962

I have had several jobs that the priest here finds for us, such as mowing lawns, cleaning an office but once you finish you are up in the air, but since it is a small town one doesn't spend much. . . . And as for the boys, they cannot ask for more we are living like kings with a harem each. The only thing that has me very impatient is that here we don't hear from Cuba, our Cuba and I can't stand it.

I would appreciate it if you can tell me anything because I am in the darkness and I want to get out of it. But I know there is a God up above who sees everything and he is my only hope. Please send me some advice, as it never hurts to receive them. I pray to God to bless you for having been so kind with all the young men like me, who have gone through that camp.

From F. González, Marquette, Michigan:

Marquette, Michigan

I will tell you that this place is wonderful. Nuns take care of us and they go out of their way to know how they can make us happy. We live with the monsignor in a house and you might not believe it, but we are considered members of the high life here. We had a party yesterday, all Americans and they invited us to their homes. If you could see how they take us out! They like us here. Snow is beautiful from here you can see the whole town and it looks gorgeous.

From Hector, York, Nebraska:

My life here is spending all day inside the house, since there is nowhere to go and one doesn't have a circle of friends. The Americans deal with us but they somewhat avoid us, I know that our English must

tire them. Whether it is that or whatever it is, I am dying to go back to Cuba.

You know what it is like to be inside a house from sun up until I go to bed? No one can take it.

From Regino, Brooklyn, New York:

St. Vincent's Home, 66 Boerum Place, Brooklyn, NY.
December 1, 1962

The boys here are Puerto Rican, Italians, Americans and blacks. I don't feel right here. I'm resigned to this martyrdom.

PS Our mail is opened.

January 3, 1962

I'd like to ask you for a favor. When my parents' visas arrive, please send them to me as soon as possible. I don't even know if it is possible to leave Cuba anymore, or when Fidel is going to topple. About this I have a bad feeling that never, because he is very strong and every time I think of that I get crazy and so furious and I start giving speeches! The only one who puts up with me is Pedro who also encourages me.

I haven't joined the invasion army because I promised my parents in Cuba that I was going to study here, otherwise I would have enlisted.

From Jorge, Louisville, Kentucky:

3201 Bardstown Road, Louisville, Kentucky
December 15, 1961

We go crazy here every time we run into Latin Americans or Americans who speak Spanish. We end up talking to them for two or three hours. I get desperate when I don't get letters from you and I haven't received mail from home for over two weeks. Tell Father Walsh that we are very happy to be living where we are living.

From Heraclio, Spokane, Washington:

Spokane, Washington

The scholarship has turned out to be wonderful. They look fondly upon us and every time they see us they wave and make conversation.

From Jorge, Denver, Colorado:

October 31, 1962,
Denver, Colorado

It has been six days since I arrived in this city where I feel very happy, since people are wonderful here, they have provided us with attentions and privileges. As I write they have given us a radio, a good coat for me, and besides, $20.00. We have a large house, it has three bedrooms, with heat, since it gets cold here. It is all furnished and without paying a cent. Yesterday my godfather and I went to work and we made $25.00 in five hours. I have a lot of opportunities here so don't worry about me.

I only get sad and worried when I think of the problem of our homeland, which is really huge now, and my whole family is over there. A cousin of mine was leaving last Friday and he couldn't because the flights were suspended. I hope when you read these lines you'll have good news about Cuba.

CHAPTER 7

Orphanages: It's the Hard-Knock Life

The first orphanage in what is now the United States opened in 1729 in the French colony of New Orleans, and these religiously motivated institutions became common in the nineteenth century. In 1800 there were approximately six orphanages; by 1880 more than six hundred.[1]

Because the Cuban refugee children needed places to live that provided year-round care, Catholic orphanages became home for many. Although the orphanages did not provide a perfect environment, they *were* open twelve months a year. Many of the children living in these institutions were not technically orphans but had parents who had problems or who simply didn't want their children.

Abraham Ribicoff, secretary of health, education, and welfare, said in 1962, "We know from long experience that with children separated for long periods from their parents a foster home is far preferable in most circumstances than individual care. Moreover there is a limit to how many children can be accommodated by existing institutions. I cannot urge too strongly that citizens cooperate in the fine efforts of the voluntary agencies to provide suitable homes for these children."

With this sort of sentiment prevalent in the 1960s, there was a shift from institutionalized orphanage care to home foster care. However, many Cuban children had the misfortune of being exposed to people not unlike the mean Miss Hangman in *Little Orphan Annie*. Some stereotypes regarding these institutions were fitting during those final years of institutionalized orphanage care in the United States.

THE ALVAREZ AND MENDIETA SISTERS, DUBUQUE, IOWA

The Alvarez and Mendieta sisters' destinies merged at Miami International Airport on October 5, 1961. Both pairs of girls were embarking on a new chapter of their lives in America, a country as unfamiliar to them as the concept of Soviet astronaut Yuri Gagarin's circling of Earth that same year.

The Alvarezes, Lissette and Olguita, were the daughters of Olga and Tony, a singing duo that had reached first-name-only superstardom status, not only in their native Cuba but also throughout Latin America. The couple performed live at concerts throughout Cuba and abroad and had made many recordings and starred in their own radio show on Radio Progreso. Voted "Mr. and Mrs. Television in 1955," they had broken ground in Cuba's newest medium with *El Show de Olga y Tony*, at CMQ-TV. It was a variety-style show that incorporated snippets from their personal life. They also owned a lucrative marketing venture, a store in the La Rampa section of Havana. Most Cuban little girls owned Olga and Tony look-a-like dolls, and Cuban women wore Olga-designed crinolines to flare their skirts.

Ana and Raquel Mendieta's family tree is laden with Cuban history. Their father's uncle, Carlos Mendieta, had been Cuba's

president in 1934. Their maternal great-grandfather was General Carlos María de Rojas. At the maternal estates in Varadero, or Cardenas, sit-down dinners for fifty were not unusual. Their father, Ignacio Alberto Mendieta, was a lawyer, and their beautiful mother, Raquel, was once "Miss Varadero," the belle of the beach resort. During their university days Ignacio and Raquel joined the Student's Federation alongside Fidel Castro.

On the New Year's day that brought Castro his victory, the Mendieta sisters were startled to see their father tearing apart their living room sofas and chairs. Inside, an arsenal of weapons was waiting. Ignacio Mendieta had been working for the underground. A picture of Fidel went up in yet another Cuban living room, and Mendieta received a post in the Foreign Ministry under the new government.

In 1960, a security check revealed that during World War II, Ignacio Mendieta had been a major in the national police, tracking down outlawed clandestine Cuban communists. That didn't sit well with the new regime, and Mendieta was asked to join the communist party. He refused and went underground. He would eventually be imprisoned.[2]

When the order came down that all school children fourteen and older had to go teach peasants in the countryside for a period of seven months, Raquel, who had just turned fourteen, would have been recruited. Their mother suggested sending the girls to the United States, while their father said the family belonged in Cuba, together.

The girls got involved in distributing antigovernment leaflets. When an older friend of theirs was caught and given thirty years in prison, Ignacio Mendieta acquiesced. The girls were sent to Miami on September 11, 1961.

Today, sitting in a souvenir-laden office with a wall full of mementos, awards, and photos in his Miami townhouse, the still-handsome Tony Alvarez says, "We have to admit that women sometimes have an extra sense. When Olga asked me whether we should leave, I told her, 'Are you crazy? And do what, start all over?'" While trying to convince Tony to leave, Olga decided that at least her daughters could find safety in the United States. She got their exit permits from Mongo Grau, whose house they often visited, and somehow she managed to get Tony's reluctant permission. "When she told me the girls were leaving, my heart just sank," he remembers. It was especially hard to part with Olguita, who was only five at the time.

Lissette had also been involved in antigovernment pranks. Tony admits that if they hadn't sent Lissette away, they would have all been jailed. Olga agrees, claiming that her daughter was "fearless and somewhat violent." Lissette was in boarding school and many afternoons she would escape and roam the streets of Havana, sticking political flyers on walls. They read, "Ideas are argued, not shot down," referring to the infamous *paredón,* or firing squads.

In her modern and elegant Miami living room, a blonde Lissette, now a one-name only singing superstar herself, remembers the fear that ran through her as militia searched their home on Cuba's posh Fifth Avenue one day when her parents were not home. She had hidden her illegal flyers between the upper and lower halves of a cabinet. To her relief they were not found, but the militia did take her mother's bath soaps, saying it was illegal to stock up on merchandise.

When her parents returned, Lissette accompanied an irate Tony to police headquarters, where profuse apologies were issued, claiming a mistaken search. Lissette remembers seeing a mountain of goods piled up that the police had taken away from *los gusanos,* the worms.

Lissette's parents sent her to the beach resort of Varadero to keep her out of trouble. However, the doorman at their apartment building alerted them to the fact that the feisty teenager had been scrawling anti-Castro slogans, such as "Fidel murderer," in the building's elevators. She would also go to the beach and shout aggressively at youngsters being trained by the government to teach peasants to read and write. Her parents had little choice but to send her away, or they knew they'd be visiting her in jail.

Now, in America, the sisters were embarking on a different sort of adventure. They were off to Dubuque, Iowa. Both the Alvarez and the Mendieta sisters had been at Miami's Camp Kendall, grudgingly awaiting relocation to their new home in America. Lissette remembers seeing their names on the bulletin board at Camp Kendall where daily chalk notices posted who was leaving, when, and to where. She recalls looking in a map for Dubuque and not being able to find it. The Mendieta sisters also saw their names on the fateful bulletin board. "We had never heard of Dubuque, we didn't even know how to pronounce it. We started reading and to us it was Doo-boo-ke, Ee-o-guua," says Raquel. "We really didn't want to leave Kendall, we felt safe there, we felt we knew the language. There were six of us scheduled to leave, three sets of sisters, and none of us wanted to leave, but we had no choice, we were not asked whether you wanted to leave."

The Mendieta sisters were painted a rosier picture of Iowa than were the Alvarez sisters. They were told that they were going to spend one or two weeks in a home and that afterward they would be placed in a foster home with a family with a similar background to their own family in Cuba.

"I remember the airport. It remains in my mind like a movie," says Raquel Mendieta. "One of the older girls didn't want to leave, so she locked herself in the ladies' bathroom. The person with us at the airport was a man, so he couldn't go in the bathroom. There was all this screaming and carrying back and forth. Finally a stewardess came and got her out. They wanted to put these tags on us; we felt we weren't dogs, so we ripped them off very quickly."

Their flight from Miami to Dubuque had a ninety-minute scheduled stop at Chicago. To the petrified Cuban girls Chicago was a city run by Al Capone and his gangsters. At the airport, they found chairs around a column and sat back-to-back watching out for gangsters during their entire transit stop.

Raquel remembers:

When we got on the plane, an older girl, the only one who spoke English, had her mouth stuffed with chocolate. The stewardess was asking for the tickets and we didn't know what she was saying. My sister who was very forward and assertive decided she must be asking for her name, so she looks at her and says, "My name is Ana María Mendieta." The stewardess replied, "Tickets, please." She insisted "My name is Ana María Mendieta,'" so this went on three or four times while the girl with the chocolates was spitting chocolate all over because she was laughing so hard. Some of the memories that I have are hysterically funny when you think about it, although at the time they were not very pleasant at all.

Just as the girls thought there were gangsters in Chicago, local Dubuque residents had their own ignorance about Cubans. Raquel recalls:

They thought that people in Cuba lived in trees and didn't wear clothes and didn't have television and had never seen a ballpoint pen. So we were on equal terms. It was very difficult to adjust to the idea that these people had never heard of Cuba. I said to some classmates, "I am from Cuba," and they asked, "Cuba, Illinois?" I would reply negatively and they would ask, "Cuba, where is that?" So there was a lot of cultural misunderstanding.

The girls were sent to live in St. Mary's orphanage, which occupied a large, modern two-story building along the Mississippi River on Kaufman Avenue in Dubuque. In 1960 Dubuque had a population of almost 40,000.

Lissette and Olguita were separated because children were grouped according to age. "Orphanage sounds human, but this was a school for troubled children. Strangely, there weren't many children around," says Olguita. "At five, I think I was the youngest of our little group of Cuban girls. We arrived during the winter. I remember mountains of snow. It was so cold! The floor was like a hospital, made of granite, with no rugs and very, very, cold. There were very tall beds, like in a hospital, or they seemed very tall to me, one next to another."

Their cultural shock was made twice as hard because the girls didn't speak English and didn't understand what people were saying. To make matters worse, the orphanage housed mostly juvenile delinquents. "One of the girls in our dormitory had stabbed her mother with a pair of scissors. Another had thrown someone down a well. Another one had tried to strangle a counselor and push her over the balcony," says Raquel. "One had committed armed burglary of a gas station, one had been raped by her stepfather, ran away from home, and requested to be taken in. Another was severely mentally retarded, I never knew why she was there. Another girl was picked up in the streets for having switchblade fights with men.

"These were the people that we went to live with. We came from middle-class homes in Cuba and we had lived a very sheltered life. Our culture calls for young girls to be chaperoned everywhere they go. We went from living that kind of life to living in this kind of environment where every second you didn't know whether you were going to be killed or someone was going to beat you up or what was going to happen to you," recalls Raquel.

Lissette remembers vegetating days, filled with inertia, sitting around a lounge listening to 45-RPM records at a time when "Mr. Postman," "Where the Boys Are," and "Moon River" were the rage. "We'd have breakfast, go to school across the way, and return to that lounge. On weekends we also moped around. We didn't do anything." Anything, that is, except pick up bad habits from their companions. "One day Lissette was wearing foam rollers on her hair and she was sitting on a chair and I had no place to sit," remembers Raquel Mendieta. "She got up and went to the bathroom and when she returned she told me to get up and I refused. So she sat on my legs. I bit her back, and we ended in a fist fight on the floor."

"I think the negative atmosphere there was rubbing off," says Lissette. "The other delinquent girls there would take our chairs in the dining room when we sat, so we imitated them." She remembers another incident that happened while she was in the bathroom, getting ready for school. A younger girl assigned to clean the area wanted her to hurry up and leave, telling her, "Get the fuck out of here," and since Lissette didn't understand, the girl proceeded to scream at her, "God damn you, God damn you." So Lissette answered the same thing back, and the girl beat her up, and continued to do so down a hallway. "The nun saw it and did absolutely nothing," Lissette adds.

Lissette and Raquel were occasionally roommates because of the policy at St. Mary's to switch roommates and furniture around every couple of weeks. "It was like they didn't want us to get used to anything," says Lissette. "A Chinese nun would tell us that we were never going to see our parents again, because that is what had happened to the children in China, and that soon we would see that family mail would stop coming. Can you imagine someone saying that to a child?" she asks indignantly.

Lissette recalls:

> One night I got a letter from my dad and Raquel got a letter from her family, and we both started crying. The nun came and told us to shut up but we couldn't, so she grabbed us and took us down this hallway and shoved us in a closet where all the heating units were. I went to grab the interior handle and there wasn't any, so I shoved her before she bolted us in and I started screaming, so they locked us up in a kitchen instead, where we cried for about five hours.

Lissette also recalls everyone being sent to see a psychologist who wouldn't ask questions or talk, but instead gave the girls mud to make figures. "I had no trauma," she now says, underrating her situation, "only that I was taken out of my country."[3]

Olguita, who also pursued a singing career for a while, currently works as a reporter for Spanish language television in New York. She is a pretty blonde with hazel, Bambi-like eyes and a soft demeanor. She talked while sitting in a noisy Cuban coffee shop across from the Telemundo television station in Miami. Olguita cannot remember Cuba, although she tries, but Iowa is still clearly branded in her mind.

The sisters were forbidden to see each other. Olguita claims that the nuns never understood that they were merely refugees, not the kind of troubled children the nuns were accustomed to dealing with. They would tell Olguita that she didn't speak English because she didn't want to, when in reality she couldn't. "I went mute for three weeks, since I didn't speak English, I didn't speak anything. I don't know what the nuns must have thought. Finally, I started associating. If they pointed to a table and said "table," I would remember. So I grabbed a word here and a word there, but in school nobody helped me."

Among the indignities that the girls had to bear, Olguita recalls how she was allowed to bathe only once a week. This was unheard of for persons coming from a tropical country where daily showers are the norm.

She says, "My parents would call every Sunday. "They tell me that I would become more silent every week, speaking less and less. By the time I returned to Miami, five months later, I had forgotten my Spanish."

Tony filled the house in Cuba with speakers so that everyone could hear the conversations when they called the girls. He remembers Olguita's trying period. "From the terror that she went through, Olguita practically stopped talking. One had to fill the telephonic void with words," says Tony. "She used to be like a cascabel and her character changed totally." Olga would lock herself up in the bathroom and cry after every call.

"I imagine that for me it must have been a great shock," says Olguita. "Coming from a picture-postcard life, to walk into a life with those cold people. Everyone and everything was so cold! My character changed completely. I became extremely shy and had to work to overcome it. When I got home, I would ask for permission even to drink a glass of water."

Olga worried that she might never see her daughters again. Lissette wasn't helping the situation. She would write letters with drawings depicting the girls as prisoners behind bars with "Help" coming out of their mouths, cartoon style. Olga says she would tell her, "Mami, these nuns are very cruel, there is a Chinese nun that hates us, they make Olguita clean toilets," which Olguita now claims wasn't true. "Lissette would also tell us the nuns wouldn't let Olguita wear a coat," says Olga. "I felt so impotent."

Whereas Olguita became shy and withdrawn, Raquel Mendieta's reaction was just the opposite. From being a very timid young girl she became her sister's mother, becoming very protective of her. Ana, the younger sister, was not adjusting well. She was homesick and crying all the time. "I felt I had to be very strong, I had to be the role model. I had to make sure that I showed that there was nothing to worry about so that she was able to carry on. I was the one who spoke to all the people in authority, to all the nuns, to social workers. I was the person in charge of all that. It was a very difficult situation for both of us."

On September 8, 1985, Ana Mendieta plunged from her New York Greenwich Village apartment window to her death at age 36. Her husband, Carl Andre, also an artist, was accused and acquitted of her murder.[4] Raquel says, "My sister Ana, who is now deceased, at one point in her artistic career was asked, 'When did you know that you wanted to be an artist?' She answered 'After a year or two in the United States I knew that I was going to grow up to be either a criminal or an artist. So I decided to become an artist.'"

After a series of different occupations, Raquel has become an artist who works mostly on installations that reflect her Cuban heritage, as did her sister's work. Ana's work drew inspiration from her homeland and used many Cuban aboriginal motifs, some of which were carved in trees, others in the soil. Her work can be found in the permanent collection of the Metropolitan Museum of Art and was recently featured in the Museum of Modern Art's "Latin American Artists of the Twentieth Century" exhibition.

ST. VINCENT'S ORPHANAGE, VINCENNES, INDIANA

While awaiting their relocation in Florida City, the Iturralde sisters, Virginia and Iraida, lived in fear of being sent to the orphanage at Denver, Colorado, the most infamous of all.

Instead, they were sent to St. Vincent's orphanage in Vincennes, Indiana. "The one in Denver was more famous, but ours turned out to be just as bad," says Iraida, recalling the hardships she encountered in Indiana.

The Iturralde sisters' flight to Indiana was recorded by *Miami Herald* reporter Gene Miller in a March 9, 1962, piece titled, "'Peter Pan' Means Real Life to Some Kids." He wrote: "This is the underground railway in the sky—Operation Peter Pan. Maybe it should be Operation Pedro Pan," coining the catchy name by which these children's exodus would come to be known.

The article had two photographs, one of two boys embraced by an adult upon their arrival at Evansville and the other of a little girl sleeping, her head on an armrest, clutching tightly a *pequeña Lulú,* or Little Lulu doll. The caption under the photo reads, "New Life in a New Land Awaits Sweet Sleep." Although unidentified, the little girl was Iraida. The article says:

> The children are refugees of Castro's Red Cuba. Their parents are 1,000 miles away. For 15 months, the Catholic Diocese of Miami quietly helped relocate 7,778 children, all fleeing Cuba without their parents. Nearly 3,000 have flown north.
>
> The Communists are certain to call it child-smuggling. No one is telling exactly how it is done. No one will. The risk of reprisal is too great.

The Delta Airlines flight from Miami to Evansville made a connection in Atlanta. Twelve-year-old Virginia was proudly wearing her first pair of nylons, given to her as a farewell gift by her Florida City foster mother. Unsure how to keep them up, she tied them with shoelaces. An airline clerk in Atlanta noticed the problems she was having keeping the stockings up and presented her with a pair of garters, her first. They were black with red roses; one said "Yes," and the other said "No."

St. Vincent's orphanage, now closed, was in Vincennes, a town with a population of 18,046 in 1960 and located 60 miles north of Evansville. The children were divided into wards according to their sex and age. Iraida and Virginia were assigned to a dormitory for girls up to age thirteen. "There were eight Cuban girls in ours, there were two sisters Yolandita and Esperancita that were only about four and six years old. Every ward had some Cuban children." Virginia, the oldest of the Cuban group, became a den mother.

Upon arrival, all but a couple of everyday outfits and a Sunday outfit were taken away. Iraida remembers having her possessions "confiscated" as a cruel and unnecessary act. Virginia, however, rationalizes the action in retrospect. "The children there were very poor. It wouldn't have been nice to have us parading around in different outfits every day. These nuns were not used to dealing with children like us, they were used to dealing with children that had no familial love, whereas we were overspoiled. Additionally, we were rootless at the moment. But the nuns had no insight or psychology in dealing with us."

Susan Garrandes, a nine-year-old girl at the time and older sister of twin brothers, recounts, "When I left Cuba with my brothers, I was told by my parents 'You are the eldest.'" She felt the enormous burden of responsibility on her young shoulders. Suddenly, she was in charge of her twin brothers, Tony and Jorge, who were eight. Having been protected all her life, now she was doing the protecting.

"The nun who was in charge of their dormitory would beat my brothers' heads against the wall. When she was eventually replaced it was by another nun who punished the boys by dressing them in girls' clothes. You just don't do that to little Cuban boys." One day, the nun tried to dress them as girls. Susan, protecting her brothers like a lioness, clobbered the nun over her head with a chair. Susan doesn't remember the result of that action.

For many years, Matilde Aguirre couldn't talk without crying about a violent incident she had suffered in St. Vincent's. One day she watched in horror as a nun grabbed her little brother,

José, by the throat, as if to strangle him. Her voice still cracks as she recounts the scene.

Matilde was assigned the chore of cleaning bathrooms. She says that she had been so spoiled in Cuba that she didn't even make her own bed. The shock of cleaning bathrooms made her physically ill. "I was so nauseated. The nun in charge of our ward, who was, in my opinion, the worst one of all psychologically, not physically, that one was the one my brother had. She wanted to force me to clean the bathrooms. I became a rebel, when I had always been a calm and quiet child. She had such a struggle with me that I was given over to another nun for my chores." Matilde became the toddlers' dishwasher, a job she did not dislike, and remembers the elderly nun that cared for the little ones as the only kind nun in the building. Her defiance had paid off.

Virginia recalls that they ate their meals with long smocks on, because after their meals they were to help clean in the kitchen. Iraida remembers a time that she needed to go to the bathroom while the group was watching television. She asked the girl next to her how to ask the nun for permission in English, and the girl replied, "Can I go to the bathroom?" Iraida went up to the nun and repeated the question, to which the nun replied, "May I," correcting her grammar. Iraida thought to herself, "What is she saying?" and she repeated her request. The nun again replied, "May I?" Thinking that the nun had said "maybe," Iraida went into a stupor, for she could not believe anyone could be so cruel as to tell a person that *perhaps* they could go to the bathroom. "How can this woman be torturing me like this?"

Iraida started to walk away toward the bathroom, and the nun asked her to come back while repeating "may I, may I, may I," and Iraida replied, "Si, a mear"* while wondering where a nun had learned such a vocabulary. "There were no doors in the bathrooms, so I thought that maybe she was asking what I was going to do there." The language barrier coupled with the nun's

---

* *Mear* is a vulgar way of saying to urinate. May I sounds like *mea,* third person singular.

harshness made the environment particularly difficult for the Cuban children at St. Vincent's.

When twins Tony and Jorge Garrandes arrived at Indiana, it was winter. At bedtime, they didn't know the word for blanket. So the twins huddled together in one bed to keep warm. "If you didn't know how to ask for something in English, you didn't get it," says Jorge. "The first months were terrible. Of course we learned English in two months. We'd have to ask the other boys how to say things. All the Cuban kids would stick together as we were all living the same misery. St. Vincent was child slave labor," he adds, emphasizing his negative memories of the place. "They would take us to pick corn, apples, or strawberries and we would see that the farmers would pay the nuns."

José Aguirre recalls a couple of nuns who would "smack us for not knowing the right word in English. Our bathing experiences were somewhat traumatic, because the nuns would be standing there. If I stepped into the shower and I didn't say soap, she'd smack me and say 'soap.'"

Because of the language and cultural barrier, Susan remembers the Cuban girls bonding more easily with the black girls than with others, as they were the only two minorities in the orphanage. Even in 1996, only 1.8 percent of the population of the Hoosier State is Hispanic. "When I think of Indiana, the two girls that I remember the most are black. The Cuban girls and black girls were able to connect." Jorge remembers his exposure to overt racism at the orphanage and how the American boys referred to him and the other Cuban children as "spics."

There was no privacy at the orphanage. Even their mail was intercepted by the nuns, who read all mail sent to the children. Both the Iturralde sisters, Susan Garrandes, and Matilde Aguirre remember asking their parents to please send for them. Matilde even wrote secretly to Catholic Charities in Miami, condemning their treatment at the orphanage.

After two months in Saint Vincent's, the Iturralde sisters went to a foster home. Some weekends they would be taken back to visit the remaining Cuban girls. One of the girls still at the orphanage gave Virginia a secret letter to mail to her parents. Virginia feared that the letter might be returned to the orphanage by the post office, so she wrote her own name and return address on the letter.

At the time, Virginia didn't know the content of the letter. She didn't know that the girl was telling her parents that she didn't mind communism or Fidel as long as she could leave St. Vincent's and be with them in Cuba. She had drawn a sickle and a hammer in the letter. Upon receiving the letter in Cuba, the enraged parents wrote to the orphanage wondering what kind of communist political indoctrination her daughter was being subjected to.

A government agent was called in, and since Virginia's name was on the envelope, the nun sent for her. When the agent saw the accused girl, he burst out laughing. "I'll never forget his face and although I didn't understand what he was saying, he was gesturing as if asking 'Is this what you brought me here for?'" recalls Virginia, who doesn't know what punishment the letter's author received.

QUEEN OF HEAVEN ORPHANAGE, DENVER, COLORADO

Denver, Colorado, was a large city with 493,887 inhabitants in 1960. Queen of Heaven orphanage at 4825 Federal Boulevard was a spacious compound run by the Missionary Sisters of the Sacred Heart since 1905. St. Francis Xavier Cabrini designed the neoclassical building with a curving entrance staircase. Mother Cabrini, who was canonized the first American Catholic Saint in 1938, founded the Institute of the Missionary Sisters of the Sacred Heart of Jesus. She and other sisters helped in the construction of Queen of Heaven by carrying brick and mor-tar.[5] The compound included the living quarters, dormitories, school, church, and large playing fields that adjoined a lake and pool.

As far as María Cristina Romero was concerned, Queen of Heaven Orphanage might as well have been the center of the moon. She had no idea about what she would find in Colorado. She assumed that if Colorado was geographically next to Kansas and Oklahoma, where cowboys and Indians lived, then it also had to be part of the Wild West. When she was told she was going to Denver, the image that immediately flashed through her mind was that of Indians. Being blonde and blue eyed, the twelve year old was sure she was going to be scalped. "I was petrified. When we landed I expected the Indians to come. Going from the airport to the orphanage you went by a stockyard. And it smelled." María Cristina was one of a group of approximately thirty children destined for Queen of Heaven on May 1962, and at twelve, she was the eldest.

Other Cuban children had been arriving at the orphanage since 1961. "I think the ones before us had broken in the nuns for us," María Cristina says. Just as her image of Colorado was accompanied by ignorant stereotypes, she soon found herself subjected to the same type of negative stereotypes. "The nuns had told the other children in the orphanage that Cubans were wild, that we were black, that we didn't know how to wear shoes."

Monsignor Elmer Kolka, director of Catholic Charities, was quoted in the March 18, 1962, issue of the *Rocky Mountain News* explaining about the fifty-three Cuban children then being cared for at Queen of Heaven: "It's a little hard for them to adjust at first. Most of them come from upper middle class families and are accustomed to being waited on. But we don't pamper them. While most of them have never had to do chores or pick up after themselves, they do here. And it should be a good experience for them."

Lourdes Lopo, then eleven, doesn't agree about the worthiness of the working experience. She recalls being assigned a floor polisher, the kind with a large polishing disc on the bottom. Never having seen one, much less used one, she had

no idea how to operate the polisher. When the machine ran away from her spinning in circles, she was beaten.

The language barrier as well as her lack of experience seemed to raise Mother Ignatius's ire. Lourdes tells of a time when Mother Ignatius asked her if she was fresh to nuns in Cuba. Lourdes understood only part of what was being asked. She thought the nun was asking her if there were nuns in Cuba, so she answered "yes," only to receive a slap across the face. "She loved to slap across the face," Lourdes recalls.

At thirteen, Lourdes's sister, Ana Gema Lopo, felt herself changing as a result of her stay in the orphanage. It wasn't just how she was treated. She felt that as an older sibling, she was responsible for her sister, Lourdes, who was two years younger. Ana became a very rebellious against the nun's autocratic rule. "There was one little Native American girl, Beverly, who was my sister's age. She was a tough bully. One time she beat my sister up and my sister came upstairs to my dorm and she had a bloody cut lip so I asked her who had done and she replied, 'Beverly.' So I ran downstairs and I got Beverly and I beat the living crap out of her. From that day on they didn't bother my sister, nobody bothered any of the other little Cuban girls. The nuns had a fit. I didn't care."

Ana's defiance continued throughout her stay at Queen of Heaven.

> I fixed them. I wasn't about to take abuse. I became a very tough kid. That is one thing that came out of this, and because I had my sister. I wasn't going to tolerate anything. They were afraid of me. One time Sister Ignatius said to me, "We are so sorry, but we are sending you to a juvenile delinquent's home." Ana thought that this time they were actually going to send her away, but instead of cowering, the feisty teenager looked straight at the nun, laughed, and said, "You go ahead and do that. I know the number for Catholic

Charities, why don't you go right ahead." She opened her eyes wide and I never heard anything else about that move.

Lourdes remembers Ana as a "spitfire" in those days. "My sister is 2 inches shorter than me, it doesn't seem at all like her, as she is very petite, but in those days she would protect me and beat up all the kids that tried to hurt me. She was always there for me. And to this day I always look up to my sister, and when I am in trouble or a difficulty, it is always her I call."

Most girls assumed a more docile position when facing their woes. "I went along with the flow. It wasn't easy," says María Cristina. "Once I was standing in line to go to chapel and someone said something. It wasn't me, and this nun turned around and whacked me in the neck. I passed out. They were very strict. It wasn't easy."

Denver welcomed not only children but also adult Cuban refugees, who sought jobs the overcrowded Miami area could not offer. Catholic Charities resettled an average of 2 or 3 adults a week and had resettled 375 Cuban refugees in Denver from March 1961 to October 1962. Additionally, 129 unaccompanied children had found shelter in Denver.[6] Monsignor Elmer J. Kolka spearheaded the effort, working closely with the council of churches and the Jewish Family and Children's Service.

Occasionally, Cubans residing in Denver would try to cheer the children at the orphanage with a social call. On May 20, 1962, the Committee of Exiled Cubans, a group made up of 150 adult Denver refugees, celebrated the anniversary of Cuba's independence from Spain with a Mass and then a visit to the then forty-eight Cuban children at Queen of Heaven.[7]

Most of the girls who attended senior high school went to public schools, although some had scholarships to a private Catholic school, Mount Carmel. The younger girls would give the older ones money to bring back items from the "outside world," such as transistor radios.

When the girls got their allowance, they used to go up the

street to a drug and grocery store called Miller's. "I used to buy Cheetos. Most people bought hair curlers or toiletries that they didn't give you," says María Cristina. "Once I saved and I bought one of those Brownie cameras. The big thing was to get a camera so you could take pictures and send them to your parents in Cuba. We all had black and white photos, because it was cheaper."

Some of her photos of that time show summer outings at the Mother Cabrini Shrine, in Golden, a town in the mountains where the girls were taken each summer. There, a spring flows and is claimed to be miraculous. Mother Cabrini had arranged large white stones in the shape of a heart, surrounded by a smaller stone cross and a crown of thorns. Three hundred and seventy-three steps lead to a 22-foot statue of the Sacred Heart. Many of the girls remember cleaning the floors of the shrine and even cleaning the road. All of them recall it as a place of great physical beauty and a delightful diversion from the monotony at Queen of Heaven.

Lourdes Lopo remembers racing up to her sister with the wonderful news that they were leaving Queen of Heaven. "She told me that she had secretly prayed to Mother Cabrini asking her that if she was real, she would get us out of there."

In keeping with a trend both within the order of the Missionary Sisters of the Sacred Heart and that was also sweeping the nation, orphanages were phased out and refashioned as private schools. In March 1966, Mother Elizabeth spoke excitedly about her "new" school, Cabrini Memorial School, formerly Queen of Heaven, to a *Rocky Mountain News* reporter: "Don't mention the orphanage. It is a school now, a private school for girls and some boys."[8] The home and school were closed and demolished in 1969.

MISSION OF THE IMMACULATE VIRGIN, MOUNT LORETTO, STATEN ISLAND, NEW YORK

Manuel Ponte, then fifteen years old, arrived with several other Cuban teenage boys in New York in early 1961. They were met by a priest and taken for a ride on the Staten Island Ferry en route to their new home, a mostly black and Puerto Rican orphanage. The beautiful Manhattan skyline bewitched the boys. Ignorant of their destination, they stopped for a nice meal of roast beef. The boys' first clue about their future was when the priest warned them no to get used to the nice food because they would not be getting it where they were going.

The Mission of the Immaculate Virgin, Mount Loretto, was situated in the southern part of Staten Island. The steeple of the 1891 church of St. Joachim and St. Ann was the prominent landmark in a sprawling, bucolic 375-acre-plus setting by the sea. From the waterfront the land stretched to Amboy Road. Hylan Boulevard bisected the property, boys on one side and girls on the other. It had its own cemetery where some of the orphans raised there who served in World War II rest, as well as Father John Drumgoole, its founder.

In 1961, Xaverian Brothers and the Sisters of St. Francis, with the help of lay teachers, cared for 880 children ages six to eighteen. When the Cuban boys arrived, Mount Loretto or "The Mount," was celebrating its ninetieth birthday. It was the largest child-caring institution in the United States.

The teenage boys at Mount Loretto attended a vocational school on the premises, St. Joseph's Trade School, where they learned drafting, printing, carpentry, auto mechanics, tailoring, printing, and electronics.

Upon arrival the Cubans were placed in living quarters separate from the rest of the boys, according to Conrado Forte, who recalls that the Cuban boys quickly demanded to be placed with the rest since sooner or later they would have to face each other. They also insisted on attending a regular high school, not the trade school. A concession was made in their case, and they were allowed to go to Totenville High School. "We were adamant about it and we even led the way for other bright blacks and Puerto Rican students who would be later allowed to go to regular high school," says Manuel. This proved correct, as by 1964, fifty-two of the older boys and girls attended high school outside the mission.

"My brother Roberto and I escaped the first night, but then

we had to turn ourselves in. Where were we going to go?" says José A. Arenas, then a distressed sixteen year old. "We arrived and we didn't like what we saw there and I told my brother, 'This is not for us, let's get out of here.' It was very cold and they caught us right away. We thought somebody was going to give us a ride to Miami. We had no sense of where we were, but we were in a town called Tottenville in Staten Island."

José remembers getting into a fight with a black boy his first week there. There were roll calls at certain hours. "They would call your name, you'd stand against the wall and you would answer, 'Present.' And while being in roll call a black guy told me something that I didn't understand, and of course I replied, 'your mother,' and a Puerto Rican wise guy translated for him. So he put his fists up, and I punched first, but it was the only hit I landed." It didn't take José long to realize that fighting was not to his advantage because he didn't have the fighting experience of the rest of his streetwise companions.

Another one of the boys told him that the only people the orphanage residents feared were crazy people since they were unpredictable. So José hatched a survival plan. He went to the town library and stole a book, *The Rise and Fall of the Third Reich*.

"The cover was black with a white swastika. And I spent a whole year with that book under my arm." The book became his shield. "After that nobody bothered me, they thought I was crazy."

At thirteen, Conrado Forte was the youngest of the Cuban boys. He remembers arriving with a few pieces of jewelry and being asked, "Is that real gold?" Innocently he replied, "Of course, what else is it going to be?" The jewelry was stolen from him immediately. Searches for hidden weapons were part of the Mount's routine, because zip guns were manufactured from car antennas in the vocational shop. "Many of the boys were criminals. The system didn't know what to do with them and they just placed them there," says Eulogio Soto. "Many even had bullet scars."

The boys at Mount Loretto were quite hardened by life. Those who weren't orphans came from broken homes or were not wanted by their parents. "I will never forget this kid of about fifteen going on one hundred who told me that his goal in life was to find his father so he could kill him," recalls a shocked Emilio Soto, still amazed and confounded by the conversation, "And here I was fresh out of my parents' nest, parents who I loved dearly."

"The counselors, and the Catholic priests in charge, behaved as the military, very regimented and uncaring. I think in a way they were tough on us so it wouldn't seem to the other kids they were giving us special treatment, though sending us to an outside school created a lot of resentment," he adds.

Emilio's recollections turned to their weekend free time:

> We were given permission to leave the grounds on every Saturday from 11:00 A.M. to 4:00 P.M. as long you were in good standing, and all your chores were done, like mopping and buffing floors, helping in the kitchen washing dishes or helping with the grounds. With these five hours of freedom we could go anywhere but had to check in by or before 4:00 P.M. no matter what. No excuses. Of course we would always go to Tottenville which was the closest town.
>
> One cold Saturday in the middle of February, I went to Tottenville. There I met Kristine, a girlfriend from school who had been shopping and was on her way home. I walked her to the bus stop and we sat in a bench to wait for her bus. We sat and talked, held hands, and kissed as the buses went by. Somehow when you are having such a wonderful time, time has no meaning. She took the 6:00 P.M. bus and I began the walk back to the Mount. Mr. Furlong, the sadistic head counselor, a retired marine who didn't hesitate to use physical force against any of the kids from the Mount if he saw it fit, was driving around town to see if anyone had flown the coop. He saw me but didn't stop. Just before I reached the grounds of Mount Loretto the police and Mr. Furlong were waiting for me.
>
> I completely froze in place. I didn't run or try to hide. I was scared to death. Mr. Furlong came forth, grabbed me by

the coat and slapped me across the face with the back of his hand. The strap on his glove left a terrible mark on my face for several days. He then went on to remind me that I was a Cuban refugee in his country and had to follow certain rules or else he would make sure I'd end up in the street. He told the police I had run away and asked the police to take me in. I was taken to the police station in Pleasant Plains. I was humiliated and harassed by the police who made sure their tactics were consistent with those of Mr. Furlong.

Around 10:00 P.M. that evening I was taken back and released to Mount Loretto. There, I was placed in an open fenced yard. I was forced to stand with arms up from 10:30 P.M. until 12:30 A.M. My ears were in pain from the cold and my feet numb from standing on the snow. I was suspended for six weeks without my dollar-a-week allowance which meant I couldn't write my parents during that time.

Eulogio Soto, Emilio's brother, also recalls being punished in the snow with arms outstretched, but he says he always puts himself in the other person's shoes and understands that rigid discipline was necessary to keep order at the orphanage. His attitude was if you play, you pay. He claims that his brother found it very difficult to adjust to life in an orphanage, whereas he was more diplomatic about his tactics. He befriended the nun who distributed them their clothing, usually Wrangler jeans, and the relationship paid off. She would slip him extras on occasion. Eulogio also remembers fondly Father Kehan, who liked the Cuban boys and would give him extra paying jobs so he could save for his parents' airline tickets to leave Cuba. Eulogio later found out that this extra money came from the brother's own money.

The friendships and relations formed in school, outside the dreary orphanage walls, served as a much needed oasis for the boys. "Totenville High School was a blessing. We'd see normal people," says José. "We were very happy to be in the school. We made friends and they sometimes invited you to their house on Saturday. For us this was tremendous."

There was a price for this freedom, however. It earned the resentment of the other boys at the Mount. Also, it was difficult to connect with the local girls because it was nearly impossible for a boy to be accepted by a girl's family if they knew you lived at Mount Loretto. The Cuban boys had to explain their temporary circumstances and prove themselves to be different. One of the boys was actually kicked out of a girl's house, only to be helped by the girl's aunt who had visited Cuba and put in a good word for him.

By the end of 1962 important changes were occurring at the orphanage. A local newspaper, the *Staten Island Advance,* reported on September 6, 1962:

> Against the changing tides of the child welfare system, the Mission of the Immaculate Virgin, Mount Loretto, is a rock. The immigrant orphans who once milled about "The Mount," now adorn the walls of the church's photo gallery. The blind girls are gone, the waves of refugee children from revolutionary Cuba and war-torn Vietnam have ebbed. Today their beds are occupied by the developmentally and emotionally disabled, mostly black, many the victims of poverty, drugs, abuse and neglect.

Through the years the Mount has gone through several changes, adapting yet always surviving, and still serving children as was Father Drumgoole's dream when he took over a shelter for homeless New York City newsboys in 1871. Today it is a recreation center run by the Catholic Youth Organization, and half of its forty-six buildings are unused. About 145 acres of the waterfront property have been designated to be open space by New York's Environmental Protection Agency.

Of his experience at Mount Loretto, José Arenas says, "At the end you resign yourself, but at that time you wonder, why me? You realize that it is just bad luck and you have to forge ahead."

Forget injuries.
Never forget kindness.

—CONFUCIUS

CHAPTER 8

Life with the Joneses

Secretary of Health, Education, and Welfare Abraham Ribicoff appealed to American kindness in early 1962, asking them to open their homes and hearts to Cuban children. "Many U.S. citizens travelling through Latin America have received the gracious Spanish welcome 'Esta es Su Casa.' Now several hundred American families can return the hospitality each month saying to Cuban children bereft of parents, 'Make yourself at home!' Under the Cuban refugee program the department of Health, Education, and Welfare will pay for the care of the children. But homes are needed. We can think of few better ways to 'fight communism' than to care for the children who flee from it. Interested?"[1]

As the request went throughout the United States, American families opened their doors with the generosity of spirit characteristic of this nation. Placing teenage boys in foster care proved to be the most difficult; unfortunately, they were also the ones most in need and outnumbered girls two to one. The following stories illustrate the kindness of four families, from Miami, Orlando, New Mexico, and Iowa, who made a wonderful difference in a young person's life.

PETER MARTÍNEZ AND THE HUBER FAMILY
IN ROSWELL, NEW MEXICO

When Molly Huber welcomed Peter into her home, he was an eleven-year-old child, just separated from his parents. She reflects on the day two years later when he left her home to join his uncle. "You know, the day Peter walked away from me, the day he left, oh it was so hard to see him leave. And I thought, 'Oh God, I've just wasted two years of my life. I thought, 'He doesn't give a hoot, why did I put all this effort?' Because I did try, but I thought it was something that had gone down the drain."

Peter, then Pedro, had arrived two years earlier, in 1962, alone on a long flight from Miami to Albuquerque, where he was met by Mrs. Huber, her husband Patrick, and their three children, Judy, aged nine, Mary, seven, and four-year-old Philip. Somewhere along the 200-mile drive to Roswell, they stopped at a roadside restaurant to stretch their legs and eat. Pedro spoke no English at all. They served him a plate with jelly for his toast and he asked what it was. When told "jelly," he thought it was Jello and ate it with a spoon.

The change from being a spoiled only child to being the eldest of four children was not an easy adjustment for Pedro, who remembers being rebellious at the time, in large part because of all the changes he had experienced in his eleven years, starting with his parents' divorce. Mrs. Huber remembers him as a very masculine but sensitive boy. Sometimes she would hear him cry at night. "I would go in to try to console him, but he used to say to me 'the woman.' It wasn't in his scheme of things to have a woman try to console him, he was a man."

Bringing Pedro into the household originally had been Mr. Huber's idea. The priest had asked for families to take in Cuban children and he had told his wife, "Why don't we take one. We have three children of our own, but there is always room for one

more." When asked what sex and age they preferred, Mr. Huber replied that they would take anybody who needed shelter.

Today, Roswell is a city with a population of about 44,000 and a reputation for UFO sightings. Back in 1962, it was a lot smaller than Havana, and an eleven-year-old could bicycle from end to end of town, something Peter did often, much to the chagrin of Mrs. Huber who worried to death when he would be missing for long periods of time.

When Pedro arrived at Roswell in April, Mrs. Huber assigned Judy, their eldest daughter, then nine, to read books with him and help him learn English. By the time the fall semester started, Pedro was already speaking in English with all the other neighborhood children.

Coming from a different culture' and socioeconomic background, Pedro witnessed a number of perplexing situations. For instance, he used to be surprised at Mrs. Huber's workload and he'd ask her, "How come you do all these things, you drive the car, you clean the house, you take the children to school?" And she replied that they couldn't afford to have somebody come in to clean. Indeed, Pedro might have had an ulterior motive for asking about a maid, as all the children in the household had chores, something he disliked. A team made up of the three oldest children, including Pedro, would wash the dishes, rotating the duties. One week one would wash, the other would dry, and a third would put away.

As Pedro learned English he became quite a good student getting As and Bs except in conduct, because he loved to make jokes and talk. When he got a D in conduct he had to wash, dry, *and* put away the dishes for a week. When he realized, the second time around, that another D loomed in his future, he went to his teacher's home and pleaded, "Please don't give me a D. I'll do anything. They'll make me wash dishes for a month."

Pedro became Peter when Mrs. Huber tried to win the boy over by pronouncing his name in a very Spanish way by trying to

roll her rrr's. "He got really mad," she says. "So I thought, to the devil with all this. We had some real go arounds I tell you." What Mrs. Huber didn't realize at the moment was that instead of Pedro, she had called him *perro,* which means dog in Spanish. Ultimately, Pedro asked to be called Peter.

"I was very rebellious at that time, I had been rolling around for so long. I have always resented changes, not being able to have a true friend from your early childhood, not establishing roots in one place." In addition to the underlying issues, Peter faced further trauma when he learned of his mother's imprisonment while living at the Hubers'. Desperate to be with her son, she had joined a group planning to escape Cuba clandestinely by boat. "One of the organizers belonged to the government and they were waiting for them at the beach," says Peter. He claims that his mother died while in exile in the United States at a relatively young age because of the hepatitis she contracted in the Piñar del Rio jail where she completed a one-year sentence. "That was very painful to me. I rebelled, but in the long run it is a matter of adaptation."

Today Peter remembers gratefully all the lessons that he learned in the Huber home, even the seemingly insignificant ones. He remembers one day while the family was in the car, he threw a piece of paper out the window. Mr. Huber watched him from the rearview mirror and kept driving. After a distance, he stopped. "'Go pick up the paper you threw out the window,' he told me. To this day, I've never thrown a piece of paper out the window again," says Peter. "I have always been grateful to them, they accepted a challenge. I always understood it was a heroic undertaking," says Peter of his foster parents.

Mr. Huber passed away a decade ago. Today, Peter and Mrs. Huber enjoy a solid, loving relationship. "I tell you, he is easily as concerned and good to me as my own children, and he was only here for two years. He wasn't able to show me this other side of him when he was with me. So it has been a real blessing as far as I'm concerned," she says.

THE McGREGOR SMITH CUBAN BOYS, CORAL GABLES, FLORIDA

A series of auspicious events surrounded the three Cepero brothers' departure from Cuba. Events started to unfold in Cuba, where they attended Candler College, a Methodist school. When their parents decided to send them out alone, contacts were made through this school to the Methodist community in Miami. In 1962, during a Sunday service at the First Methodist Church in Coral Gables, Mrs. Elizabeth Smith heard her pastor's plea for temporary homes for three Cuban brothers.

When Mrs. Smith arrived home, she told her husband about the boys and asked if they could take them all in, since their two sons had already left home. Mr. Smith asked, "What if they are black?" and she replied, "I would want them anyway." After much pleading, crying, and cajoling, Mrs. Smith got her way.

Mr. Smith's eventual acquiescence guaranteed the Cepero brothers—Pablo, sixteen; Eloy Guillermo, fifteen; and Eloy Mario, eleven—a luxurious life upon their arrival at an elegant two-storied home located at 1132 South Greenway Drive, facing the Granada Golf Course in Coral Gables.

Their new life included a swimming pool and the services of a butler and a maid. Coral Gables, a city within the Miami metro area, was the richest neighborhood in the area, certainly outside the reach of the average Cuban refugee. The area had been designed by George Merrick in the mid-1920s, built on his family's former citrus plantation, and patterned after a Mediterranean village. The houses were Spanish and Italian in architectural style. Even authentic gondolas once traveled a series of canals.

McGregor Smith was a dynamo of a man, and like Merrick, a visionary. A native of Tennessee, his usual attire, even for work, was a short-sleeved shirt and a straw hat. He was the chairman of the board and chief executive officer of Florida Power and Light Company, member of the board of directors of both the Federal Reserve in Atlanta and Eastern Airlines, and one of the five mem-

bers of the Atomic Energy Commission. He oversaw the building of Turkey Point, South Florida's first nuclear energy plant.

The boys brought a new lease on life to Mr. Smith, who was undergoing regrets about not having spent enough time with his own children. The boys arrived with three changes of clothes, the amount allotted by the Cuban government in June 1962. Shortly after their arrival, he took them shopping for clothes. "You have to look nice, because you are now my sons," he told them. Never one to have something as trivial as a foreign language interfere in his communication with the boys, Mr. Smith immediately took a cram course in Spanish.

The middle Cepero brother, Eloy Guillermo, was not only a gifted athlete but also a gregarious, outgoing person. Mr. Smith bonded with the boy, seeing in him a reflection of himself. When Eloy Guillermo entered Coral Gables High School he ran the track-and-field course in his regular sneakers and broke the school record. The athletic coach enrolled him on the basketball team. "I spoke no English, they had to translate the moves for me," Eloy Guillermo explains. "Mr. Smith told me, 'You have a lot of talent. We have to exploit it.' So he became my trainer. He'd get me up at 6:00 every morning and make me run in the golf course across from the house. After six months I was the best runner in the city. I was made an all-city athlete."

"He was so proud of us, he bought a stack of *Miami Herald* newspapers to give to all his friends." When Eloy Guillermo played basketball he had his own cheering squad as Mr. Smith, the cook, the butler, and the whole family attended.

During one of the games a rival player was elbowing Eloy Guillermo. Mr. Smith charged down during a break to admonish Eloy Guillermo, "How are you allowing yourself to be pushed?" Because of this meddling, the coach threw Mr. Smith out of the game, only to have to apologize to him the next day. Mr. Smith gloated, "I'm right, because he has to learn that nobody can push him around." He was echoing a philosophy that extended well beyond basketball. Eloy Guillermo failed mathematics, and

Mr. Smith took over his summer tutoring making sure he achieved an A in the fall semester.

Younger brother Eloy Mario bonded with Mrs. Smith. "She taught me English and helped me make the adjustment to a new culture, she was so sweet and helpful," he says. "She was a real southern lady, had never worked and had gone to finishing school. She was a gifted artist. I still have a portrait she made of me." The Smiths were in their sixties when they took in the Cepero boys. They asked the boys to call them *tía y tío*, or aunt and uncle. "We brought them joy. They tried to teach us English, and we made them laugh."

During their first summer together Mr. Smith decided they were going to see some of the country while camping. He packed a station wagon with the butler and the three boys, and they traveled his home state of Tennessee and also to Georgia and South Carolina, hardly ever camping along the way because the car was so stuffed that getting things in and out of it was a chore, so they stayed in hotels. One night they did stop at a campground. The boys had played musical instruments in Cuba and discovered that music transcended language barriers. Eloy Guillermo played the conga drums, younger brother Eloy Mario a pair of maracas, and Pablo the harmonica. Mr. Smith also played the harmonica. The foursome enjoyed playing together and did so regularly. One night Mr. Smith and the McGregor Smith Cuban Boys treated stunned campers to a live performance.

As part of the camping trip they spent more than two weeks on Mr. Smith's property in Blue Springs, Ocala, in the north-central part of Florida, which Smith later donated as a wildlife preserve. However, memories of that summer of swimming in a clear lake, boating, and campfires are etched in the minds of the Cepero brothers.

The brothers remember the fun and excitement of that summer, just as they remember other inspiring moments. Eloy Guillermo recalls one Sunday morning when McGregor Smith told them to put on their suits because they were going to

church. Since Mr. Smith was not a typical churchgoing person, the boys were surprised. They started walking through the woods, Smith with a bible in one hand and a machete in the other. Their surprise grew even more when he took the machete and partly cleared a path to a hilltop.

Once there, after taking in the view, Smith read aloud from his bible for about half an hour. When he finished reading, he wept. He told the boys, "I'm crying thinking of how much your parents must be suffering without you." All four joined in a teary, sweaty embrace, wearing suits and ties under the fiery Florida sun, surrounded by God's amphitheater.

During the year, there would be other occasions, including the time they flew to the company's camp in Palatka, northeast Florida, on the corporate plane. Eloy Mario thought life in his new homeland was wonderful, "I thought everybody lived this way."

It was not unusual for the Smiths to entertain senators, governors, and the "Who's Who" of Florida in their Coral Gables home; the Cepero boys were involved in these events. Everyday dinners were elaborate events with fresh flowers on the table, and Mrs. Smith discreetly summoning the butler by pressing a floor button. He would then enter the dining room carrying silver trays from which the boys served themselves.

Eloy Guillermo recalls with amusement the fun-loving personality of Mr. Smith. One night they saw Mr. Smith dressed in red from head to toe and wondered where he was going in such attire. He looked at the boys and surprised them by saying, "Get your musical instruments, we are going to play tonight." Mr. Smith was the featured keynote speaker at the American Banking Association banquet in Miami Beach. A walking cayenne pepper of a man and the McGregor Smith Cuban Boys entertained the astonished convention.

A few months after the Cepero boys arrived in the United States, direct flights between Cuba and the United States terminated. Because Mr. and Mrs. Cepero had not been able to get their exit visas in time, they had to find a third country to leave Cuba. They chose Mexico. Their exit permits were granted two years after their sons' arrival. Mr. Smith was in the Soviet Union, attending a meeting of the Atomic Energy Commission. As soon as he received a message that the Ceperos were arriving in Miami from Mexico he asked the Soviets to fly him to Helsinki where he boarded a plane to New York and then connected to Miami. He made it in time to greet them at the airport.

"You should have seen that reunion! My mother, my father, the three of us, Mr. and Mrs. Smith, the butler, it was amazing," Eloy Guillermo remembers. The Ceperos also found shelter with the Smiths for a month, until they decided to move to Tampa where they had friends. McGregor Smith helped the Ceperos buy a home and a business. Eloy Guillermo stayed at the University of Miami, living at his fraternity house and spending weekends at the Smith home. He never lived with his parents again, because he was already on his own.

In Miami, on the way to Key Biscayne, by Turkey Point, there is a sign that reads "McGregor Smith Recreational Area." On the wall of Eloy Guillermo Cepero's office at the mortgage banking company that he co-owns, there is a large oil portrait of McGregor Smith. "When he died, his wife and I were with him," says Eloy Guillermo, who remained a true son to Smith to the very end.

"Looking back, it was like a fairy tale," says Eloy Mario, realizing how lucky they were.

CARLOS PORTES AND THE HOCKETTS, MARSHALLTOWN, IOWA

Carlos Portes was having a difficult time assimilating to his new life in the center of America, in Marshalltown, Iowa, where he was living with his uncle's family. However, the eleven-year-old boy found much needed refuge and comfort in his Catholic faith. He claims that his belief in God gave him strength in those days. Church provided Carlos with something comforting and familiar. In order to be closely involved in his religion, he

became a fanatic altar boy, serving every single Mass he could possibly serve. In church, language was not a problem for young Carlos, since Mass was universally said in Latin and he knew the words from Cuba.

"I used to meet the priest at Saint Luke's hospital every single day at six o'clock in the morning, bring Holy Communion to all the sick beds and serve Mass every morning," Carlos explains. "Then we ate breakfast in the hospital and the priest would drive me to the local school where we'd say Mass for the entire student body. Again, I was the altar boy. On Sundays I was always the altar boy for every Mass because I stayed very, very close to the church all the time."

Mr. and Mrs. Leon Hockett were regular church attendees and they took a strong liking to young Carlos. One Sunday they invited him to their home for lunch and to spend some time with them. They repeated the invitation the following Sunday, and a relationship began to grow. Carlos found himself spending more and more time with the Hocketts, in whose home he even had his own room with a desk and bookcases.

Carlos recalls:

> They had never had any children, so here was a challenge for them, to help raise this young boy, whose culture they really didn't understand. But I had this bubble of joy, or whatever you want to call it, that threw a different feeling into the household. It was very, very interesting because they didn't speak Spanish and I didn't speak English, so all of our communication was in sign language. And all of a sudden I started becoming the all-American boy.

Kay Hockett would spend hours sitting with Carlos, correcting his English, teaching him proper diction and sentence structure, manners, and the importance of being a gentleman. "He was so eager about everything that was American; he liked American expressions. Anything that was American, he just wanted it and craved it," she says.

Carlos says those teachings have stayed with him throughout his life. As a successful businessman today, he says that in business situations he is often the only one addressing people as "Sir" or "Madam" and that this respectfulness has made him stand out in his profession. However, those American idioms that he loved and picked up easily also got him in trouble. Mrs. Hockett says that her late husband Leon used to collect these expressions to tell Carlos, who would never forget them. One day Leon taught him, "If the shoe fits, wear it." The next day in school a nun was calling Carlos's attention to something, and he replied, "If the shoe fits ... " He was reprimanded and that night at the PTA meeting, Mrs. Hockett went over to the nun and told her she should be reprimanding her husband instead for not explaining to Carlos that these expressions cannot be used all the time.

Carlos knows he was fortunate. He regrets that immigrants that go to a large metropolis like New York or Chicago or Los Angeles do not really get to know what American generosity is all about, because people are thrown into melting pots where competition is severe and everything is about survival. He observes:

> When you actually share in Middle America you find that people do care about your development and when you talk about a little town like Marshalltown, everything there has to do with the children, with the education of the child. You could have a little league baseball team or you could have a Tom Sawyer play in school and everybody from the town comes to see it, because they want to give you their support. All of a sudden I became integrated into that whole process.

Mrs. Hockett remembers a time when they had bought a new, more powerful tractor, and Carlos immediately asked to drive it. Mr. Hockett refused, so Mrs. Hockett intervened asking Carlos if he knew how to drive it. He replied that he did. She convinced her husband that the boy couldn't harm the machine, and Carlos was allowed. "After several turns back and forth, the next thing I know he hit the magnolia tree and took one-third of it

out. As he was heading to the back edge and I said, 'Carlos Carlos, what happened, you told me you knew how to drive?' 'Yes,' he replied. 'But I do not know how to stop.'" Mrs. Hockett laughs at the memory more than thirty years later.

Carlos was a determined and resourceful boy and always seemed to be able to make money. When other teenagers were saving for records or a car, he was saving money to get his parents out of Cuba. He worked as a movie theater usher, mowed grass, cleaned yards, and performed all sorts of jobs. In order to get around, Carlos needed transportation. "He bought a bicycle from some people who wanted to help him, but he had to pay one dollar for it. He knew the value of it," remembers Mrs. Hockett. "And that bicycle was the greatest love of his life. And I remember one night it was stolen and was he broken-hearted! Someone told him to pray to one of the saints and if he prayed hard enough it would be returned in some way. The phone ran that night, and it was the police department. They had found his bicycle!"

She remembers:

> Money was quite a touchy thing. We were so careful not to give him money, because it would be so easy to win him into our family, if he was free to have things. My husband would often buy things, and have extras, so Carlos and he would share them. But just to give him money, we never did. We did not want him to ever care for us because of that money part because we were alone, and it was so easy ... I enjoyed him so much!

Once Carlos felt like an American youth, he, like many teenagers in the sixties joined a rock-and-roll band. Carlos appointed himself as lead vocalist, singing, with a Spanish accent, "She Loves You," "Twist and Shout," and other Beatles tunes. The band practiced in one member's garage, but one day when the neighbors complained, Carlos said, "I know where we can go," and off to the Hocketts they went. "So they came over," says Mrs. Hockett. "It didn't make any difference to me and he knew it. It

was a good outlet for them. My husband made some tape recordings. They weren't too bad, and got a lot of jobs, although a lot of
it was pretty wild and pretty noisy."

While the Hocketts' influence on Carlos and his American
experience was indelible, there is one incident in particular that
has branded itself upon Carlos's memory, a representation of the
affirmation that he found in his road to becoming an American.
Carlos went to an old soldier's home in Marshalltown. He knew
how to sing "La Cucaracha," and the old soldier knew how to
play it on his harmonica, but didn't know the song's words. "An
old American soldier makes me, a Cuban boy, feel part of the
fact that now we are going to do something together," he says.
This isn't something he envisions happening in a big city. He
believes Iowa did play a very important role in the acceptability
process. Middle America helped him establish his roots.

In 1997 Carlos Portes received the Ellis Island Medal of
Honor given to immigrants who have contributed to America.
He flew Kay Hockett to New York to stand by him. Back in his
home, after the touching ceremony, she called him aside and
told him, "When I was a little girl my mother, brothers, and sisters pitched in to buy my father a gift. When he died, my mother
gave it to Leon, your foster father. I think it is only proper that
you have it," and handed him a beautiful ring made of petrified
wood, with a conquistador carved on it.

"He is a wonderful son to me, I don't know how I could ask
him to be better. I'm alone, and he always tell me, 'Kay, I'm only
three hours away. I can be there any time you need me.' And
that just tells the whole story. He's quite the love of my life. So
Cuba gave me quite a bit."

JULIO NUÑEZ AND THE SAGAN FAMILY, ORLANDO, FLORIDA

A group of boys sat waiting at the Greyhound bus station in
Orlando, Florida. They were coming from Camp Saint John in

Green Cove Springs, Florida, after having been in Camp San Pedro in Orlando, which was being closed. The teenagers were on their way to live with foster parents in the Orlando area.

When the boys heard they were being placed in foster homes they were relieved, as life in the camp had not been easy. Believing that they were being placed in rich homes and hoping for new wardrobes, some had thrown out their old clothes and filled their suitcases with rocks.

Clutching their rock-laden suitcases, Julio Nuñez and Tony Ardavin, who were going to live with the same family, eagerly looked out for the car picking them up. They saw a beautiful, large, shiny car pull up, and their mood lifted, thinking it had come for them. Their hearts sank, however, when they saw one of the boys, Cesar Calvet, get into the car. Then they saw another such car came to pick up Mel Martínez. "Then we saw an older car, and it was for us. But we were the winners in the end," says Julio Nuñez. "They all went to good homes, but we went to an outstanding one."

The outstanding home belonged to Mr. and Mrs. Joseph Sagan, whose life intertwined with the Cuban boys one Sunday when they attended Mass with their four daughters. During the sermon the priest told his flock about the need for foster families for the boys from Camp San Pedro. Joseph Sagan admits, "I figured that they would not be talking to me, because I had four daughters, so I was only halfway listening."

But daughter Eileen had been listening. During the drive home from church that day, she asked her father about being a foster family for the boys. He answered, "But you are girls, four girls in a family, and those are hot-blooded young men. I don't know if it would be a good thing." Eileen persisted, reminding him of the extra bedroom available in the new addition they had recently built onto their Dial Drive home.

Meanwhile, Mr. Sagan was thinking he should have been paying more attention to the priest for details, since after all, they were barely getting by economically; how could they take on two more persons? He told his family that he would have to think about it. Eileen didn't let it go. "Well Dad, you are always talking about doing a Christian duty. Now we have a chance to go ahead and do something about it." Mrs. Sagan, who had been silent up to that moment, joined in, "Joseph, what do you say to that?"

Mr. Sagan lost the battle against the five women, and Julio and Tony moved in. Back in Cuba, Julio's relationship to his own parents had not been close, so in the Sagans he found the family he had been searching for. "He was an Air Force person, very American and strict. She was a truly remarkable person, she became my mother," Julio explained. He called Mrs. Sagan "Missy." Eileen's role with Julio was that of an older sister and confidant. While Julio also got along well with the other two sisters Kathy and Peggy, he had conflicts with Tricia because they had the same personality.

Upon their arrival Mr. Sagan immediately spelled out behavior boundaries and rules. Julio remembers being told, "I don't want you to touch my daughters and you have to behave like gentlemen," he says. "And that is how it always was."

The boys shared a room and as part of the family they were assigned responsibilities such as dish washing and lawn mowing. "We lost about two mowers, as they used to run over the lawn sprinklers with the mowers. We went through a pump that was turned on during the freeze, and it cracked," says Mr. Sagan. "We used to call it the Cuban invasion. They were good citizens all around, no question, their upbringing was solid as they all had families who were professional people. And although they were somewhat spoiled, they learned to eat Ukrainian dishes—pirogies—which my wife had learned to cook for me."

As part of the family, the boys were allowed to drive the car if they paid for their own insurance. Both had accidents. Tony ran over a neighbor's palm tree and mailbox, confessed to it, and made amends. Julio was upset at the unfairness of the American system when he failed to halt at a stop sign and totaled the coral-and-black station wagon. He objected because his insurance rate

TO BAGGAGE CLAIM
→
PARA RECLAMAR
EQUIPAJE

George Guarch receives unaccompanied children at Miami International Airport. Photo courtesy of the Guarch-Pardo family.

The Cuban flag flies over Florida City. Photo courtesy of Barry University Archives and Special Collections, Miami Shores, Florida.

Unaccompanied Cuban children arriving in Miami, met by George Guarch of the Catholic Welfare Bureau. Photo courtesy of the Guarch-Pardo family.

Left: A group of girls in Florida City. Photo courtesy of the Perez Plana family, gifted to the author.

Above: Daydreaming of the United States. Photo courtesy of the Perez Plana family, gifted to the author.

Florida City girls on an outing. Photo courtesy of the Perez Plana family, gifted to the author.

Yvonne Conde happily reunited with her brother Pepe, her mother, and a friend in Bayfront Park, downtown Miami, months after their arrival. Photo from the author's collection.

Monsignor Walsh speaks to newly arrived Cuban Boys at St. Raphael's Hall. Photo courtesy of Barry University Archives and Special Collections, Miami Shores, Florida.

U.S. Secretary of Health, Education, and Welfare Abraham Ribicoff and Father Walsh. Photo courtesy of Barry University Archives and Special Collections, Miami Shores, Florida.

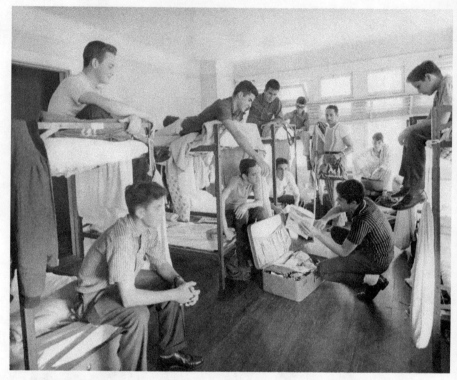

Boys unpack in a dormitory. Photo courtesy of Barry University Archives and Special Collections, Miami Shores, Florida.

Above: Unveiling of the street sign for Pedro Pan Place, City of Florida City. Photo courtesy of Clemente C. Amezaga.

Left: Closeup of Pedro Pan Place street sign, City of Florida City. Photo courtesy of Clemente C Amezaga.

Group of Pedro Pan women holding a sign that says Operation Pedro Pan Av, designated by City of Hialeah. Photo courtesy of Clemente C. Amezaga.

Right: Historic marker in Florida City. Photo courtesy of Clemente C. Amezaga.

Below: Operation Pedro Pan Historic Site, Camp Matecumbe. Photo courtesy of Clemente C. Amezaga.

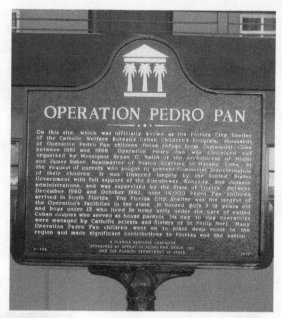

Street sign for Las Muchacitas de Villa María St. Photo courtesy of Luisa Talavera.

went up while Tricia, who had also had a car accident, did not have her insurance increased. He couldn't understand why. With all of the cultural adjustments and adherence to American laws, Mr. Sagan explains, "You could not make him see or make him understand that insurance companies had different rules for teenage boys and girls."

Julio acknowledges all that he learned about responsibility and the value of a dollar from his American foster family. Conversely, however, Julio couldn't make the Sagans understand other ways in which adapting to the United States was more difficult. As Cuban refugees Julio and Tony faced prejudice and discrimination in school and in their personal lives "The football team would gang up on you in the school bathroom, they wanted to burn you." Then in his personal life, he tells of his devastation, "I fell in love with a beautiful Irish girl, we had a romance something like Romeo and Juliet's, but her father didn't want her dating me because I was Cuban and an 'orphan.' So she married the star quarterback, divorced shortly thereafter, and died of a Lithium overdose. I'll never forget her, I loved her very much."

To counter the discrimination he endured, Julio threw himself into his studies. His hard work paid off. After years of study he went on to become a physician. "He wanted to receive acceptance by his peers in school. He wanted to wear the clothes that they wore. But, there was a little animosity on the part of some of the young men in school towards him and the others. He never said anything about it until later on in years," remembers Mr. Sagan.

According to Mr. Sagan, Tony has a different reaction to his U.S. experience. As Mr. Sagan explains, Tony "didn't seem to be hip to the trends. He had his own ideas, but he was not a studious person. He did very poorly in school." He speaks of how they were considering taking him out of the program because he was failing his grades. They suggested to Tony that he get involved in a trade such as mechanics. Tony would have none of that, however. For him, these types of positions were beneath his

family's. Mr. Sagan recalls, "We told him that here it was considered to be a very good occupation and that it was higher type of thing in this country. So he went to some of the dealerships to talk to the foreman and asked very pointed questions about the occupation. Then, when he had asked, he decided that he would become a mechanic and went to vocational school."

Tony served the United States in the Vietnam War, where he was shot down twice in a helicopter. He went on to get a bachelor's degree in construction management.

These four stories are a very small sample of the kindness of the American people toward the unaccompanied Cuban children. Thousands of Americans responded "yes" when asked to open their hearts and homes to strangers. Their generosity of spirit and support eased the way for displaced Cuban children to adapt to their new home.

It were better for him
That a millstone were hanged about his neck,
And he cast into the sea,
Than that he should offend
One of the little ones.

—Luke 17:2

Chapter 9

Flight of Innocence

Being forced to leave your home, your country, your family, everything you know, love, and trust is a jolting experience. Learning to adapt to a new culture surrounded by strangers is certainly one of the most difficult things a child can experience. But the loss of innocence experienced by some of the children was so horrific that they were forced into a world of silence and shame. These were the kind of experiences that are never forgotten, of innocence that can never be reclaimed.

"I've always resented that he stole my first kiss," says Dulce María Sosa, referring to her repulsive foster father. After six months in Florida City, the Sosa siblings, Mari, twelve, Dulce María, ten, and Pastor, nine, had been placed in a Spanish-speaking foster home in Long Beach, California, where the family eccentricities were only part of the picture.

"You would have to actually see this place to believe it," Dulce explains. "It is the oldest house in Long Beach. To us, it seemed like a place right out of the Munster family. The foster mother was a concert pianist with long, unruly hair, sprinkled with gray. She met us at the airport with a floor-length fur coat. I had never seen a fur coat in Cuba. I come from the countryside, to me it seemed like she was wearing animals. She looked like a witch," Dulce recalls. And though her new foster mother chose to wear animals, she also kept animals as pets—three monkeys in cages, which the Sosa children met as they first entered their new temporary home. Dulce remembers her initial fear when she and her siblings were given some ice cream. "We were so afraid to taste it because we were certain we were going to be poisoned."

Bizarre as the home may have been, it was also quite roomy. The foster family's eldest boys were in college and the two younger girls were at home. The three Cuban children shared the vacant bedroom.

Dulce's time out of her room was spent at music lessons and school. It was during the rides to music school that her foster father continued his abuse. As it turned out, before Dulce had ever had the chance to acclimate to her new surroundings, she was forced to confront a terrifying reality. As she describes it, she was sitting in the kitchen when her new foster father told that he was desperate, that he was so anxious to be able to touch her breasts and kiss her. She tried to change the subject. She tried to figure out what to do, but as in cases of sexual abuse, she was powerless. "He started fondling me and kissing me and told me not to say anything."

But this was something she couldn't live with alone. The constant dread and fear was too much for the little girl to endure. When Dulce told her sister Mari about her perverted foster father, Mari reported it to the nuns at school. Instead of getting support, Dulce was accused of lying and offered a choice: she could either go to another out-of-state foster home by herself or stay where she was. Choosing between two evils, she chose to stay with her sister and brother. At home, Mari was punished for "lying" as her foster mother stood by her husband. As penalty she wasn't allowed to leave her room, so she retaliated by going on a hunger strike. Dulce and Pastor would steal money from the couple's daughters and buy food for Mari, which they would deliver by climbing a tree and reaching into the bedroom.

So for almost three grueling years, Dulce, resigned to her fate, endured her abuse. As she explains, "My only choice was to remain silent and put up with it, and I had to do it for almost three years."

While the perverted foster father did not physically fondle twelve-year-old Mari, she was not spared perversion. Dulce explains. "With her, he would stand by the bathroom window, watch, and masturbate, which he also did with me," says Dulce. The irony, as she sees it, is that, "They had a reputation for being the best family, a religious family."

As a child, Dulce was a gifted singer, winning every weekly talent show while the siblings were in Florida City. One of her performances survives in a David Suskind documentary, produced for the United States Information Office about the children's exodus.

Today, Dulce is still a gifted singer and songwriter who pours her heart's content into her emotional songs. Some years ago, she became involved in metaphysical concerns as well as self-help. Through her new insights she realized that she had to face her abuse head-on and started talking about it, which she found helped her to shed her private burden and its effects. She also found solace and a channel for her feelings in her profession. "Luckily, singing saved me. It was my liberation," says Dulce.

FAUSTINO'S STORY

Faustino Amaral was six years old and innocent when he first arrived in the United States. An only child to a Spanish-born mother who remembered the Spanish Civil War and the effects of communism there, Faustino was sent alone out of Cuba with his mother's hope that she would spare him some of the horrors she had endured. Little did she know. He was sent to live with family friends in Miami, but when this arrangement did not work out, Faustino was sent to Florida City, then on to a foster home in Albuquerque, New Mexico, where the torture began.

His new foster father was a police officer; his foster mother, a

housewife with two children. He describes the animal-like treatment he received at the hands of these inhuman beings: "Whenever one of the children did something wrong I was the one who got beaten up," he says. "I had asthma. I have sinus problems. Because I couldn't eat and breathe at the same time and because I wheezed when I ate, they would put me to eat with the dog. They would actually set my plate next to the dog's plate, and I had to fight the dog off for my food."

This was just one example of the abuse to which Faustino was exposed. Anything that was his was taken from him. The little money his mother had managed to send was never delivered to him. All he received was a statue of the Virgin Mary—his only possession and remembrance of his mother.

Recorded in the files kept at Catholic Charities, Faustino's abuse was finally discovered after seven or eight months by a social worker who saw through the foster family's lies. Detecting that something was wrong, the social worker moved the boy to a new foster home to live with the Henry Fitzgerald family.

Now withdrawn, frightened, and locked in his own self-contained world, Faustino moved to yet another home. "I'll never forget when I arrived at the Fitzgeralds. I had this shirt on and it was a little bit torn, and I was told, in a very sensitive way, 'That is a nice shirt, but let me take it off and I'll give you a clean shirt to wear.' I went to take the shirt off, and you know how when you feel pain you tense up? And she noticed and said 'What's wrong?' and I said, 'Nothing, nothing, it doesn't hurt.' And she sat there, and said, 'My God!' I had bruises all over me."

Mr. Fitzgerald remembers the boy as having been badly abused by the other people who had taken care of him. So does Mrs. Fitzgerald, but she discretely chooses not to discuss that situation. She does discuss Tino (as she calls him), however, and her early days with him. She describes him as having been a quiet boy, one that looked smaller than his age and who was always thankful for everything.

At the Fitzgeralds' home, Faustino found the ideal family,

where there were four other boys and plenty of love to go around. Mrs. Fitzgerald recalls one of the reasons the social worker chose her family: "They wanted to place him in a home with boys so he would grow out of his mistreatment."

Coming from a broken home, Mrs. Fitzgerald too had been in and out of orphanages during her childhood. She empathized with the plight of the Cuban children and would eventually take care of a total of six unaccompanied Cuban children. "It worked out well. We understood their problems. We had had them ourselves. We did for them what we ordinarily do for our own children, let them know we cared for them, make sure they went to church, go on picnics. It was just everyday affairs," she explains.

Faustino's appreciation of the Fitzgeralds is boundless. "She worked with me," says Faustino. "They had just done away with phonetics, and she took out the old phonetic books and she told me, 'You will learn to pronounce properly.' And she would say, 'Your tongue goes like this,' and it worked, my speech is very clear. The last years were real good." Faustino still calls Henry and Patricia mom and dad. Like the Fitzgeralds' two older boys had done before him, Faustino joined the air force, following in his foster father's footsteps.

"When I left the first family, the only thing that I kept is the Virgin Mary that my mother sent me. I took it to the Fitzgeralds' house and when I went to leave, I told her I wanted her to keep it. She still has it to this day."

VILLA MARÍA, SAN ANTONIO, TEXAS

In 1962, San Antonio was a city with a population of just over half a million and was very racially divided: Mexicans on one side, gringos on the other. Villa María, an old, massive, dark brick structure on Flores Avenue, was a home for Hispanic señoritas, young ladies who worked during the day and lived on the second and third floors under the supervision of nuns of The Daughters of Mary Immaculate Order. This religious order operated more

than one hundred homes for girls all over the world. The fourth, or top, floor of the house was occupied entirely by Cuban girls. Some rooms slept one, some two, some three, some more. In all, forty teenagers were to share only three baths.

Diana Alonso, one of the Cuban first arrivals, recalls her first summer at her new residence. "The nuns had forty kids under their care and they had to be strict because some of us were very rebellious. They had to set severe rules. Some of us didn't like that, but I found them very caring. They bent over backwards to make us as happy and comfortable as they could."

This opinion was shared by Mirta Almeyda. "I can't complain about the treatment we received. We cannot forget that we were charity cases. They were not loving nuns, but I got along with them just fine. I respected them, they respected me."

The girls had few complaints. They were cared for. They had minor issues on occasion until the incident occurred. One night, when most of the girls were out for awhile, one of the girls who had her own room was raped. The attacker climbed up a fire escape, climbed in a window, and attacked. No one heard him. No one saw him except the victim.

After the attack, the police came to speak to the victim. She spoke to them that night, then never talked about the incident again. Silvia Alfonso remembers finding out about the incident when the nuns came to check her room. The victim was taken to the doctor to be examined, and then again a month later to determine she was not pregnant. "The thought of pregnancy had never entered her mind," says Esperanza Rodríguez, who accompanied the victim to the physician. "Frankly, it didn't enter mine either. We were so innocent. We blame the nuns. We had asked for a guard because on other occasions, men had tried to break in. Of course, we got a guard after the incident."

Silvia Alfonso remembers the great empathy they felt for the raped girl. The fact that this horrible incident could have happened to any one of them made the girls bond closer, forgetting any petty differences. They refused to tell a curious high school

teacher the identity of the victim. They all closed ranks on the matter, protecting the victim and realizing how alone and vulnerable they were. The only family they had was each other.

JOSEFÍNA SANTIAGO

Josefína Santiago* was ten years old when she left Cuba in May 1962. During her five and a half years away from her parents she was shuffled between an orphanage in East Orange, New Jersey, and four foster homes before finally moving in with her aunt and her husband. She recalls all of the foster homes as pretty "horrific," except the last one before moving with in her family: "I don't know why I went to four foster homes. The first foster home had six or eight of their own kids and I felt at the time like I was just one more. I didn't get a lot of attention except to be corrected, but I was kind of a loner anyway."

But no place felt like home and she had no sense of belonging. "I remember a situation where I wanted to sleep in the lower bunk and a big fight ensued," she explained. "I went to bed on the top bunk and I took with me a letter from my parents. I found out through the letter that my sister had an eye operation and she could possibly go blind, so I cried and they kept calling me 'Cry baby.' They thought I was crying because of the fight, and pretty much everything was like that."

She remembers feeling that no matter what she did she couldn't win. She was willing to live with that, however, just so she didn't have to go to another foster home. "I didn't want to go to anymore foster homes, I really didn't. I'd just as soon stay put in the orphanage. But this Argentinean caseworker talked me into trying one more home. The family was very well off and they had a swimming pool. The caseworker really pushed the pool. I had a room of my own which was very different. They had a daughter the same age as I was, and they tried very, very hard to be fair.

---

* a pseudonym

They didn't want their daughter to be an only child anymore because she was beginning to show signs of being difficult, so I was there to prevent her from being the only one."

By this point in her life, Josefína was very unhappy and was having a hard time being civil. "I was treated well, but really was not shown a whole lot of understanding. I was such a nasty person, I was so sarcastic, cynical to the nth degree and I couldn't stand myself that way. I really couldn't stand to be so cynical, but I didn't have any other way out. And I started acting out and nobody noticed. Nobody paid any attention."

When she was told she was moving with her family because her aunt had arrived from Cuba, Josefína thought that maybe things would finally improve for her. She was finally going to be with her own family. She was going back to familiar faces and to a Cuban household.

She couldn't have imagined the appalling circumstances she was about to face. "I can tell you there were thirteen steps up to my bedroom; I used to count them every night," she recalls. Her aunt worked nights and as soon as she was out the door, her husband would climb those thirteen steps to Josefína's room. "My uncle sexually abused me, and physically abused me. It was the worst thing that had happened to me in my life at that point."

Following the behavior pattern of most abused children, Josefína kept her abuse a secret, even when her parents arrived. "In my own childish way I thought it was best not to tell, I kept it inside for four years. It wasn't until my aunt died that all of a sudden it just erupted; now I was free to tell. I had not done it for consideration to her, but now the stopper was gone, so it all came out."

Josefína expected relief. She hoped for compassion. At the very least she wanted understanding and solace from her mother. Once again her hopes were dashed as her mother flat out denied that what Josefína was telling her was remotely possible.

Josefína's mother first response was, "I don't believe you, you must be making it up." Josefína's relationship with her mother had been poor since their reunion, so she was prepared to take whatever her mother had to say.

Josefína had kept the secret long enough. It was time to let it out. As she explains, "It didn't matter whether she believed me or not. I was emotionally prepared, I didn't let her get away with it. I called again a week later, went back into the same conversation, and this time she said, 'Yeah, but it wasn't that bad.'" This wasn't what Josefína wanted to hear.

"Another week went by. I told my mother again. She said, 'Well it only happened once right?' No mother, it happened every night for the entire time that I was there."

Josefína, who was no longer living at home at the time, claims that her mother kept her away from her father for about three years after her confession, so he wouldn't find out. "Because she knew my uncle was a pedophile, and my father had no idea. She knew where she was sending me. This uncle-in-law had done this to two other young ladies in my family at the same age."

Josefína persisted in her weekly confrontational calls to her mother, hoping that she'd finally get through—that finally her mother would understand. But she never heard anything more than, "Well that was so long ago, you have to forget about it, make believe it never happened."

Says Josefína, "And that has been our relationship ever since." Josefína was not about to give up, however. She knew the damage and pain her uncle-in-law had caused. She demanded that it be acknowledged. "If you won't respond as my mother, you are not my mother. And she knows it," Josefína says emphatically. "There are times that she'll call and say, 'Well I know you don't love me but ...' And I guess she expects me to say 'Oh, no mother yes, I love you.' And I won't do it. She didn't earn it. She might be my mother biologically and I respect her, because that is my upbringing, I owe her respect, I don't feel that I can owe her love."

Josefina's mission of affirmation continued. She explains: "Years later I went to Cuba with my mother and we went to see an aunt that I consider my real mother, and I told my aunt that I had been sexually abused, and she fell all over me crying. My mother never did that."

BACK TO CUBA

To leave Cuba alone as a child and endure parental separation and adaptation to new circumstances and a new country is very difficult. To return to Cuba after three years and adapt again to yet a different system, is even harder.

Like all Pedro Pan children, Mildred Carrido* was sent out of Cuba alone. She was ten years old. Her parents were divorced and her mother had sole custody of the child. Her father, who had left Cuba already, was somewhere in South America. As far as Mildred was concerned, he had fallen off the face of the earth. He did not participate in his daughter's upbringing and made no effort to keep in touch.

Once in Miami, Mildred went to live with friends of the family, a couple living with their two-year-old son and the woman's mother. Mildred was apprehensive. During a past encounter with this family, when she was six or seven years old, the man had groped and fondled her. She never told anyone. Now here she was, moving into his home—on his turf.

Things were not too bad at the beginning, Mildred wasn't happy about the chores she given to do, such as cleaning and washing her own clothes, tasks to which she was not accustomed, but it was manageable. But then her daily existence became formidable. She recollects: "Then that man started molesting me again. Thank God that he never went all the way. I think he was afraid of his wife, but he made my life very difficult, he would

---

* a pseudonym

pursue me everywhere, he would touch me at every corner of the house, I lived in a permanent state of anxiety."

In order to escape her situation and to make some money so she could call Cuba and buy clothes, Mildred started working when she was eleven. Down the street, a friend's parents brought factory work home so Mildred would go there every day after school to help out.

Unfortunately, this situation didn't seem to solve her problems. When she'd return home, she'd confront another member of the family. She explains. "The woman's mother gambled and she would ask me for money. She said that if I didn't give it to her, she would kill herself in front of me. She also threatened me not to tell her daughter. She would have fits and throw herself in bed. Then I would have no money and the daughter would question me as to what in the world I was doing with my money."

The abuse to which Mildred was subjected took many forms. She was criticized every day by the wife for what she wore and was told over and over that she looked like a prostitute. She was a tall statuesque brunette and had the body of a fifteen year old at age eleven. "Looking back and analyzing things, I think she was jealous of me." Once, unprovoked, the woman opened her closet, threw everything to the floor, and stomped on it.

In addition to their constant persecution, Mildred was excluded from the family's social life. Her role was as a babysitter when they did go out. Meanwhile, Mildred had been waiting and hoping for her family to come to the United States, but those hopes were dashed: Mildred's stepfather decided that he wasn't leaving Cuba, and her mother, a person with feeble convictions, decided she wasn't leaving either. Instead of saying to him, "I have a daughter over there, I have to go," her mother started making arrangements to return Mildred to Cuba, something that wasn't easy at the time. With the help of an uncle who was in the government, an entry permit for Cuba was secured and the child returned via Canada.

Once in Cuba, Mildred's mother told her that she would not be attending school, "since Castro's regime would topple soon." But Mildred had endured enough. The teenager stood up to her mother telling her that she was not going interrupt her life and that she was going to study. The first day of school with her American clothes, Mildred was the center of attraction. At the beginning she was vetoed from activities because she was a repatriated child, but Mildred decided to join the system. She explains, "I did a lot of voluntary work. You have to, otherwise you cannot achieve anything, a good profession, a good job. I tried to see the positive side of things and got enthused."

Trying to fit within the revolution, Mildred found some predicaments. Her beloved aunt and grandmother left Cuba and Mildred couldn't even write to them, as any form of communication with exiled "worms" would reflect badly on her. When her father died she had to ask for permission to write to her grandmother.

Mildred married young, at seventeen, and had a daughter. She became a university professor. She divorced. She remarried in 1980, but was by then disenchanted with the Cuban system and wanted to leave the island. She continued to be a prisoner, a victim without the freedom to leave a repressive government, but she persevered in her quest for liberty. In 1995, Mildred and her family landed at Miami International Airport again. She was starting life as a refugee for the second time. It took her thirty-four years to come full circle. But this time it was her choice.

To lose your language is a tragedy.

—ROSARIO FERRÉ

CHAPTER 10

From No Hablo Inglés to
I Don't Speak Spanish

While living with an American foster family in Tomah, Wisconsin, near Canada during a five-year separation from her parents, Alicia Brito went from a childish nine-year-old Cuban girl who didn't speak English, to a fourteen-year-old all-American teenager, who didn't speak Spanish.

Upon hearing the news that their parents had left Cuba, Alicia worriedly told her older sister, "Yolanda, I don't speak Spanish anymore." So, in preparation for their reunion, they started practicing Spanish at night before going to sleep. She recalls, "We'd start laughing because it sounded so funny." Hearing the commotion, their foster parents asked what was so funny and the girls replied, 'We are speaking Spanish!' And they would also laugh.

"We met our parents at the airport in San Francisco and everything was fine, the kisses and the embraces, but when we went to get our luggage, they started asking more questions and I would say, 'Yolanda, tell them that . . .' and my mother started crying, they were totally traumatized from all the changes. The principal change was physical, as I could now look at my father in the eye and I was taller than my mother."

After the girls left Cuba, their mother had two more girls, ages one and three at time of the reunion. Their elder sisters had chosen their names from the United States, but now the babies curled around their mother's ankle wondered who these strangers were. "When we left our parents they were young, now they had gray hair. When we got in the car, the three-year-old asked our mother when the company was leaving."

Alicia started getting headaches from trying to speak Spanish. "I could understand but I couldn't speak, although they had to explain some words. I could understand everyday talk, but when my brain started readjusting I would get horrible headaches! I would talk to the gringos in Spanish and to my parents in English!"

Four years in an all-American environment had elapsed since the day Faustino Amaral left Cuba alone as a six year old. Now as a ten year old, he was getting off the plane at Miami International Airport to reunite with his mother. "I saw her and I went running, and I screamed, 'Mom, mom,' and she is yelling in Spanish, and I'm like, 'Oh my God' and I ran back toward the plane." Faustino says he picked up his lost Spanish very quickly, because his mother didn't let him out of her sight for a minute. "She would always be pushing Spanish down my throat so I had no choice. I learned by the time my father came over in February, two months later."

Susan Garrandes's language problems also went from one extreme to the other, from no English to no Spanish. She left Cuba at age ten. "It got to the point that when my mother called we couldn't communicate at all, we began having language problems," she says. A friend of the family in Cuba who spoke some English would translate for Susan and her parents what they were saying to each other over the phone.

When she got to New York, her older brother, who spoke no English, picked her up at the airport. At the baggage claim area, he asked her the color of her suitcase, "I could only say *roja*, or red, although it was orange and gray."

The next three months in a New Jersey school were also try-ing for Susan as everybody around her was streetwise. "I was so naïve having come from this sheltered orphanage life, there were also a lot of Cubans all around, and my brother and his wife did not speak English." Dealing with yet a new adaptation got to be so difficult for Susan that she would pray at night to be sent back to the orphanage.

> If you associate our life to a repeat offender's, who always ends up in jail, for better or worse, he knows the system. When you know the system you are comfortable, as you learn to live with it. And all of a sudden things were new to me again, even the food I was now eating.
>
> Once you get back to your family, you didn't really know those people. I remember when my mother got here from Camarioca, she flew to New York and I went to the airport and I was hiding behind my aunt. I was afraid to see my mother. I didn't know if I was going to recognize her. I didn't know what I was supposed to do, it was a freak-out experience it was all too new too complicated and my mind just couldn't accept it.

Having been separated from his parents at age six for almost six years and immersed in an English-only environment, Mario Sánchez totally forgot his Spanish. He was "encouraged" not to speak it by the nuns at Mount Saint John Academy in Gladstone, New Jersey. "The nuns at the orphanage would smack you if you spoke a word of Spanish. My brother didn't forget his Spanish because he was a rebel, and when the nuns hit us for speaking Spanish, he would take it in stride and continue talking in Spanish with the other Cuban children, whereas I would take it seriously."

His parents would write and he didn't understand anything, and his older sister had to translate. He now compares family life after his parents' arrival to a *Benny Hill* or *Monthy Python* televi-sion sitcom.

He could not speak to his mother or his grandmother. His father spoke English and could communicate with the boy, but would speak to his brother and sister in Spanish. Unfortunately the father was working night and day to support the family of six. He worked in a grocery store during the day and a canning factory at night. "One day my mother wanted to give me soup for lunch and when she told me, I turned so neurotic that she had to call my father at work. He rushed home and I told him I didn't want soap. It was a strong reaction, since the nuns used to wash our mouth with soap at the orphanage." *Sopa* is the Spanish word for soup.

"I was the official translator for my whole family during all my youth, but not only for my immediate family, but for all our cousins and uncles, and we are a very extensive family," says Luis Ramírez. "One day when I was about fourteen or fifteen I said, 'No more translating,' except for my immediate family, and they already spoke English." Luis was eight when he left Cuba and went to live with the Varelas, a foster family in Delaware. He felt very loved and accepted by this family, who had five girls and made Luis their toy. However, even as a young boy he recognized that he was losing his Spanish. He would lie awake at night talking to himself in Spanish or trying to recite poetry in Spanish.

When his parents arrived, their financial situation was precarious. Four persons lived in a studio with a Murphy bed. Knowing that Luis was well taken care of, they asked the boy to stay with his foster parents a bit longer, until they could have a better economic situation. Luis rebelled since he wanted to live with his parents, so five persons ended up living in the studio apartment.

Luis could understand Spanish but could not speak it; however, he picked it up again very quickly. That is when his career as the official family translator began. "My father was a lawyer and he made me translate things literally, even when he was cursing someone. I would ask him, 'Do you really want me to say that?' and he would sternly reply, 'Tell him.'"

One day Luis had to translate for a cousin who was having his eyes checked for a prospective job. However, he was blind in one eye and asked Luis not only to translate but also to tell him the letters in the eye chart. Luis answered, "I don't tell lies."

Antonia Martínez went to a New Mexico foster home at age nine with her fifteen-year-old sister. Her foster family would take kindergarten books from the library to teach her English. She remembers people in New Mexico as being very nice, but reacting as if the girls were from another planet: "They didn't now where Cuba was." Nobody spoke Spanish in the household, and they didn't want them to speak in their native tongue to each other so they could learn to speak English quickly. The sisters would sneak conversations between them. "I guess when you are small you pick up things a lot faster, and you learn things pretty fast when you don't get to speak the other language," Antonia says.

Her parents arrived three years later in 1965, leaving Cuba through Mexico. They found a younger daughter that could not speak Spanish although she could understand it. "My mother cried for days, because I guess she was feeling like she sent one child out and she was getting something back which is not what she sent out. I'm sure it affected her greatly. I did understand, I would talk to her *como una americana,* a word here and there, my sister would translate a lot."

Antonia had another surprise in store, as the family moved to Puerto Rico, a country where Spanish is the official language. "The school and everything there was in Spanish. You had English as a second language, as a subject. I had a hard time there. I had always been a good student, so math and science were easy for me, but the language was not." Luckily for her, the family moved to Miami shortly. "My sister got together with a boyfriend that lived in Miami and decided to get married. My father said, 'We have been apart too long already, we are not going to be separated again, if she is moving to Miami, we are all moving to Miami.'"

When Mariana Prats put her four older children—Lola, six, Benito, seven, Margarita, eight, and José, nine—on a flight to Miami on September 1961 and kept her youngest two, she thought she would be joining them in fifteen days. It would be four long years before she would see them again. "We got scared for our children when they started closing the churches. In Camagüey we had no priest for fifteen days. They kicked out the priests and the Salecian nuns from their school. There was a panic."

Once they had their passports and police approval to exit, a new regulation was created that the exit had to be approved by the police from Havana, in case there were any charges against them in Havana. The Havana police held passports for months. Another regulation was issued regulating the exit of physicians since too many had left the island. Doctors could not leave Cuba without the approval of the Medical Association and without leaving a substitute in their place. Because Dr. Prats was a physician, their exit plans were again shattered. He went to Havana during a weekend only to be told that the Medical Association was open only Wednesdays and Thursdays. Days, weeks, and months went by. The family would eventually leave through Mexico.

Meanwhile, the four Prats siblings were sent to an orphanage in Syracuse, New York. They made the *Syracuse Herald* as the first Cubans there. Shortly thereafter, they went to separate foster homes, the two girls to one, and the two boys to another. The girls went to the home of the Clough family. Mrs. Clough had two children, but she wasn't "finished mothering," so she asked her church for foster children. "We were so accepted there and we were made to feel very welcome," says Margarita Prats, who was then eight. "They really loved us as their own kids. She was really a family kind of person who wanted to have kids around. They were very nurturing." Mrs. Clough says that the children were accepted by her parents as well as her siblings.

Living among Americans in Syracuse, the four Prats siblings forgot their Spanish completely in the four years they were separated. What is even more tragic than the loss of a language is the loss of the familial connection. Lola, the youngest, who was six, forgot not only her English but also her parents. "I wrote to my parents while they were in Cuba, but they were just somebody I had to write to. My foster parents made me write, otherwise I don't think I would have. I really didn't understand why I was leaving, and once I got here I'd forgot about them. I remember my foster parents used to make me write letters and I didn't know who I was writing to. They said they were my parents, but I would say, 'No, you are my parents.' It was kind of confusing."

The age difference of only two years was crucial in the girls' reaction to their parents. "I missed my parents," says Margarita. "Whenever there was talk of their coming and there was always a rumor, I would be looking forward to it. When it happened, I wanted to see them, I wanted to be back with them." The day the girls left their foster home was another traumatic event in their young lives. Margarita was twelve and Lola ten. "I didn't want to leave my foster parents. They were my parents and I didn't want to go to these strange people," says Lola. My sister understood more, even though it was a two-year difference. She understood that we had other parents to go to. It was a gut-wrenching separation from them. We screamed and cried at the airport. It was another separation again."

The Prats family settled in the Washington, D.C., area, because they had many friends there. The kindness of strangers followed the new arrivals. Dr. Font, a dentist who owned several homes in Bethesda, heard about the Cuban family with the six children and offered them one of his houses until Dr. Prats could revalidate his medical license.

Mariana Prats had studied two years in Canada, so she spoke English well. Her husband's language skills were more limited, but he had some knowledge of the language. When she reunited with her children she followed the advice of a psychiatrist friend who advised her not to sever the relationship with the children's foster parents, but rather to encourage it. He told her that she was going to want them for herself but that she would have to share them for a while. "As soon as they arrived, I made them call their foster parents; they talked for about half an hour, and long distance was such an expense for us at the time," she recalls. "That evening I made them write letters." Mrs. Clough remembers being invited to visit as soon as the family was settled.

The four Prats siblings who had left Cuba alone spoke no Spanish and the two youngest spoke no English, but their mother remembers them understanding each other somehow. "Somebody had given us a large conference table, it was our dinner table too and we would sit around it and my father would hold up a shoe and say, *Esto es un zapato* and everyone in the family had to repeat it," says Margarita. "We still have that joke in the family about *esto es* something."

Mariana remembers that one of their first purchases was a television set, as the children came from homes where they had been used to a television. "The house was barren we had no furniture, but they quickly learned *mira* and look, as they pointed to the television. We understood them and never forced them to speak any language. Their grandparents, who spoke no English, would baby-sit and they would all laugh and try to teach them English and the grandparents Spanish."

Margarita remembers, "We all arrived and spoke English at home. I don't remember that it was a problem with the little ones, that we spoke English and they spoke Spanish. After a while the whole family started speaking whatever language they were comfortable [with] verbally. And then you would answer in whatever the other person wanted to answer. To this day I greet a Spanish person and I start speaking a little Spanish and then I throw in English and I don't notice." Lola says that to this day she continues to speak to her mother and father in English and they answer her in Spanish. She understands Spanish but doesn't speak it that well.

The girls have kept in constant touch with their foster family, visiting each other every year. "As soon as Lola left she started putting LLMND in all her letters. She still does. It means Lola Loves Mom and Dad. It was just a blessing that time they came into our lives because they certainly filled a gap for me and through the years," says Mrs. Clough. The Cloughs have attended weddings and important family occasions. They consider the girls' children their grandchildren also. "I am just so proud of that family," she says. "Whenever I get the chance I tell the story of how their mother loved them so much to send them here not knowing what was going to happen to them."

At best,
the reunion of broken relations
is a nervous matter.

—HENRY BROOK ADAMS

CHAPTER 11

Reunion with Parents

Parents who had sent their children out of Cuba tried to follow them out through various channels. There were the lucky ones who were able to leave the island shortly after their children, thus making the dreaded separation only a few months long. Others were stranded in Cuba after flights stopped on October 23, 1962, left to wonder how to leave the island that had turned into a prison.

After the failed Bay of Pigs invasion, Castro realized that he had a source of cash sitting in Cuban jails. Because the United States wanted the brigade-member prisoners released, Castro formulated a plan whereby he would benefit from their release. He demanded and bartered, asking for $62 million for the release of the brigade members.[1] Just before Christmas 1962, two months after the flights stopped, 1,113 members of the 2506 Brigade were exchanged for an agreed-upon $53 million ransom of food and medicine, the distribution of which was supervised by the Red Cross.[2] On December 23, 1962, the freed prisoners arrived in Miami.

A National Sponsors Committee worked with the Cuban Families Committee to raise the money. American companies, among them forty-three railroads, forty-four trucking compa-

176

nies, eleven shipping companies, and four shipping lines, cooperated. One hundred and thirty-eight concerns contributed medicine and other items.

Planes or ships that carried the supplies to Cuba delivered human cargo on the return trip, among them many parents of Cuban children alone in the United States. The exchange ended on July 3, 1963, with 9,703 persons having been brought out of Cuba, among them the Bay of Pigs captives along with twenty-three American prisoners, Americans living in Cuba, and 1,500 Cubans holding American citizenship.[3]

José Rodríguez was on the waiting list to leave Cuba, because his daughter was in Miami, when he and his wife were notified that he was leaving in the *Maximo,* a Red Cross ship. He says, "I got on line at 4:00 A.M. and made it to the ship in the afternoon. It brought over 1,204 persons, even children, who were crying. We left Cuba at 6:00 P.M. and arrived at Fort Lauderdale at 1:00 P.M. the next day. There were about fifty buses waiting for us. The first thing they asked me in immigration was if I had belonged to the Communist Party, to which I answered loudly, 'Never.'"

After the glimmer of hope of leaving on a ransom ship or plane disappeared, many parents chose the dangers of the sea as an escape route to join their children. "I decided to leave on a boat," says Lolita Madariaga, whose children María Dolores and Juan had left in May 1961. "A friend of ours canceled his trip and I took his place on the boat. We hid in the patio of a house, squatting for a long time. We left the port of Caibarién at night, all of us hiding below deck, while the skipper, who was undertaking the journey only for money, was alone on deck."

She remembers the horror of that journey. "His engine broke down and that man cursed. He even cursed God and I told him, 'Shut up, what we have to do is pray.' There were about seven of us and we drifted for six days, and ran out of food. I bonded with a couple who also had their daughter in the United States."

Fear overtook her and her shipmates toward the end of her journey. "On the last day, we saw a boat full of army types and

one of our young men was going to jump overboard, as we were terrified, thinking it was the Cuban militia, but I talked him out of it. It turns out that they were Alpha 66,* and they had been following us. We were put ashore on a key near Florida and the skipper returned to Cuba. The men from Alpha 66 gave us flares and provisions and called the Coast Guard. A U.S. destroyer picked us up."

Peter Martínez's mother was not as lucky. She also tried to leave in a boat, but unbeknownst to her, it was a government agent who had planned their escape. They were ambushed at the beach and she was sentenced to a year in jail for trying to leave her country. Her health deteriorated in prison and from that point on she remained sickly and weak. She died years later in exile as a consequence of the hepatitis contracted in jail.

Other parents left through third countries, usually counting on the charity of family or friends for their survival while living in immigratory limbo for weeks, months, or years, waiting to get a U.S. entry visa.

On September 28, 1965, Castro, then Cuba's premier, promised to open the doors to Cubans wanting to leave for "the Yankee Paradise." He said, "Now they are leaving in small boats, many of them drowning and they [the Americans] use this as propaganda. Now those who want to leave can leave, because there are many here remaining who struggle for the people."[4] Those leaving would "undergo no risk from us," he added. "Now we will see what the imperialists would do or say."

On October 4 the "imperialists" replied. While signing a reform of U.S. immigration law in New York City President Lyndon Johnson announced to the people of Cuba that "those who seek refuge here would find it." He also said that he would ask Congress for $13.6 million to carry out this undertaking.[5]

Diplomatic negotiations ensued through the Swiss embassy and the Americans proposed that first priority be given to the

---

* Alpha 66 is an organization of Cuban exiles who on occasion have been involved in guerrilla landings and commando raids in Cuba.

15,000 to 20,000 Cubans with relatives in the United States and second priority to the 15,000 to 30,000 political prisoners.[6]

October 10 was the starting date designated by the Castro government for the Cuban exodus; by October 9 a small flotilla was heading toward Cuba.[7] Camarioca, a small fishing port west of Havana, was determined to be the embarkation point.

On the third boat from Cuba, Mrs. Osvaldo Bazo was told that "Cuba was not allowing youths near draft age to leave." A militiaman almost forced her to leave her fourteen-year-old son behind. Mrs. Bazo said the militiaman grabbed her son just as the boat was ready to sail. She and her husband struggled with the militiaman and threw the boy into the boat, which put out at once, before the youngster could be recaptured according to the *New York Times* on October 25, 1965.

By October 17, 1965, 500 Cubans had arrived in the United States. Reports continued to circulate that men ages fourteen to twenty-six were not allowed to leave due to the military draft. Castro had sent a note through the Cuban delegation to the United Nations in which he offered to exchange 70,000 political prisoners for Cubans being held prisoner in other Latin American countries. His note further said that Cuban minors would not be forced to leave with their parents if they felt they did not want to go to the United States.[8] Finally, he stated that youngsters between fifteen and twenty-six years of age would not be permitted to leave Cuba.

On October 28, 1965, the Cuban government ended the small-boat traffic between both countries, after more than 3,000 refugees had made the crossing, while negotiations continued for an orderly exodus. Reports of the negotiations suggested that two flights a day out of the airport of Varadero would be allowed.

The immigratory agreement was reached on November 6. It allowed for 3,000 to 4,000 Cubans to immigrate each month to the United States; however, men of military age were excluded. The highest priority was given to parents whose children in the United States were under twenty-one. The Cuban government made a list of Cubans who wanted to leave and the United States

made a list of Cubans who were to be claimed by their relatives. The Swiss were responsible for collating the two lists.[9]

There were seven airlines that flew the Freedom Flights, as they were called. They started on December 1, 1965. The U.S. federal government provided a $100 grant for each family or $60 an individual and paid for the cost of the flights to and from Cuba. It also assumed the cost of transportation for those resettling outside Florida.[10]

During the month of December 1965, parents of 128 children arrived via the Freedom Flights. By January 4, the Cuban government had authorized the exit of 6,000 persons.[11] By January 28, parents of 456 children had come into the United States. At that time there were still 1,353 unaccompanied children under care.[12] These twice-daily, five-days-a-week Freedom Flights lasted until February 1, 1970, and cost the federal government $50 million.

FAUSTINO AMARAL

Faustino Amaral's mother arrived on the very first Freedom Flight, a Pan Am flight, on December 1, 1965, with seventy-four other refugees, fifty-one of whom were women and children. "You see her on the old newsreels, wearing a plaid coat," he says, laughing. "She had lined the coat with four or five layers of wool material in case there was no material in the U.S. or she couldn't afford it."

Faustino remembers the reunion as a confusing blur, but the sense of happiness he felt is still with him. "There is this feeling—she is my mom, and after all the homes I went to, this is refreshing. But I wouldn't dare open the refrigerator door without her permission. I didn't feel totally at home."

His mother reacted to seeing her son again by overprotecting the boy, smothering him. "I couldn't play with kids, as I would get scratched. Heaven forbid I would break a leg! I used to roller skate, ice skate, snow ski, I had lived at the foot of Skandia Peak in Albuquerque. I would try to explain to my mom that I did

those things all the time, that it was normal.

"One time my aunt and uncle who lived in New Jersey came to Miami. They took me to a store, gave me $20 and told me, 'We want you to spend it right here, right now because if it gets to the house, your mother is not going to let go of it.' I wanted roller skates and I bought a pair. My mother was so mad! But then she saw me on skates, she said, 'He knows how to skate!' It was difficult to convince her that four years had gone by."

JULIO NUÑEZ

Julio Nuñez was at work at the airport, where he was responsible for taking apart and putting together propeller accessories for Vietnam-bound military planes. This was among the many jobs he had held after leaving the Unaccompanied Cuban Children's Program at age eighteen. Suddenly on his own, he went to Miami to live with family. "After two weeks, when they realized that they weren't getting any money for me, they kicked me out," remembers Julio bitterly. "I had to stop my education as I didn't even have enough money to eat."

Julio moved in with two friends from the camp who were in the same circumstances; they shared an apartment on SW Twelfth Avenue and Fifth Street as well as an old clunker of a car.

"I was listening to the radio as I worked, and I heard a list of persons arriving in the Freedom Flights and my parents were among them. I had been separated for six years, always hoping that after all the suffering, we were going to be a happy family once united. "When I went to the airport to greet them, my mother took one look at me and said, 'You are not my son!' I was no longer the well-dressed boy she knew; I was full of grease, I was a man who had gone through hell; some very difficult years. 'You are not my son, you are not my son,' she kept repeating—a phrase she uses to this day."

When he saw his father, Julio thought that he had less than two months to live; he looked like a cadaver. A worried Julio moved in with his parents and worked twelve hours a day to

make money so his mother could pass her medical boards and revalidate her Cuban physician's degree. His father, who had been a lawyer in Cuba, got a job at the airport tying bundles. He would come home with his hands all cut up. Julio says, with pride in his voice, "My father would tell me, 'This is the price of dignity. As long as you can work never accept coupons.'" Julio's dream of a happy family was slipping away, as his father slipped further away. "He was a zombie, he didn't talk, he was like catatonic from suffering so much."

Julio, meanwhile, desperately wanted to pursue a medical degree but had no money to seek a U.S. education. He ended up going to Spain where university studies were free. He left with $80 in his pocket and nobody to help him out financially. As Julio had suspected upon seeing him, his father was ill. He died nine months after arriving in Miami, and Julio could not return to the United States for the funeral since he had no money for a ticket home. "My family has never been the same," he says ruefully.

WILLY CHIRINO

Like so many other families who came to the United States to reunite, the Chirino family was strapped for money. While the family of six—the parents, an aunt, two young girls, and fifteen-year-old Willy—was close-knit, they were suffering from the stress of the situation. With only $100 to their name when they arrived in Miami, they had to start anew. Both parents had been professionals in Cuba, but without the ability to speak English, their career opportunities were limited.

Willy Chirino remembers his parents' arrival as being difficult for him and his family. "I feel tenderness for my younger sister, who was then nine, when I think that we used to sell doughnuts door-to-door." To supplement his income, Willy took on a newspaper route, distributing three hundred *Miami News* newspapers in the Bal Harbour section of Miami Beach. He recalls, "What I really hated was collecting money Saturday mornings. But I had

to do it. It was my way of helping the family."

That was before his music career. "In tenth grade I had a rock band and we would play in parties on Friday and Saturday nights. But then I started playing the drums in an orchestra in nightclubs." Working six nights a week he earned $70 dollars a week, a hefty salary back then. And all cash.

"I tell my daughters and they don't believe the schedule I kept. They say it is not possible. I would get up at 7:00 A.M., my father would take me to school until 3:00 P.M. I would sleep from 4:00 to 8:00. I would shower, eat, and go to work until 4:00 A.M. I'd come home and sleep and start all over. Sometimes I had to give up my afternoon nap for rehearsals. This went on for two years, but I did it with pleasure because I really love music. However my head felt really heavy, like a rock, from lack of sleep."

RAFAEL CARVAJAL

In 1967, the Vietnam War was tearing the nation apart. U.S. bombers attacked Hanoi. Muhammed Ali was indicted in Houston, Texas, for refusing to be inducted into the U.S. Armed Forces. In New York, 700,000 persons marched in support of the soldiers in Vietnam, and Martin Luther King led an anti–Vietnam War march. More than 50,000 demonstrated against Vietnam at the Lincoln Memorial.

The 1967 arrivals met the same fate as previous arrivals. The world was changing, but Cubans were still coming to United States as political refugees to start life all over again. Rafael Carvajal explains, "My parents had no money." So, like many Pedro Pan children, Rafael had to help out. "The first job I held after arriving from Albuquerque was cleaning the floor at the Americana Hotel from midnight to 6:00 A.M. I didn't like it, but I had to do it. It was a bit demeaning, as you would see a young woman and there you were, cleaning floors. Then I got a job as a busboy at the then Vizcaya Restaurant, now Casa Juancho, and I had a problem with an older Spanish waiter who thought that I

was going to take over his job, so I went to work at another restaurant, Toledo. I started going to school at night so I could finish the few courses I needed to start college."

THE ZALDIVAR BROTHERS

Aware of the financial hardships that would face their parents when they arrived in the United States, some children, such as the four Zaldivar brothers, Osvaldo, Alvaro, Raúl, and Roberto, worked very hard to save money for their parents. "We would paint houses, do anything," says Roberto. "I became an altar boy so that I had the right to the glass votive candle holders. They could be drinking glasses for my parents."

Roberto also distributed newspapers, on foot. "On Sundays the guard at St. Raphael's would wake me up at 3:00 A.M. and I would walk from Biscayne and Twenty-first Street to Twenty-third Street and Second Avenue. I would pick up my papers and walk to Thirty-sixth Street, distribute them all, and walk back to get my second batch."

The boys worried about the future with their parents. "With Father Walsh we had a secure life. We had food, clothing, and shelter. We attended private schools. But where would we live and how would we manage? The boy's fears were not unfounded because their parents could not work. His father had become blind at age forty, and his mother was in frail health and had to wear an iron corset. Since they arrived in the United States through Mexico, with U.S. residency status, they did not qualify for refugee assistance. "We would go from church to church, to all of them, Catholic, Lutheran, to pick up the bags of food they would give out as well as clothes," Roberto explains.

The family's first home was a $55-a-month dilapidated one-bedroom wooden apartment. "It had no shower, just an ancient bathtub, the kind with feet," says Roberto. The family bought a $5 sofa that was missing a leg, which was supplemented by a brick. A relative gave them a booklet of supermarket stamps, which were redeemed for a four-person set of china, so the family

only needed to buy one more plate, as Osvaldo, the eldest, had moved to Venezuela. And they already had the glasses. Roberto recalls that when his mother would clean the ancient kitchen on Saturdays, roaches, bugs, and even mice would come out. "But it was bright and airy and we were happy there," says Roberto.

In a reversal of roles, the brothers became their parents' keepers in their new homeland, all four of them working and pooling their money to support the household. At the time of their parents' arrival Roberto, the youngest, was fifteen. He worked at odd jobs and at church on Saturday in exchange for his tuition. The oldest brother went to work for IBM in Venezuela. Alvaro, then nineteen, worked in a cruise ship. He later made a career in the airline industry. Raúl, who was eighteen, also made a career in the airlines. Roberto became an architect and then switched careers to become a physician.

LOUIS LAGUARDIA

Meanwhile, in New Jersey, Louis LaGuardia resisted sending for his parents until he could make sure he could provide for them financially, without anyone's help. He describes his method, "I worked part-time through high school, and managed to graduate in the top 5 percent of my class. Then I got a job a Palisades Amusement Park, which was a big thing in those days. You could earn $75 a week working eighty hours, but $75 in 1964 or 1965 was a lot. I saved over $1,000 and then I started the paperwork for their immigration. I knew that at least we could live for three months with the money we had."

Louis knew that his parents, who were in their fifties, would have a difficult time adapting to the American system. His mother, Fé, remembers looking for her son at the airport and not recognizing him. Her cousin had to tell her, "Here is your son," because the twelve year old she sent to the United States was now a man of seventeen. He had rented an apartment for them. "My son had worked in an amusement park, mopping floors, selling clothing in the street," Fé said. He got them off to a manageable start.

However, shortly after his parents arrived, Louis lost his job. "My father had to go to the Jersey City welfare office where he got $15. The following week he got a job and returned the $15. And what a mess, as the bureaucracy wasn't set up for returns! He just left the $15.00 on the table."*

Fé, who beams with pride as she speaks of the accomplishments of her son, who has a Ph.D. in psychometrics, the educational arm of psychology, remembers how hard her son worked through high school and college. "When it snowed, he would come back from school, where he also worked, and ask me to hurry with his food. He would bundle up, gather up two shovels that he had, and run off to Fort Lee where they would pay well to have their snow removed."

Unfortunately, not all parents beam with pride as they look back on their reunions with their children. And not all children look back at their reunion with their parents as a positive memory. In many cases, children who were separated from their parents idealized them; however, the parents, in reality, didn't always measure up to their children's image. Time and adversity had changed both the children and their parents. It was impossible to expect that family life could just pick up and continue like it had been in Cuba. The distress and hardships of exile were life altering for everyone.

MARIO SÁNCHEZ

Mario Sánchez had a very hard time readjusting to life with his parents. "My sister had a fight with my father and left home. It was a very difficult readjustment; I really didn't know who these people were! I had lived without them half of my life and I had to learn to love them. And I never really loved my mother. To this day I don't. I respect her. I loved my father because I gained his

---

* In a February 2, 1962, article the *New York Times* reported that Cuban refugees had returned $250,000 of the assistance they had received.

respect, but I didn't know who these people were," says Mario.

JOSEFÍNA SANTIAGO

Josefína Santiago was totally unprepared for her mother's bizarre behavior the day they met. During the five and a half years without her parents, she had survived four foster homes, several stays in an orphanage, and sexual abuse by an uncle-in-law. The hardened fifteen year old sat in the airport during a snow blizzard, anxiously waiting for her parents' plane to arrive. Just after the plane landed, the airport was closed due to the heavy snow.

"My mother took off her shoes, and she was walking around barefooted, and I am trying to convince her that she couldn't do that. I'm telling her, 'Snow is cold, you are going to get sick.' And my mother insisted on doing this because she had made a promise to the Virgin of La Caridad del Cobre. I thought it was the most insane thing, and I was sitting there thinking, 'I don't believe that I have a crazy woman for a mother.' I was so embarrassed, so ashamed! All those years I had been waiting for my mother to come and this is what I get?"

She continues, "My father had been a professional in Cuba and we had been well-to-do. When my father got to the United States he was literally digging ditches and guess what? He snapped. And guess who he took it out on? He started giving me black eyes and beating up on me. He came over here when I was fifteen and I left home when I was seventeen. It was like I didn't ever really get to go back home."

Like some other children in similar situations, Josefína's disappointment turned to anger: "To this day I resent being a parent to my parents. No kid should ever have to go into a bank and fill out loan applications and that kind of stuff, that is just not age appropriate. I did so many things that were adult, because I had to do it for my parents. Part of me said, 'This is absolutely not fair, you weren't there when I needed you, and I have to be

there when you need me! I had to teach not only the language, but also all the customs and the intricacies. I have to do all this for you? Where were you when I started my period?

"Even when they were in Cuba I had to constantly lie to them on the phone and tell them that I was okay. I couldn't tell them the truth, they couldn't have handled it. Besides, what could they have done about it?"

Josefina apologizes for becoming passionate as she speaks. She says that being a parent to her parents is one of the things that makes her angry. She is particularly hurt that they never tried to understand all the horrors she experienced during her time away from them. While she tries not to hold anything against her father, since she knows he had her best interest at heart before he snapped, it is different with her mother.

To this day she sees her mother as a maternal failure. She also resents the fact that her younger sister was kept in Cuba while she was sent away. This much she has resolved, "I am never sending my kids away. My kids are better off where I am. I will not part with my children. After I became a mother that is when it hit me most. I could never allow anyone to take my child away from me, and yet how did I get here? It couldn't have been without my mother's consent. I hold her responsible.... My mother should have been the one not to let me go."

As far as her mother's reaction, Josefina says, "She doesn't offer any excuses, she refuses to talk about it. That's fine. If you are happy with the way things are we'll deal with it this way."

Josefina's mother is one of the many who will not talk about the separation from their children. This seems to be a common thread among the Pedro Pan parents. While many families have not talked about it to this day, some children feel they have the right to an explanation. They feel the need to understand why their parents took the drastic action of sending their children away. Instead of explanations, however, they are met with an I-don't-want-to-talk-about-it attitude.

Reunion with Parents / 189

ELISA AND MARI VILANO

Elisa Vilano's younger sister, Mari, suffered the trauma of separation by temporarily rejecting both Elisa and her parents. The girls lived with the Galanti family, their second foster family in Buffalo, New York. After graduating from high school, Elisa had moved out of the foster home with a college scholarship. She also worked as a receptionist. "I went to visit the family one day and Mrs. Galanti says to me that my sister didn't want to come downstairs to see me because she was now part of her American family and didn't want to see us anymore. I thought I would die. What had I done? Here I was supposed to be responsible for my sister and be her mother, and she didn't even want to see me!"

Mari remembers how happy she was in Buffalo. She became a popular all-American girl, changing her name to Billie. "It was my nickname from Vilano and I kept it. I got very engrossed with the school and I desperately wanted to blend in. It was very hard when I had to see my parents again; it was three years and eight months. At the time I just wanted to be an American girl, I didn't want to go back with the pain, I was afraid to be dragged down to Miami again."

Elisa went to the airport alone when her parents arrived because her sister still refused to see them. "I told them she had a very bad cold," says Elisa. "I just couldn't tell them that she didn't want to see them. I don't remember how she received them. I've blocked it out. I was in such a state of fear that I had been a disappointment to my parents because I felt responsible for what had happened to her."

Just as they had opened their doors to Elisa and Mari, the Galantis opened their doors to their parents. It was Christmastime and the Vilanos stayed with them for a few days until they found an apartment. A local reporter in Buffalo, Peg Pitillo, had found the Cuban girls' story interesting. She had followed Elisa's adaptation to Buffalo and her new country in a series of articles such as "Williamsburg Girl Prays Her Parents Will Attend Her Graduation," "Cuban Girl Wins Scholarship," in the *Buffalo*

Evening News. Finally, the reporter was able to write, "Girl's Prayers Are Answered" when Elisa's parents arrived. The article had a photo of Elisa, her sister, and their parents decorating the Galantis' Christmas tree. Happily, the perfect family shown in the photo reflected reality, as the family was truly blissful. Mari had warmed up to her parents immediately, and being in the Galanti household eased the transition. "As soon as I saw them, I was fine." Because of the article, a benevolent reader offered Mr. Vilano a job and a car, and the family moved together.

Elisa thinks her sister's reaction was a resistance to having her life disrupted again. "It was the fear," she says. "Her reaction was that she couldn't face it; she couldn't face yet another change, she was already set in a household." But, another change was in store as the newly arrived parents couldn't get used to the frigid winter in Buffalo. The family left for Miami soon thereafter, a change the girls viewed as negative. Elisa gave up her college scholarship, going to work, as she felt responsible for her parents. Mari's fears of being uprooted came true. "I was very angry, it was worse than the initial separation. I was uprooted once again, I had rebuilt a life for myself and I was very angry that I had to give it all up." Ironically, Mari found in Miami the prejudice that eluded her in Buffalo. "It was horrible, they spit at me in school. I took night courses so I wouldn't have to endure that. To me it was a surprise, I didn't take it very well. So I got married very young, it was an escape marriage," she says.

DULCE MARÍA SOSA

When Dulce Sosa's father came to the United States he suffered greatly with the changes in his life going from Cuba to Spain to California. Then having his wife work outside the home for the first time was the final stressor. His daughter explains, "He developed a paranoid persecution complex. Then they started divorce proceedings and they were so involved in it that they couldn't assume their proper role as our parents. On the contrary, we became their parents," says Dulce speaking, about her

sister and brother. "The family unity direction was lost in the true sense of having an emotional and psychological focus. It was a struggle for survival."

Once back with her family, Dulce was enrolled in a public school for the first time. This was her first real exposure to gangs, racial variety, and social complexity in Los Angeles. As difficult as it was to adjust to a new school, she says, "My parents breakup was the worse hell for me. You can't blame anybody, but I thought we were going to be happy again."

JUSTO RODRÍGUEZ

Justo Rodríguez lived his own particular kind of emotional limbo for two decades. He was deprived of ever having the dream of a happy family as his parents never left Cuba. "They apparently didn't want to leave. I didn't see them for twenty-one years. It is difficult without the support you find in your parents. The first time I saw them was truly great. After twenty-one years, I spent Mother's Day with my mother in Cuba in 1983. My father died that July. My mother came to Los Angeles in 1990 and met my daughter, who was 19 at the time." Justo visited Cuba again in 1996.

Justo does not know why his parents didn't leave Cuba. He says that it might have been because of his maternal and paternal grandmothers, but he just doesn't know. "When I was at Matecumbe and I would ask them to come, they never said yes."

ANTONIO PRIETO

Antonio Prieto is another one of those who was never reunited with his family and can't understand why. As a fourteen year old he was told that he was going to the United States for a week. He was also told that things were about to change in Cuba. He surmises, "They didn't leave because they always thought that the regime was going to be over." But he also reproaches his mother for her materialism. He believes that as she didn't want to lose their possessions, which they would have had to surrender if they left the country. "It wasn't like we were millionaires or anything," says Antonio. "My father is a Spaniard from Galicia who owned a small grocery store, some other small rental properties, and our house. I don't know, I can't understand that."

One Christmas, around 1978, more than sixteen years after leaving Cuba, Antonio got a phone call telling him that his mother was in Hialeah, a city that is part of greater Miami. Antonio had previously asked someone who went back and forth to Cuba to please visit his parents. This person arranged the trip, unbeknownst to Antonio. His memories of his mother's visit and the long-awaited reunion are not pleasant. She spent very little time with him, preferring to stay at her sister's. She was always questioning the behavior and choices of her grandchildren, who were total strangers to her. Antonio's memories of his mother are that she was never an easy or pleasant person. "She wanted a lot of material things, we gave them to her, and she was gone."

When Antonio's father arrived the following Christmas, Antonio felt like he reverted to his childhood. Together with his children, he rejoiced in this parental encounter. "I would wake up and look for my children, and they weren't in their beds. They were sleeping with grandpa. I would come home after working the midnight shift, and he would tell me to go to bed and I would say, 'No, let's go out, let's talk.' I felt pretty good that he was here. It was Christmas and it was a happy time."

Since that blissful holiday, neither parent returned to visit. Antonio went back to Cuba for the first time a few days before his mother died in January 1995. He returned shortly thereafter to discuss with his father where he wanted to be in light of his wife's death and he wanted to stay in Cuba. Now, at ninety-two, he is changing his mind.

"What do I think of this experience?" says Antonio. "I am happy that they sent me out of Cuba, but not that they never came. I'm still paying for some of the memories I have."

The revolution is like Saturn,
It eats its own children.

—*DANTON'S DEATH*, 1835,
GEORG BÜCHNER

CHAPTER 12

The Children in the Sixties
and Seventies

While the young Cuban exiles, sheltered in foster homes, orphanages, or group homes, were assimilating to the United States, the Cuban government knew their whereabouts.

During his stay in the port of Mariel awaiting his mother's release, Javier Jiménez had long talks with Colonel Tony de la Guardia. De la Guardia, head of the *Departamento de Moneda Convertible*, or Department of Convertible Currency, and his twin brother, Patricio, had been students of Javier's mother, a physics professor.

During one of these talks, de la Guardia confessed he knew that Javier was one of "Monsignor's children." He admitted that the Cuban government had always followed the children closely and had spies among the workers of the temporary shelters in Miami. De la Guardia proceeded to give Javier details about the camps, such as names of teachers, even details of the suicide of an instructor.

The insidious watch of the Cuban government over the children was frightfully evident to Josefína Santiago's father. Josefína recalls her father telling her that during a police interrogation

in Cuba, "As part of the interrogation, they showed him pictures of me, playing in the yard when I was at the last foster home."

Dr. Martínez, who was jailed for "terrorism" shortly after her daughter left Cuba, confirmed these tactics. During her interrogations she was told that they knew the whereabouts of her daughter and that the child was going to be kidnapped and returned to Cuba unless Dr. Martínez talked about her counter-revolutionary activities. "When your hands and feet are tied, you believe that they have the power to do anything," she says.

Besides all the upheaval that the children had endured, leaving their parents, their homeland, and their language and being immersed into a new country and culture, the context within which this was all taking place was evolving. Cuban youths along with American youths were entering an untamed social period without precedent, one that had young people as its protagonists. It was the sixties, a decade synonymous with political and social change.

Many of the teenagers joined the various social movements, expanded the ranks of the peace and love files, and wore flowers in their long hair. This all meant a rejection of a large part of the traditional values embraced by the family in Cuba and, in many cases, even a rejection of their families' political beliefs.

MY SIXTIES

I was one of these teenagers. After my family arrived in Miami we moved to Puerto Rico. I arrived there as a teenager, a lanky and too-tall thirteen year old desperately looking for peer acceptance. In order to gain this acceptance, I embraced Puerto Rico as my own, foolishly shunning my Cuban identity. I copied the Puerto Rican style of talking and refused to go to any activities at La Casa Cuba, the Cuban social club in Isla Verde, a beach resort area in San Juan. I found my Cuban contemporaries too traditional, too "square."

During my high school years Carnaby Street and Haight

Ashbury became my Meccas and rock-and-roll bands, both local
and foreign, my mantra. I endured white go-go boots and cor-
duroy mini-skirts in the tropical heat. I had a lot of problems at
home and became a rebellious teenager, not speaking to people
for days at a time. Chaperoning me to dances didn't last long; I
won that battle. But I lost my battle to my long bangs à la Cher;
my mother cut my hair one night as I slept. In those culturally
schizophrenic days, I wore frayed bell-bottom jeans and sandals
some days, but on others I enjoyed wearing tailored clothes, having manicures, and sweeping my hair in curls.

I discovered marijuana in college and my studies went down
the drain; I would spend long hours groovin' at the university's
social center. I marched at protests in favor of Puerto Rico's
independence. These temporary rejections of norms were without a defined political basis; they were just expressions of rebel-
lion. I finally left home at age nineteen in 1969.

AREÍTO AND THE ANTONIO MACEO BRIGADE

In the late sixties a group composed of young Cubans published
a magazine, *Areíto*. In the seventies they formed the Antonio
Maceo Brigade and would be known as Maceitos. They made several trips to Cuba, the first one on December 22, 1977, after
President Carter lifted the ban on travel to Cuba in March of
that year. Once on the island, the group was granted a meeting
with Fidel Castro.

Membership in the brigade had three requirements: one of
them was "To have left Cuba as a minor or to have been born
abroad of Cuban parents." This rule excluded a large segment
of the more conservative exile group. Other requirements were,
not to have participated in counterrevolutionary activities and
not to have a violent attitude toward the revolution; to support
the end of the U.S. economic blockade against Cuba; and to support the normalization of relations between Cuba and the
United States.[1] Most of the Brigada Antonio Maceo founders

were young Cuban students and university professors living in the United States and Puerto Rico.[2]

One of the Pedro Pan children, Alex López, was involved in paving the way for these trips to Cuba, which were repudiated by the majority of the exile community. In an interview granted to *Areíto* magazine, he explained that as a travel agent he had made a specialty in tourism to socialist countries. This specialty led to a trip to Cuba on November 1976. He says about his return to his homeland, "I walked back in through the same door that I had left. You feel scared, you feel confused. You want to absorb everything, because in the back of your mind you are fearful that this might be the only time that you'll have this opportunity. . . . The departure from Cuba is the hardest part. When you leave for the second time, you are not leaving your home, you are going home. And that is very strange, because I really had felt like a stranger there." Alex took his first group to Cuba in May 1977. In his second tourist group, one of the passengers was his mother. When she landed in Cuba he told her, "Here is Cuba. I give you back what you took from me."

Alina Bermúdez,* who was nine when she arrived alone with her sister in the United States, went from a right-wing Alpha 66 member to a left-wing Brigada Antonio Maceo member. When she rebelled against parental authority by leaving home at eighteen, she also rebelled against their beliefs and started trying to find her own. She moved in with two Uruguayan roommates. "We would have get-togethers and drink *mate,* play the guitar, and sing protest songs, the whole works. I would talk about Cuba and they would say to me, 'What do you know about Cuba, you left when you were nine? You only know what your parents tell you.'"

Wanting to find out for herself, Alina went to Cuba with the Antonio Maceo Brigade in 1980:

> My trip to Cuba was so incredible and so painful. When I arrived, we were put in camps and then given three or four days to see our family. My family didn't know I was coming

---

* a pseudonym

and on the way home I started getting scared, thinking, "What if I kill my grandmother from the emotion when she sees me?" A thirteen-year-old cousin that didn't know me greeted me and I said, "I'm Alina," and he ran to me and said, "Cousin!" and cried. Then I saw my grandmother and we hugged and cried and cried, and she sat down and had shortness of breath and I'm thinking, "I came to Cuba to kill my grandmother."

The house was like a museum, everything exactly as we had left it, with the pictures we had sent through the years everywhere. I cried from the time I got off the plane, I cried so much in Cuba. I didn't want to leave. I kept saying, "I'm breathing Cuban air," or "This is Cuban sky." When I went back to the camps, I had such a sadness inside.

When I returned to Miami, I was very anti-Cuban exile. I made declarations that ended up in a communist newspaper and became the traitor of my community in San Francisco. My parents called me a communist. My father died in 1989 and we never made up. I would go back to Cuba in a minute, I wanted to but I got scared. I've come to terms with the fact that I do not belong here nor do I belong there.

For Nelson Valdés, Cuba had been a present reality in his mind since he left in 1961 as a fifteen year old. He felt his departure had been a total eradication from his culture, family, and identity. He explains his feelings once in Cuba in an article in *Areíto*: "At last we were able to feel up close the total human dimension and dynamic of the Cuban revolutionary people: ethical, happy, popular and mythical as well as its great cultural and mythical riches. This trip had personal, political and existential consequences for me."[3]

CONTRA VIENTO Y MAREA

Nelson was not the only one experiencing cultural eradication in the United States. *Contra Viento y Marea*, or *Against Wind and Tide*,

was an anonymous book written by members of the Grupo Areíto in 1978. It chronicled the "voices of these youths who, against wind and tide, have defined themselves with Cuba," and tried to explain, through the nameless narratives of forty-seven persons, the phenomenon of radicalized Cuban youths in the United States and Puerto Rico whose priority was to "reinsert themselves somehow in the historic process of the Cuban Revolution."[4] This book won a special award in Cuba at the XIth Youth and Student Festival at Casa de las Americas. Some of the writers are Pedro Pan children. They remember their departure from Cuba, the glass wall, the uncertainty. One recalls, "Some parents suggested that we would be sent to Russia if we stayed. The sad reality is that they lost us when they turned us over to the United States." Another young woman wrote, "With all of the fear of the *patría potestad* they had sent us out, without a course, to this country . . . it was the same as being sent to Russia or Patagonia."

These youths asserted that they became disenchanted with the United States, felt like they didn't belong anywhere, and longed for a spiritual reunion with Cuba as a panacea for the feelings of alienation both against their parents and the Americans. One of the Areítos remembers the shock of blatant racism in the South, the horror of watching blacks having to sit in the back of buses and drink from separate water fountains. "When the happenings occurred in Selma,* I joined a protest march and I wound up in a black church singing 'We Shall Overcome.'"

One Pedro Pan youth, who could not bring himself to pledge allegiance to the American flag in school, felt deep within him that he didn't belong in the United States. He returned to live in Cuba as soon as he was legally able to do so. His brother claims that, ironically, this youth has never been able to fit totally in Cuban society, because he was shunned for not going through the same developing revolutionary process that his peers underwent. "When they started telling him all the things he had to do,

---

* In 1965, Alabama state troopers and local deputies stopped and clubbed black activists as they marched peacefully from Selma to Montgomery, Alabama.

he said 'I just came to live in my country' and they told him, 'Well, then let's see how you survive.'"

Many members of the Brigada Antonio Maceo and Areíto have changed through the years, mellowing with age. As their parents hoped, they matured and overcame their rebelliousness as they watched the ideals of the revolution crumble.

ABDALA

> *The love, mother, for the homeland,*
> *Is not the absurd love for the earth,*
> *Nor to the grass we trample upon,*
> *It is the invincible hate for who oppresses it,*
> *It is the eternal rancour for those who attack it;*
> *And such love awakens in our bosom*
> *The world of memories that call us*
> *To life again*
> *When blood flows from the anguished soul;*
> *The image of the love comforts us*
> *And the sweet memories it stores!*

—SPOKEN BY PRINCE ABDALA, FROM THE
EPIC POEM *ABDALA* BY JOSÉ MARTÍ

Romantically and idealistically linking themselves to the Prince who sacrifices his life for his homeland, a character created by Cuba's greatest nineteenth-century hero, José Martí, the Abdala Student Movement originated on January 28, 1968, and was propelled by those same lofty ideals. "Abdala was founded and conceived as a student movement within American universities in defense of the sovereignty and democracy of Cuba," says Leo Viota, "vis-à-vis the Venceremos Brigade, and the Antonio Maceo Brigade that had a propagandist movement defending the [Castro] regime."

Leo left Cuba as an unaccompanied eleven year old in 1961. He joined Abdala at age twenty-one, after finishing his volunteer service in Vietnam, where he went following his ideals, thinking it was his duty to fight the communist enemy. "In Abdala, I

found a group that was doing even more directly what I had gone seeking in Vietnam. It was a young, Cuban organization and I liked the idea."

Abdala had no age requirements, but it attracted mostly young college students of both sexes and many Pedro Pans. In its zenith it had around 600 to 700 members. There were chapters in throughout the Unites Sates, Puerto Rico, Costa Rica, Santo Domingo, Spain, and other countries. They also worked closely with Cuban student groups at various universities. Eventually, they were able to have several Abdala "cells" within Cuba.

About 300 Abdala representatives from fifty universities attended Abdala's first congress in 1971, where the Abadala Study Group was born. Is purpose was to increase in members the pride of being Cuban through awareness and their ability to Cuban issue in an informed manner.

The group published a monthly journal, *Abdala*, with a distribution of thirty-thousand, from Elizabeth, New Jersey. In its first issue, Abdala stated its mission: "The Abdala Student Movement was conceived principally for that task [to take a new course of action]. This is the work of students which, disillusioned with the negative positions of both sides, decided to try to search for a solution that really serves the people of Cuba.... We want to create a national conscience. 'Terrorists of the mind' can be a precise definition of our intentions. We have to mine the consciences of our fellow students."

Leo recalls that the group's principal public function was to face off against Castro's representatives at all levels, through demonstrations, picketing, or confrontations. "We were an activist group," says Leo. Many of the confrontations against those persons supportive of the Castro regime ended in arrests.

On October 1970, the Soviet flag was lowered at the United Nations, protesting Soviet intervention in Cuba. The United Nations became an Abdala target again on March 13, 1971, when a group of sixteen members took over the Security Council protesting what they saw as the United Nations' lack of attention to human rights violations in Cuba. After exclaiming, "We are Cuban students and in the name of the Cuban people, we are taking over the Security Council of the United Nations. We demand to see a diplomatic functionary to hand him a document,"[5] the demonstrators chained themselves to delegates' chairs. The group was thrilled to be arrested because they generated news coverage for their cause. "It was our launching pad," says Ángel Estrada, who is a Pedro Pan child and was one of the participants.

Luis Reina found his Cuban roots in Abdala. In an article he wrote for the journal, the then twenty-one-year-old freshman at Rutgers College says, "Today it is my decision to be Cuban.... In the United States, where I was sent so I wouldn't fall in the hands of the treacherous and murderous Communism, and where I saw my personality get mixed up, almost forgetting my native language, thanks to Abdala the Cuba that I carried inside, the one lay dormant in my soul, was reborn. And I didn't think about it, without a doubt, I said 'present' to my homeland and I am willing to offer all I have for its liberation."[6]

Abdala acquired a reputation for being very a physical, even terrorist, group, but their principal aim was to debate and inform. They also published flyers, distributed and plastered throughout colleges and universities, stating, "The Venceremos Brigade* does not want to Debate," listing twenty-three points they wanted to discuss, such as Soviet bases in Cuba, the takeover of the universities, 30,000 executions, and others.

Abdala interrupted a Cuban Film Festival, in March 1972, where the group used stink bombs and mice smuggled in cigarette packs by thirty Abdala members. Half an hour into the screenings the scurrying mice created panic among the attendees.

In June 1972, fourteen members chained themselves to the Statue of Liberty and draped a Cuban flag across the statue's

---

* The Venceremos Brigade was made up of radical left American college students who would go to Cuba to cut sugarcane and work in the fields.

forehead. They were protesting the death in a Cuban prison of Pedro Luis Boitel, a student leader who opposed Castro in 1960.[7] The group patterned themselves after Cuban freedom fighters like slain student leader José Antonio Echevarria, Castro's rival in the war against Batista.

Abdala grew and attracted others who were not students. They branched into lobbying and reached out to international organizations. Joining the Youth Congress, members traveled, scattering their vision worldwide.

With a hidden transmitter in Miami they broadcast more than 800 programs to Cuba.[8] This transmitter was burned down by Castro agents, according to Abdala. However, they regrouped after the loss, coming back with three transmission plants.

Lolita Cardenas,* also an unaccompanied Cuban child, was attracted to Abdala because she found kindred spirits, "a bunch of people who thought, went through the same experiences, and were attacked like I was. Going to school in the north was not the same as going in Miami. Here you were a minority. I got a D in an English literature class because the professor was very leftist and wanted me to write a paper about the reasons for the triumph of the revolution. I refused." Lolita claims to have been under that kind of pressure every day. "It was the time of Vietnam and the peace movements, you had to defend yourself and your beliefs every day. Abdala was a wholesome way for young adults to spend their time. There were a lot of idealistic people, very pro-social, they wanted to help the community, but internationally they were the most right-wing you could find."

Ángel remembers his experience in Abdala as a learning opportunity. "Abdala was for us a great school, tremendous fast-track growth, both morally and in terms of human realizations." Abdala seems to have filled a void for many. It served as a place where those who in the past hadn't felt they belonged could now belong.

---

* a pseudonym

JUAN FELIPE DE LA CRUZ SERAFÍN

Juan Felipe de la Cruz Serafín might be viewed as a martyr by some and a terrorist by others, but he was willing to give up his life for his beliefs. In 1973 he was arming a bomb in a Paris hotel, aimed for the Cuban embassy, when the object blew up and killed him.

Very patriotic and defiant since his youth, he began protesting at the early age of fifteen, by setting off a bomb in an Agricultural Fair organized by the Castro government in Havana. His parents immediately sent him out of Cuba alone.

He ran for commissioner of the city of Hialeah in 1969 and joined one of the Cuban exile groups, the Directorio Revolucionario Cubano (DRC), or Cuban Revolutionary Directory, in 1970. He directed their radio program while writing for *Replica* magazine. He was married and led a prosperous life at the time of his death. After his demise, fellow member of the DRC pasted his photo on Miami streets with text that read "Juan Felipe your ideas live on."[9]

In the sixties and seventies, many of the Pedro Pan children were, like most youths of the time, drawn to causes that demanded social justice. Unlike the others, many were drawn to Cuban causes, lured by the their love for their homeland, regardless of their political orientation.

It might be miles beyond the moon
Or right there where you stand
Just have an open mind
And suddenly you'll find
Never-never land

—FROM *PETER PAN,* THE MUSICAL
LYRICS BY BETTY COMDEN
AND ADOLPH GREEN

CHAPTER 13

The Children Today

Born between 1943 and 1956, the children of Pedro Pan are now grown and leading lives which are most certainly colored by their earlier experiences. Thinking about the time alone in the United States, some believe their parents deceived them and feel somehow betrayed, while others admire their parents' courage. Some think that the experience, difficult as it was, was for the best in the long run. Some are ambivalent. Others are angry.

In response to a questionnaire* answered by 442 Pedro Pans, when asked if their experience was negative or positive and why, a majority, 69.60%, found the experience to be a positive one. They had some of the following responses:

Made me stronger
Made me a tougher person

---

* A questionnaire was mailed to the approximately 1,000 Pedro Pans who have been located; 442 responded. See Appendix 1.

Made me an independent person
A hard-working person
Taught me self-reliance
Learned to adapt to changes
Gained confidence against adversity
Taught me discipline
Became an adult ahead of time
Gave me a lot of responsibility
Became a man overnight
Allowed me to develop by myself
Became closer to my mother and father
More aware of what I have and I give thanks daily
Made me a survivor
Matured early

Surprisingly, only 7.36% of the 442 respondents found the experience to be a negative one. They had the following responses:

Made me harder
Painful
A traumatic experience
Cost me my self-confidence
A scar that never goes away
Separation anxiety
Did not enjoy my childhood
I have fear of abandonment
Sense of loss
The lack of motherly kisses at bedtime
Sense of abandonment
Like losing a limb
Mental agony
Left a big scar in my heart
Gave me responsibilities I did not need at such a young age

OPERATION PEDRO PAN GROUP

A group of the children who lived with Monsignor Walsh kept in touch informally; over the years they have reconvened to celebrate his birthday. That group evolved into what is now Operation Pedro Pan Group, a nonprofit organization whose purpose is to help children in need.

Elisa (Elly) Vilano-Chovel asked Monsignor, "If I could get a group of Pedro Pans together, is there anything we could do to repay you?" He then told her of his dream of a children's village for abandoned and neglected children. About 200 Pedro Pans signed a pledge in 1990 in which they promised to help "today's dependent children and those who arrive unaccompanied under the foster care of the Archdiocese of Miami." Thus, Operation Pedro Pan Group set a fund-raising goal, the current Boystown and future children's village. The plan for the children's village has the approval of Miami's archbishop and is to be built on 30 acres of land that was once Camp Matecumbe.

The group has monthly get-togethers and several yearly fund-raisers. It has also conducted two symposiums where Operation Pedro Pan and the Unaccompanied Cuban Children's Program have been discussed and cathartic group discussions of individual experiences have taken place.

When the political situation changes in Cuba, many Pedro Pans say they would like to help rebuild their homeland—even move there and start anew. Others, who now have American children and grandchildren, feel too settled in their new homeland, having spent almost four decades in the United States.

PSYCHOLOGICAL STUDIES

Whether the experience of leaving your family and country is repressed or forgotten, the experience is bound to change even the strongest child. The memories of these children and their

effects have been the focus of three psychological studies, all undertaken by Pedro Pans who are now psychologists.

Dr. Lourdes Rodríguez-Nogues entitled her 1983 doctoral dissertation *Psychological Effects of Premature Separation from Parents in Cuban Refugee Girls: A Retrospective Study.* After a 1993 Pedro Pan reunion, Lisa A. Suzuki, Ph.D., an assistant professor in the Department of Applied Psychology at New York University, together with María Prendes-Lintel, Ph.D., herself a Pedro Pan and the coordinator at the Lincoln Family Practice Program, in Lincoln, Nebraska, decided to conduct a study about the Cuban children titled *Unaccompanied Cuban Refugee Children: A Retrospective Examination of Adjustment Experiences.* José Manuel Goyos, Ph.D., sampled 170 of the children for a study titled *Identifying Resiliency Factors in the Adult "Pedro Pan" Children.*

Although the studies varied in gender and numbers, the three studies agree that the separation did have an impact on the children, but that the children were very resilient, perhaps because they expected that their parents would be joining them. Most appear to have moved on to successful careers and close relationships with family and social support networks.

THE CHILDREN SPEAK NOW

Statistics can only begin to tell the story. This life-altering trauma left each and every Pedro Pan child changed. It left each child wise beyond his or her years. It enlivened a survival instinct that children rarely need to rely on to survive their childhood. Without a doubt, the impact of the separation is still a vital part of the adult children. Some Pedro Pans, whose stories have been chronicled in this book, sum up the impact that their exodus had on their lives.

Through interviews and questionnaires they have revealed their pain, many for the first time. A man simply wrote on his questionnaire, "I cannot complete the questionnaire. I am sorry.

All of these memories cause me too much pain." Following are some of their voices.

ILEANA FUENTES

"This eradication is in my poetry, my activism. I would have liked to grow up Cuban inside Cuba. I have never been able to coalesce in my existence this strange dimension of being an exile.

"Where I belong has been inside that island, for better or for worse. I feel as if I have been in suspended animation. We have grown up, but our interrupted Cuban childhood still calls to us. I am terrified of finding out eventually that I do not belong to Cuba, or in Cuba, either after so many years.

"When my daughter Carisa was eleven, I sent her to Tampa for a week's vacation at my cousin's who has children her age. My aunt and uncle were going to be there, a big family affair.

"When she boarded the plane, this was the first time she had flown alone, we had always traveled together. I was on the other side of the glass and all the suffering of that separation, the anguish by default, that I felt in that moment was so horrible that I spent the afternoon crying. Suddenly I was at the other side of the *pecera*. Suddenly I was in the place of my mother and father.

"In that moment I corroborated how traumatic this separation had been for me. I knew it had been but I had no proof. The fact that I almost had a nervous breakdown at the other side of that glass wall, that it was like a transportation in time, that was proof, corroboration, for me. And we have never been the same. And I always say that having gone through the experience I would never separate from my daughter. Never."

SUSAN GARRANDES

"When I was younger I was in therapy. I needed it. You also have a feeling against your parents. To a kid five minutes is like a couple of hours. That is why you give a kid a five-minute time out. Time to children seems like a lifetime full of things. It affects

one in many ways and if you don't work on them they can be detrimental in your other relationships. You put up your own barriers according to the things you went through.

"This separation made me very intolerant with people who think it is the end of the world because they couldn't buy themselves a lipstick. Come on, wake up, smell the coffee. You've got food on the table and a roof over your head? Be happy. You become very intolerant of people who are always crying and whining about things that are not really important. You also put a lot of weight on family and unity and that kind of stuff. You don't want to be without it."

MARÍA CRISTINA ROMERO-HALLORAN

"I was in the car with my daughter one day and I said, 'You know, I am tired of being an adult who has taken care of people since I was twelve.' And then it hit me that we had to grow up all of a sudden, and we were cheated out of those years of adolescence. It hit me that there is a little kid in there that wants to come out because I was cheated of those years.

"I was the one who rented apartments for my parents. And then life settles down and by then you are an adult and you end up having you own kids. Now I have my father to worry about who lives with me. And everyone goes through that, you become your parents' parent. But, going back, I missed a bunch of years, I didn't do them in the normal way that kids live through those stages. As you come to terms with it, you can't go back to relieve the past, but it is as well that you realize that it happened, that you are missing that as part of your psyche."

JOSÉ A. ARENAS

"I do not think this experience was negative, as a matter of fact I am proud of having been a small number in this immigration, but I don't want my children to go through something like this. You try to teach them that it is a jungle out there."

ROBERTO ZALDIVAR, M.D.

"This separation has had both effects on me. As another child refugee once told me, 'We have been marked for life,' and it is true. Our experience has made us different, made us mature ahead of time. Gave us responsibilities that we did not need to have at such an early age, yet made us value many things that other people don't value at all. I have seen people my age blaming their parents for all this. And it is not the fault of our parents, but the fault of a government on our land who made us and them do what we did—decide to leave our homeland.

"Some years ago a college professor who visited my house said that this that I have done today, put my experiences in writing, people my age have not done. That all of us keep this experience of our life quiet and not talk about it and it is true. I have written all of this with many tears in my eyes that had not come out before."

MARIO SÁNCHEZ, PH.D.

"Going to play ball at the beach with my sons, I felt those were the best times of my life," says Mario Sánchez. He was separated from his parents at the age of six for almost six years. "I felt as if I was living it for the first time. Doing six-year-old stuff with them, I became six years old with them. When they were between six and eight they can act like kids, and you don't send them to hell."

JOSEFÍNA SANTIAGO

"I was thrown right into the American culture, music wise, television. It is like I don't know anything Cuban anymore. I feel like I am missing a part of me.

"I can't speak Spanish as well as I would like. I have a rudimentary mastery of the language, which makes it very difficult for me in what I do. I am a Spanish mental health counselor and

people speak to me in Spanish and I'm sitting there fighting with words, because I never learned emotional words.

"I don't feel American. I don't feel Spanish. I sometimes get upset when people ask me what are you going to do on Thanksgiving, and I say, 'There were no pilgrims in Cuba.'

"I've been teaching emotionally disturbed students for twenty-two years. I just felt the need to assist someone who is troubled and angry. I like to see results. I do it for them, but I also do it for me, for the satisfaction of seeing it work. There is one less confused kid in the world, one kid who thinks he is worth something, at least somebody does. I would have like to have had that. I never got it, at least not when it counted, when I needed it."

ANONYMOUS

"I apologize for not answering your survey as soon as it reached me. But to be honest, every time I thought about answering your survey I did not want to deal with old memories. I have such awful memories. It amazes me how I can go back to when I was fourteen and remember it just like it was last week. It still hurts too much. There was nothing good about the experience—putting it aside is what I can do best. I only hope I can still be of some help. If you need a vote for negative experience, mine needs to be ranked close to the top. I do not know when I stopped crying every night of those awful three and a half years, but I should have been drained of tears by the time my parents came. I still feel very unhappy and unfulfilled with my life. There is such a big void inside that even a husband and three wonderful kids has not filled. The light at the end of the tunnel is always so, so far away."

ANONYMOUS

"I never said much about my early years, but about four months ago I told some of my story to my twenty-seven-year-old daughter and she couldn't believe what happened. She was so moved that

she called her twenty-four-year-old sister to come to the house to hear this.

"I have tried to tell my mom, but the emotions are so hard that I can never get enough nerve to tell her. I'm afraid that she would feel bad. I just want to tell her, but not [for her] to feel bad.

"In just writing these words to you my tears are running down my cheeks. I'm glad that this survey helps release some of the darkness that still lingers in my soul. I'm glad that it happened, but it hurts. And only we know how much for the rest of our lives."

ANTONIA MARTÍNEZ

"When you are smaller you don't realize what adults are going through, and you really don't appreciate until you are a parent, and you realize the sacrifice that they made and everything that they did. I have a nineteen-year-old son and I keep thinking back to the different instances, the decisions that they had to make and the choices, they were very difficult choices I don't know if I would have been able to do it the same way or not. I guess if you are faced with that choice at that time, that is the choice that you had to make."

MILDRED CARRIDO

"I consider myself a strong person, otherwise I would not be sane. I got my mental or character strength from what I went through, because when life crumbles around you, you take survival measures. I think how different my life would be if I had had a family. I still bleed through that emotional wound of not having a happy family life. I think my personality is affected by all of this, even if I try to compensate with my profession, my family, I believe that I have personality problems. Sometimes I am not secure about things, and I realize that I have no reason to feel that way. I do things that denote insecurity and I do them again and again."

ELISA (ELLY) VILANO-CHOVEL

"The Pedro Pan experience had an enormous impact in my life. I was forced to grow up before my time, estranged from my family, my roots, and my customs and had to become responsible not only for myself but also for my younger sister who could not comprehend what had happened.

"I am thankful for the opportunity of growing up in this land of freedom because of my parents' sacrifice of parting with us. Four decades later families in Cuba continue to be forcefully split by the government's structured control of education away from home and by migration. We were the 'sweet hope of our homeland' and missed the chance of living and helping when it was our turn. Nevertheless, I believe that each one of us is part of the solution for a democratic Cuba. I pray that in the future no one will ever again have to choose between freedom and family as our parents did, they are two of our undeniable God-given rights!"

WILLY CHIRINO

"My experience was positive, you mature a bit. You see things from another point of view. To know the good things in life you have to go through the bad. It taught me to enjoy the family more. Maybe that is why I am one of those parents who give their children I don't know how many kisses a day.

"I have always enjoyed seeing the terrible pride that Monsignor Walsh feels for my successes. He is always the first on line every time I get an award. I dedicated my star on Calle Ocho to him. It is necessary that people know about his work, he didn't do it for recognition, nobody knows.

"I have always had an extraordinary love for Cuba. As time goes by I feel more Cuban and less American, more Latin American, not only Cuban. I like to visit and socialize in Latin American countries, where I feel at home. I will always be a foreigner here. I admire their ways, their discipline, certain things, but I don't identify with it.

"I dream of returning to Cuba. I am already planning the concert I am going to give."

Regardless of the impact of the experience and the effect it had on their lives, just like Chirino, the Pedro Pan children interviewed for this book share the desire to see Cuba again, whether as visitors or to start a new life there. Unlike previous historical children's exoduses, the Pedro Pan exodus, as of this writing, has not seen its conclusion.

Epilogue

Departure from our beloved homeland has left all Pedro Pan children straddling two cultures. The Tropic of Cancer is our Berlin Wall, a parallel that separates us from Cuba, a place we now can visit, after receiving the proper authority from the Cuban government.

I often wonder what my life would have been had I stayed in Cuba. I wonder about my mirror images, my schoolmates that might still be in Cuba. What has their life been like?

I remember that my father started taking Russian lessons in 1960. I would look over his shoulder and be fascinated with the Cyrillic alphabet. I too wanted to learn Russian. I am convinced that had I stayed in Cuba, subjected to constant indoctrination, I would have been a good little communist, at least for awhile. I would have been instructed, but not educated. Education implies a wide range of knowledge and being able to satisfy all intellectual curiosity. Cubans are limited by the state as to what they can read and even what careers they can study (whatever is needed by the government at the moment).

No student in Cuba is allowed to graduate high school without participating in yearly "voluntary" farm work. The hours are long and the conditions often grueling. A recent arrival told me of an eleven year old of slight build, a boy small for his age, given boots so large to work in the fields that he could not walk in them.

The government instituted boarding schools, which the top students attend. Refusal to attend these schools truncates any possibility of a college education. Children who attend these boarding schools are allowed to go home every other weekend.

With the perennial gasoline shortages, many do not see their parents for long periods of time. Is this not what our parents feared, losing their children to communist indoctrination, whether in Russia or locally? Even Castro's daughter, Alina Fernández, says that she didn't want her daughter taken from her to attend these boarding schools, and that is one of the main reasons why she left Cuba and took her daughter out of the country.

When asked if I think my parents made the right decision, I always answer, "Yes, because I was given choices." Once in this country, any one of us could have chosen to return to Cuba or to be communist.

However, other children I've talked to, a minority, under 10 percent, do not feel this way. They resent the separation and they cannot forgive the pain they went through. What we all share is a sense of empathy, a sense that nobody else can understand what that separation meant to us, the fear that the government might not allow our parents to exit.

About half of the 14,048 children went to live with friends or family once in the United States. I was among those, and that is the reason why I did not see the hundreds of other children in the shelters and why I was ignorant about the exodus.

I am so grateful that my natural curiosity led me to inquire more about Pedro Pan after reading Joan Didion. By finding out about the others, I dug up a painful part of my life that I had buried. Although I lived with two kind families and later my uncle, I felt like I was an extra mouth to feed at a time that they were in financial need. I felt I was an intruder and couldn't talk to anybody about it. My separation felt like a year, although I was separated from my mother for only six months. During that time, I changed schools three times while learning English. Everything was so unfamiliar. I felt very much alone.

Interviewing Pedro Pans, I found my feelings mirrored. I cried after many interviews and letters. I also found myself continuing on a journey of Cuban rediscovery. My apartment is

becoming a Cuban museum, with Cuban books, paintings, and maps. I thirst for more knowledge about my homeland and try to learn as much as I can. After my teenage years of Cuban rejection, I've matured to the opposite end of the spectrum. I also took advantage of the opportunities the United States has provided me and have worked as a film producer and flight attendant. I completed my studies to graduate level and have been a freelance journalist for nine years.

Many of the children feel like I do, not completely American. Not out of ingratitude, but our hearts beat to a different rhythm, one made up of rumbas, guarachas, and danzones. It is a rhythm that makes us get teary-eyed when hearing the Cuban national anthem and makes us feel patriotic when reading anything by José Martí. And we still prefer black beans to carrots. We were born south of the Tropic of Cancer, the northernmost point on the earth at which the sun can appear directly overhead. And that has made us different.

Yet, can we ever feel at home again in Cuba, a country so drastically different now from the one we left in 1960, 1961, or 1962? Have almost four decades of exile condemned us to live in never-never land forever? Refugee children bear an indelible mark. But sharing this plight with other Pedro Pans gives me a connection I've never had before—with others who know what it feels like to straddle two cultures.

For More Information

If you are a Pedro Pan child and would like more information, contact

Operation Pedro Pan Group

at

www.pedropan.org

161 Madeira Avenue

Suite 61

Coral Gables, FL 33134

(305) 554-7196

The author will continue to expand the Pedro Pan database. Please add your information, which will remain anonymous at your request:

Yvonne M. Conde

c/o Routledge

29 W. 35th St.

New York, NY 10001-2299

PedroPanNY@aol.com

REST IN PEACE

Their bodies found a permanent resting place in the United States. Their souls dwell in a homeland without frontiers, confines, or dates, in unalterable peace.

Roberto Alcantud
Luis Alvarez
Randi Barceló
Dulce María Carneado
Daisy Cuan Li
Juan Felipe de la Cruz Serafín
Zoila E. de la Paz Alfonso
Armando Echemendia
Alfonso García
Marcelino García
Francisco González Cuesta
Oscar Gregorio
Agustín Gomez
Guillermo Hernández-Galloso
Fernando Ibarbangoitia
Gisela Iglesias
Arturo Iturralde
Roberto R. López-Molne
Ana Mendieta
Luis Meso
Juan Alberto Monge
Emilio Pis
Larry Ramos
Carmen Rosa Rodríguez
Armando Rousseau
Oscar Salazar
Cesar Sánchez
Ramiro Siegler
Luis Villaverde
Jorge Viña

Appendix 1
Questionnaires

Answers to Questionnaires
442 Total Respondents
Date and Place of Birth (426 responses)

La Habana 246 (57.75%)   Outside La Habana 180 (42.25%)

What Work Did Your Father Do in Cuba?

Accountant	25	Fruit Vendor	1
Administrator	3	Government Employee	9
Advertising	1	Grocery Store Owner	7
Airline	3	Handyman	1
Architect	4	Jeweler	3
Attorney	20	Journalist	2
Banking	9	Manager	6
Baker	1	Naval Officer	4
Barber	1	Nurse	1
Bus Driver	3	Supervisor	1
Business Owner	51	Optometrist	2
Businessman	8	Pilot	1
Butchers	3	Pharmacist	8
Cattleman/Ranch Owner	5	Photographer	2
Car Dealer	3	Physician	18
Carpenter	1	Playboy	1
Chemist	3	Police	2
Cigar Agent	4	Politician	3
Factory Owner	1	Port Pilot	1
Congressman	1	Professor	5
Dentist	4	Salesman	16
Distributors	2	Self-Employed	5
Engineers	17	Soldier	1
Export/Import	3	Teacher	4
Factory Worker	1	Telegraph Operator	2
Farm Owner	5	Unskilled Laborer	2
Farmer	4	Veterinarian	1
Foreman	2		

Did Your Mother Work Outside the Home?
(437 responses)

Housewives   312 (71.39%)

If Yes, Occupation

Administrative	1	Lawyer	3
Architect	1	Nurse's Aide	1
Beautician	4	Optometrist's Aide	1
Bookkeeper	1	Pharmacies	5
Business Owner	4	Physician	5
Clerk	3	Professor	10
Census Bureau	1	Teacher	47
Government Employee	2	Teacher's Aide	2
Dentist	1	Realtor	1
Dental Technician	1	Sales	12
Domestic Servant	2	School Principal	6
Elevator Operator	2	Seamstress	2
Laundress	1	Secretary	4
Law Firm Employee	1	Tobacco Maker	1

Would You Classify Your Family in Cuba as
(426 responses)

Upper Upper	17 (3.99%)	Lower Middle	86 (20.19%)
Lower Upper	32 (7.51%)	Upper Lower	17 (3.99%)
Upper Middle	257 (60.33%)	Lower Lower	0

17 respondents wrote in "Middle Middle" (3.99%) Given that choice, I believe many more people would have chosen that option.

What School Did You Attend in Cuba and Where?

Various, mostly private and Catholic.

Religion
(417 responses)

Catholic   410 (98.32%)

Others:

Agnostic	1 (0.24%)	Christian	2 (0.48%)
Atheist	1 (0.24%)	Jewish	1 (0.24%)
Baptist	1 (0.24%)	Lutheran	1 (0.24%)

Do You Know How You Obtained Your Visa Waiver to Leave Cuba?
(424 responses)

Yes	300 (70.75%)	No	124 (29.25%)

What Date Did You Leave Cuba?
(418 responses)

1960	9 (0.02%)	1961	205 (49.04%)	1962	204 (48.80%)

How Old Were You?
(428 responses)

Age	Number of children	Age	Number of children
1	2	10	32
3	2	11	47
4	1	12	34
5	1	13	49
6	6	14	69
7	9	15	55
8	18	16	53
9	20	17	26
		18	4

Did You Understand Why You Had Been Sent Out, the Politics Involved?
(442 responses)

Yes	345 (78.05%)	No	97 (21.95%)

Once in Miami, Where Did You Go?
(427 responses)

A Camp	370 (86.65%)	Family	38 (8.90%)	Friends	19 (4.45%)

Did You Leave Cuba Alone or With Brother(s)/Sister(s)?
(427 responses)

Alone	196 (45.90%)	With siblings	231 (50.55%)

If with Brother(s)/Sister(s), How Old?

Ages ranged from 6–18

Were You Ever Separated from Them?
(200 responses)

Separated 103 (51.50%)

If You Went to a Camp in Miami, Which One¿

(Many respondents did not remember names of camps/shelters.
Others went to more than one)

St. Raphael	1	Kendall	99
Cuban Boys Home	1	Matecumbe	106
Florida City	115		

After the Miami Camp, Were You Relocated to a School, Foster Home, or Orphanage¿ If Yes, in What State¿

Alabama	2	Minnesota	2
Arizona	2	Montana	19
Arkansas	2	Nebraska	23
California	10	Nevada	2
Colorado	20	New Jersey	10
Connecticut	1	New Mexico	43
Delaware	6	New York	23
Florida	27	Ohio	13
Georgia	2	Oregon	2
Illinois	11	Pennsylvania	6
Indiana	11	Puerto Rico	1
Iowa	4	South Carolina	1
Kansas	34	Tennessee	2
Kentucky	1	Texas	24
Lousiana	5	Washington	6
Massachusetts	5	Washington, D.C.	2
Michigan	13	West Virginia	2

Did You Speak English¿
(442 responses)

Yes	77 (17.42%)	No	365 (82.58%)

How Long Were You Separated from Your Parents¿

In months
Less than one year: 130 (29.41%)

Number of Months		Number of Months	
1	2	7	7
2	3	8	17
3	7	9	8
4	11	10	8
5	7	11	14
6	16	12	30

More than one year: 103 (23.30%)

Number of Months		Number of Months	
13	61	18	21
14	1	19	4
15	3	20	1
16	4	21	4
17	4		

More than two years: 57 (12.90%)

Number of Months		Number of Months	
24	27	29	1
26	1		

More than three years: 37 (8.37%)

36	23	46	2
42	12		

Four years or more: 53 (11.99%)

48	43	54	7
51	2		

Five years or more: 46 (10.41%)

60	40	63	1
62	1	66	4

Six years or more: 21 (4.75%)

72	19	78	1
75	1		

Seven years or more: 9 (2.04%)

84	9

Eight years or more: 6 (1.36%)

96	5	100	1

Nine years or more: 1 (0.68%)

108	1

Ten years or more: 3 (0.68%)

120	3

Twelve years or more: 1 (0.23%)

144	1

Thirteen years or more: 1 (0.23%)

156	1

Appendix 1 / 225

180	Fifteen years or more: 1 (0.23%) 1
192	Sixteen years or more: 1 (0.23%0 1
204	Seventeen years or more: 1 (0.23%) 1
216	Eighteen years or more: 4 (0.90%) 4
240	Twenty years or more: 3 (0.68%) 3
258	Twenty-one years or more: 1 (0.23%) 1
300	Twenty-five years or more: 1 (0.23%) 1

Never reunited with their parents: 15 (3.39%)

Did You Forget Your Spanish During Separation?
(440 responses)

Yes   54 (12.27%)   No   386 (87.76%)

Do You Think Your Parents Did the Right Thing
by Sending You Out Alone?
(429 responses)

Yes   366 (85.31%)   No   41 (9.56%)   Unsure   22 (5.13%)

Would You Do What Your Parents Did Under the Same Circumstances?
(320 responses)

Yes   147 (45.94%)   No   104   (32.50%)   Unsure   69 (21.56%)

Are You a U.S. Citizen?
(440 responses)

Yes   426 (96.81%)   No   14 (3.14%)

Education—Highest Level

No high school	2	(.47%)
High school	54	(12.74%)
Some college	30	(7.08%)
Two or three years of college	78	(18.40%)
Bachelor's degree	116	(27.83%)
Seventeen years	7	(1.65%)
Master's degree	80	(18.87%)
Nineteen years	10	(2.36%)
Doctorate	38	(8.96%)
Twenty-one years	2	(.47%)
Twenty-two years	7	(1.65%)

Current Occupation

Accountant	15	Comptroller	2
Account Manager	1	Computer Consultant	1
Account Rep.	1	Consultant	3
Adm. Assistant	4	Contracting	2
Administrator	1	Coordinator	1
Airline	4	Counselor	2
Annalist	1	Customs Broker	1
Architect	2	Dental Assistant	2
Art Adm.	2	Dept. Asst. Sec. of a State	1
Artist	3	Developer	1
Attorney	13	Diplomat	1
Auditor	1	Director	7
Auto Tech.	1	Disabled War Veteran	1
Bandleader	1	Economist	1
Banker	6	Editor	1
Business Owner	17	Electrician	1
Business Person	3	Engineer	20
Car Agency Dir.	1	Entrepreneur	1
Car Wash	1	Executive	2
Catholic Priest	5	Filmmaker	1
Catholic Resettlement	1	Financial Analyst	1
Chair. Pharmaceutical	2	Financial Planner	1
Chemical Co. Owner	1	Firefighter	1
Chemist	1	Hairdresser	1
Claims Rep.	1	Hearing Aid Specialist	1
Clerk	2	Hi-Lo Operator	1
Communications	2	Horticulturist	1

Housewife	14	Office Adm.	1
Insurance	8	Office Manager	1
Investigator	2	Operation Manager	1
Investments	1	Paralegal	1
Intl. Bus. Mgmt.	1	Park Ranger	1
Intl.Trade Consultant	1	Personal Shopper	1
Investigator	1	Pharmacist	1
Jeweler	1	Pharmaceutical Tech.	1
Journalist	3	Phone Company Director	1
Laboratory	1	Phone Operator	1
Labor Rep.	1	Physician	11
Law Officer	3	Psychologist	1
Legal Assistant	2	Pianist	1
Library Director	1	Political Assistant	1
Manager	11	Postal Service	2
Mortgage Underwriter	1	Professor	4
Motion Picture Writer	1	Professorial Assistant	1
Navy	1	Psychiatrist	1
Network Technician	1	Psychologist	7
Nun	1	Public Relations	2
Nurse	4	Real Estate	4

Current Married Status
(421 Responses)

Single	43	(10.21%)
Married	319	(75.77%)
Divorced	50	(11.88%)
Widow(er)	3	(.71%)
Separated	5	(1.19%)
Living Together	1	(.24%)

If Previously Married, How Many Times?
(142 reponses)

Once	109	(76.76%)	Thrice	3	(2.11%)
Twice	29	(20.42%)	Four times	1	(.70%)

Current or Previous Spouse(s) Cuban?
(398 reponses)

Yes 233 (58.54%)   No 165 (41.46%)

Do You Have Children?
(377 responses)

Yes   349 (79.13%)   No   92 (20.86%)

If Yes, How Many?
(349 responses)

One	76	(21.78%)	Four	21	(6.02%)
Two	154	(44.13%)	Five	7	(2.01%)
Three	90	(26.07%)	Six	1	(.29%)

Do Your Children Speak Spanish?
(354 responses)

Yes   267 (82.41%)   Some   9 (2.78%)
No   78 (24.07%)

Do You Identify Yourself as Cuban?
(417 responses)

Very Little	15 (3.59%)	Very	219 (52.51%)
Somewhat	74 (17.74%)	Extremely	109 (26.13%)

Do You Keep Cuban Traditions?
(429 responses)

Yes   342 (79.72%)   Some   39 (9.09%)
No   48 (11.19%)

Would You Return to Live in Cuba, if the Political Scenario Changed?
(428 responses)

Yes	103 (24.07%)	Visit	2 (0.47%)
No	230 (53.74%)	Part-Time	7 (1.64%)
Unsure	86 (20.09%)		

This Experience of Being a Child Refugee—
Do You Think It Had a Positive or Negative Effect on You?
(421 responses)

Negative	31 (7.36%)	Unsure	7 (1.66%)
Positive	293 (69.60%)	Neither	4 (0.95%)
Both	86 (20.43%)		

Are You Fulfilled in Life Today?
(379 responses)

Yes	354 (93.40%)	Unsure	9 (2.37%)
No	16 (4.22%)		

Do You Think You Would Be the Same Person if You Had Stayed in Cuba?
(422 responses)

Yes	34 (8.06%)	Unsure	32 (7.58%)
No	356 (84.36%)		

Political Affiliation
(381 responses)

Republicans	207 (54.33%)	Social Democrat	2 (0.52%)
None	71 (18.64%)	Feminist/Activist	1 (0.26%)
Democrats	58 (15.22%)	Not Communist	1 (0.26%)
Independent	32 (8.40%)	Pro-Freedom	1 (0.26%)
Conservative	3 (0.79%)	Rightist	1 (0.26%)
Liberal	3 (0.79%)	Social Progressive	1 (0.26%)

Appendix 2
The Republic of Cuba in 1958

STATISTICS AND DATA

Percentages of Public Expenditure for Education in Latin America in 1958

1. **Cuba**	**23.0%**	6. Peru	14.6%
2. Puerto Rico	21.5%	7. Mexico	14.7%
3. Argentina	19.6%	8. Guatemala	11.7%
4. Costa Rica	19.6%	9. Ecuador	10.8%
5. Chile	15.7%		

(Source: UNESCO, Annuaire International d'Education)

Percentage of Illiterate to Total Population

1. Argentina	8%	6. Panama	28%
2. Costa Rica	21%	7. Uruguay	35%
3. Chile	24%	8. Colombia	37%
4. **Cuba**	**25%**	9. Mexico	38%
5. Puerto Rico	26%	10. Ecuador	44%

(Source: United Nations Statistical Year Book, 1959)

Percentage of Female Students to Total Registered

1. **Cuba**	**45%**	6. Mexico	27.9%
2. Panama	43%	7. Costa Rica	27.5%
3. United States	32.8%	8. Venezuela	25.2%
4. Argentina	30.3%	9. Paraguay	23.2%
5. Chile	29.8%		

(Source: UNESCO, Annuaire International d'Education)

Higher Education Students per 1,000 Inhabitants
(World Comparison 1957-1958)

Country	Population in Millions 1957	Students in Higher Education	Students per 1,000 Inhabitants
United States	171.2	3,037,000	17.7
Cuba	**6.4**	**86,500**	**13.5**
U.S.S.R.	200.2	2,110,860	9.5
Japan	90.9	626,736	6.9
France	44.1	180,634	4.1
Italy	48.5	154,638	3.2
Germany	51.5	153,923	3.0
England	51.5	96,128	1.9

(Source: UNESCO)

The Catholic Church and Education in Cuba in 1958

Population	6,250,000
Catholic Population	5,665,000 (94.20%)
Girls' schools, 194	34,335 students
Boys' schools, 130	33,691 students

One of 92 inhabitants received education in a Catholic School.

(Source: Pontifical Annual)

Social Benefits
Remuneration Percentage to Workers and Employees
over the National Income in the World in 1958

1. England	74.0%	6. Sweden	64.2%
2. United States	71.1%	7. Norway	62.5%
3. Canada	68.5%	8. West Germany	61.9%
4. **Cuba**	**66.0%**	9. Australia	61.9%
5. Switzerland	64.4%	10. France	59.7%

(Source: OIT Annual of Work Statistics, 1960)

Inhabitants per Television Set in Latin America in 1958

1. **Cuba**	**18**	4. Mexico	70
2. Venezuela	32	5. Brazil	79
3. Argentina	60	6. Colombia	102

(Source: Statistical Abstract of the USA, 1960)

Inhabitants per Telephone in Latin America in 1958

1. Argentina	17	6. Panama	48
2. Uruguay	25	7. Brazil	63
3. **Cuba**	**28**	8. Colombia	64
4. Chile	46	9. Mexico	75
5. Venezuela	47		

(Source: Statistical Abstract of the USA, 1960)

Inhabitants per Radio Receiver in Latin America in 1958

1. Uruguay	4.6	6. Chile	10.6
2. **Cuba**	**5.0**	7. Brazil	11.0
3. Argentina	7.0	8. Mexico	11.0
4. Venezuela	8.6	9. Costa Rica	15.2
5. Panama	9.1		

(Source: Statistical Abstract of the USA, 1960)

Inhabitants per Automobile in Latin America in 1958

1. Venezuela	17.4	6. Panama	41.3
2. Uruguay	23.2	7. Costa Rica	47.3
3. **Cuba**	**27.3**	8. Mexico	52.4
4. Argentina	30.9	9. Brazil	62.4
5. Chile	34.6		

(Source: Statistical Abstract of the USA, 1960)

Inhabitants per Physician in Latin America in 1958

1. Argentina	840	6. Mexico	2,200
2. **Cuba**	**980**	7. Brazil	2,500
3. Uruguay	1,000	8. Nicaragua	2,600
4. Venezuela	1,700	9. Costa Rica	2,800
5. Chile	1,900		

(Source: U.N. Statistical Year Book, 1959)

Notes

PROLOGUE

1. Dorothy Legarreta, *The Guernica Generation—Basque Refugee Children of the Spanish Civil War* (Reno: University of Nevada Press, 1984).
2. Interview by author with Olga Levy Drucker.
3. Olga Levy Drucker, *Kindertransport* (New York: Henry Holt and Company, 1992).
4. *New York Times,* 11 Oct. 1998.
5. Nicholas Gage, *Eleni* (New York: Ballantine Books, 1984).
6. Monsignor Walsh, who ran the Unaccompanied Cuban Children's Program, says 14,048 children left Cuba through Operation Pedro Pan. Ruby Hart Phillips reported on March 9, 1962, in the *New York Times* "14,072 Children Sent Out of Cuba."

CHAPTER 1 ADIÓS CUBA: 1959–1960

1. *America* magazine says 66,000 Cubans had left by February 18, 1961. According to Fagen, Brody, and O'Leary, approximately 43,372 Cubans had sought passage out in 1959 and 1960, and 80,928 more would leave in 1961. The authors cite 1,705 employable Cuban refugees departing in 1959 and 9,138 in 1960, or a total of 8,508. The number increased to 20,323 in 1961. They suggest multiplying the employable numbers times four for a rough estimate. 8,508 x 4 = 34,032 for 1959 and 1960 and 20,323 x 4= 80,928 for 1961. Since these figures are from the Refugee Center in Miami, those Cubans that did not register there are not counted, therefore the figures are underrepresented. See Richard R. Fagen, Richard A. Brody, and Thomas J. O'Leary, *Cubans in Exile—Disaffection and the Revolution* (Stanford: Stanford University Press, 1968), 63.

    Paul Bethel, press officer at the U.S. embassy in Havana, says that 100,000 had fled by the end of 1960. See Paul D. Bethel, *The Losers* (New York: Arlington House, 1969).
2. Robert E. Quirk, *Fidel Castro* (New York and London: W. W. Norton and Company, 1993).
3. Ibid., 81.
4. Bethel, *Losers.*
5. Quirk, *Fidel Castro,* 214.
6. Hugh Thomas, *Cuba* (New York: Harper and Row 1971), 1080.

7. Ibid., 1081.
8. Horace Sutton, "How to Lose Tourists," *Sports Illustrated*, Jan. 1959.
9. *New York Times,* 2 Jan. 1959, 1; 3 Jan. 1959, 2; 4 Jan. 1959, 1; and 5 Jan. 1959, 3.
10. United States State Department, *Zenith and Eclipse: A Comparative Look at Socio-Economic Conditions in Pre-Castro and Present Day Cuba,* Bureau of InterAmerican Affairs, 8 Feb. 1998; and *Contacto* magazine, July 1998.
11. Jorge I. Domínguez, *Cuba—Order and Revolution* (Massachusetts and London: The Belknap Press of Harvard University Press, 1978), 197.
12. *New York Times,* 5 Jan. 1959, 3.
13. *Chicago Sunday Tribune,* 4 Jan. 1959.
14. *New York Times,* 18 Jan. 1959, Editorial.
15. *New York Times,* 4 Jan. 1959.
16. Nikita Khrushchev, *Khrushchev Remembers* (Boston: Little, Brown, 1970), 489.
17. *New York Times,* 9 Jan. 1959.
18. Bethel, *The Losers.*
19. Quirk, *Fidel Castro,* 218.
20. *New York Times.* 13 Jan. 1959, 1.
21. *New York Times.* 13 Jan. 1959, 12.
22. *New York Times.* 16 Jan. 16 1959, 3.
23. Dr. Juan Clark, *Religious Represssion in Cuba* (Miami: Cuban Living Conditions Project, 1998).
24. *New York Times,* 11 Jan. 1959, 8.
25. *New York Times,* 20 Jan. 1959, 1.
26. *New York Times,* 13 Jan. 1959, 1.
27. *New York Times,* 15 Jan. 1959, 1.
28. *New York Times,* 22 Jan. 1959.
29. *New York Times,* 25 Jan. 1959.
30. *Facts on File,* 5–11 Mar. 1959, 79, 80.
31. *Facts on File,* 16–22 Mar. 1959, 131.
32. Aleksandr Fursenko and Timothy Naftali, *One Hell of a Gamble— Khrushchev, Castro & Kennedy 1958–1964* (New York and London: W. W. Norton & Company, 1997), 11. (From Folio 3. List 65, File 874, APRF, Ponomarev, Mukhitdinov to the Central Committee of the Communist Party of the Soviet Union.)
33. Ibid., 12. (Resolution from Protocol 214, Presidium meeting of 23 Apr. 1959, Folio 3, List 65, File 871, APRF.)
34. Domínguez, *Cuba,* 438.
35. *Facts on File,* 14–20 May 1959, 164.
36. Ibid., 3 Mar.–4 Apr. 1959.
37. Dr. Juan Clark, *Mito y Realidad-Testimonios de un pueblo* (Miami and Caracas: Saeta Ediciones, 1990).
38. Quirk, *Fidel Castro,* 248.
39. Ibid., 249.
40. Ibid., 249, 250.

41. Fursenko and Naftali, *One Hell of a Gamble*, 22.
42. Christopher Andrew and Oleg Gordievsky, *KGB—The Inside Story* (New York: Harper Collins, 1990), 467.
43. Quirk, *Fidel Castro*, 354.
44. *Facts on File*, 6 Aug.–12 Aug. 1959.
45. *The Reporter*, 4 Aug. 1960.
46. Quirk, *Fidel Castro*.
47. *Facts on File*, 15–21 Oct. 1959, 339.
48. Ibid., 12–18 Nov. 1959.
49. *Facts on File*, 19-25 Nov. 1959, 86.
50. Leovigildo Ruíz, *Diario de Una Traición 1960* (Miami: The Indian Printing, 1970). Also *Revolucion*, 4 Jan. 1960.
51. *Facts on File*, 1–6 Jan. 1960.
52. *New York Times*, 3 Jan. 1960.
53. Congressional Record-Senate, 2 Feb. 1960, 1736.
54. Ruíz, *Diario de Una Traición*.
55. Ibid., 42.
56. *U.S. News and World Report*, 29 Aug. 1960.
57. *New York Times*, 15 Feb. 1960.
58. *Revolución*, 10 Nov. 1960.
59. *Revolución*, 6 June 1960.
60. *U.S. News and World Report*, 4 July 1960.
61. Ibid.
62. *U.S. News and World Report*, 20 June 1960. *The Reporter*, 7 July 1960.
63. Domínguez, *Cuba*, 346, 347.
64. Carbonell, *And the Russians Stayed*.
65. Domínguez, *Cuba*, 146.
66. Ruby Hart Phillips, *The Cuban Dilemma* (New York: Ivan Obolensky, Inc., 1962).
67. Andrew and Gordievsky, *KGB*, 467.
68. Hart Phillips, *The Cuban Dilemma*, 269.
69. Carbonell, *And the Russians Stayed*, 123, 124. Juan Vives, *Los Amos de Cuba* (Buenos Aires: Emece 1982), 98–100.
70. *U.S. News and World Report*, 31 Oct. 1960.
71. *Revolución*, 1 Nov. 1960.
72. Fursenko and Naftali, *One Hell of a Gamble*, 71.
73. Hart Phillips, *The Cuban Dilemma*.
74. *Revolución*, 12 Nov. 1960.
75. *Revolución*, 18 Nov. 1960.
76. Hart Phillips, *The Cuban Dilemma*.
77. *The Encyclopaedia Britannica*, 11th ed.

CHAPTER 2 ADIÓS CUBA: 1961–1962

1. *New York Times*, 3 January 1961.
2. Hart Phillips, *The Cuban Dilemma*, 293.
3. Ibid.

4. *New York Times*, 5 Jan. 1961.
5. Ibid.
6. Ruíz, *Diario de una Traición*.
7. *New York Times*, 6 Feb. 1961.
8. *New York Times*, 8 Feb. 1961.
9. Ruíz, *Diario de una Traición*, 16–17.
10. *New York Times*, 30 Jan. 1961.
11. *Facts on File*, Feb. 1961.
12. Ruíz, *Diario de una Traición*.
13. *New York Times*, 9 Mar. 1961.
14. *New York Times*, 28 Feb. 1961.
15. *New York Times*, 29 Mar. 1961.
16. *New York Times*, 5 April 1961.
17. Hart Phillips, *The Cuban Dilemma*. Also *Newsweek*, 3 Apr. 1961. *New York Times*, 20 Mar. 1961.
18. *Newsweek*, 3 Apr. 1961.
19. *New York Times*, 20 March 1961.
20. Enrique Encinosa, *Cuba en Guerra* (Florida: The Endowment for Cuban Studies of the Cuban American National Foundation, 1994), 72.
21. Nestor Carbonell, *And the Russians Stayed* (New York: William Morrow and Company, 1989), 146.
22. Edward B. Ferrer, *Operation Puma—The Air Battle of the Bay of Pigs* (Miami: International Aviation Consultants, Inc., 1975).
23. *New York Times*, 20 Apr. 1961.
24. Ibid., 20 April 1961.
25. Ruíz, *Diario de una Traición*. Also *Time*, 12 May 1961, 25; *New York Times*, 2 May 1961.
26. *New York Times*, 12 June 1961; Ruíz, *Diario de una Traición*.
27. Ruíz, *Diario de una Traición*.
28. *New York Times*, 6 Aug. 1961, 1.
29. *Facts on File*, *23* Feb.–1 Mar. 1961.
30. *New York Times*, 23 June 1961.
31. Ruíz, *Diario de una Traición*.
32. *New York Times*, 8 July 1961.
33. *New York Times*, 18 June 1961, 3.
34. *New York Times*, 15 Sept. 1961.
35. *Time*, 6 October 1961.
36. *New York Times*, 17 Sept. 1961.
37. Clark, *Religious Repression in Cuba* (Miami: Cuban Living Conditions Project, 1988), 11, 12, 15.
38. Ruíz, *Diario de una Traición*.
39. *New York Times*, 23 Dec. 1961.
40. Clark, *Religious Repression in Cuba*.
41. José Duarte Oropesa, *Historiología Cubana Desde 1959 hasta 1960* (Miami: Ediciones Universal, 1993).
42. Fursenko and Naftali, *One Hell of a Gamble*.

43. *New York Times,* 4 Feb. 1995.
44. *New York Times,* 15 Feb. 1962.
45. *New York Times,* 8 Mar. 1962.
46. *New York Times,* 1 Apr. 1962.

CHAPTER 3   CUBAN CHILDREN'S PROGRAM, MIAMI: 1960–1961

1. Gene Miller, "'Peter Pan' Means Real Life to Some Kids," *Miami Herald,* 9 Mar. 1962.
2. U.S. Department of Health, Education, and Welfare, *Cuba's Children in Exile* (Washington, D.C.: Social and Rehabilitation Service, Children's Bureau, 1967), 1.
3. Ibid.
4. Hart Phillips, *The Cuban Dilemma.*
5. Bryan O. Walsh, "Cuban Refugee Children," *Journal of Inter-American Studies and World Affairs* (July–Oct. 1971): 391.
6. Ibid., 397.
7. Ibid., 398.
8. U.S. Department of Health, Education, and Welfare, *Cuba's Children in Exile.*
9. *New York Times,* 7 Jan. 1962.
10. Joan Didion, *Miami* (New York: Simon and Schuster, 1987), 122.
11. U.S. Department of Health, Education and Welfare, *Cuba's Children in Exile.*
12. Walsh, "Cuban Refugee Children."
13. Ibid., 388.
14. Ibid.
15. Tracy S. Voorhees, *Interim Report to the President on the Cuban Refugee Problem* (Washington, D.C.: Government Printing Office, December, 1960), 10.
16. *New York Times,* 2 Feb. 1961, 5.
17. *New York Times,* 2 Feb., 4 Feb. 1961.
18. U.S. Department of Health, Education and Welfare, *Cuba's Children in Exile.* Also *New York Times,* 4 Feb. 1961.
19. Katherine Bronwell Oettinger, "Services to Unaccompanied Cuban Refugee Children in the United States," *The Social Services Review* (Dec. 1962).
20. Ibid.
21. U.S. Department of Health, Education and Welfare, *Cuba's Children in Exile,* 3.
22. Walsh, "Cuban Refugee Children."
23. K. Oettinger, "Services to Unaccompanied Cuban Refugee Children in the United States."

CHAPTER 4   OPERATION PEDRO PAN, CUBA: 1961–1962

1. Ramón Grau Alsina and Valerie Ridderhoff, *Mongo Grau-Cuba desde 1930* (Madrid: Agualarga Editores, 1997).

CHAPTER 5   THE TEMPORARY SHELTERS IN MIAMI

1. *New York Times,* 27 May 1962.
2. Walsh, "Cuban Refugee Children," 393, 394.
3. Ibid., 393.
4. Ibid., 396.
5. U.S. Department of Health Education and Welfare, *Cuba's Children in Exile,* 1.
6. Ibid.
7. Ibid., 397.
8. Hebrew Immigrant Aid Society.
9. *The Voice,* 9 Mar. 1962.
10. *The Voice,* 25 Jan. 1962.

CHAPTER 6   ASSIMILATION AND ADAPTATION: WHEN PEDRO BECAME PETER

1. Clifton Fadiman, *The Little, Brown Book of Anecdotes* (Boston: Little, Brown and Company, 1985).
2. *El Miami Herald,* 18 Oct. 1987.
3. Sara Yaraballi donated these letters to the Otto Richter Library of the University of Miami, Special Collections, Cuban Archives.

CHAPTER 7   ORPHANAGES: IT'S THE HARD-KNOCK LIFE

1. Marvin Olansky, "The Real Story of Orphanages," *Philanthropy Culture and Society* (May 1996).
2. Robert Katz, *Naked by the Window: The Fatal Marriage of Carl Andre and Ana Mendieta* (New York: Atlantic Monthly Press, 1990).
3. *Exito Magazine,* Miami.
4. Katz, *Naked by the Window.*
5. *Rocky Mountain News* (Denver), 12 Mar. 1966.
6. Ibid., 24 Oct. 1962.
7. Ibid., 20 May 1962.
8. Ibid., 12, Mar. 1966.

CHAPTER 8   LIFE WITH THE JONESES

1. *The Christian Century,* 4 Apr. 1962.

CHAPTER 11   REUNION WITH PARENTS

1. Carbonell, *And the Russians Stayed.*
2. *New York Times,* 26 Jan. 1963.
3. *New York Times,* 4 July 1963.
4. *New York Times,* 30 Sept. 1965.
5. *New York Times,* 4 Oct. 1965.
6. *New York Times,* 8 Oct. 1965.
7. *New York Times,* 9 Oct. 1965, supplement.
8. *New York Times,* 20 Oct. 1965.
9. *New York Times,* 7 Nov. 1965.

10. *New York Times,* 2 Dec. 1965.
11. United States Government Memorandum, 4 Jan. 1966, from Dr. Ellen Winston, Commissioner of Welfare, to John F. Thomas, Director, Cuban Refugee Program.
12. United States Government Memorandum, 8 Mar. 1966, from Dr. Ellen Winston, Commissioner of Welfare, to John F. Thomas, Director, Cuban Refugee Program.

CHAPTER 12   THE CHILDREN IN THE SIXTIES AND SEVENTIES

1. *Areíto,* 3–4 (1978), 4.
2. José A. Cobas and Jorge Duany, *Cubans in Puerto Rico—Ethnic Economy and Cultural Identity* (Gainsville: University Press of Florida, 1997), 115.
3. Nelson P. Valdés, *"Encuentro con los Familiares," Areíto IV,* vol. 3 and 4, 1978.
4. Anonymous, *Contra Viento y Marea* (Mexico: Siglo Veintiuno Editores, 1978).
5. *Abdala* newspaper, 1971.
6. *Abdala* newspaper, May 1971.
7. Enrique Encinosa, *Cuba en Guerra, Historia de la Oposición Anti-Castrista 1959–1993* (Florida: The Endowment for Cuban American Studies, 1994), 244.
8. Ibid., 246, 267.
9. *Abdala,* vol. 23, Aug.–Sept. 1973.

Bibliography

Alarcón Ramiréz, Dariel. *Memorias de un Soldado Cubano—Vida y Muerte de la Revolución*. Madrid: Tusqetes Editores, 1997.

Carbonell, Nestor T. *And the Russians Stayed—The Sovietization of Cuba*. New York: William Morrow, 1989.

Castro, Fidel. *La Revolución Cubana*. Mexico City: Ediciones Era, 1972.

Cobas, José A., and Jorge Duany. *Cubans in Puerto Rico—Ethnic Economy and Cultural Identity*. Gainsville: University Press of Florida, 1997.

Didion, Joan. *Miami*. New York: Simon and Schuster, 1987.

Duarte Oropesa, José. *Historiología Cubana—Desde 1959 hasta 1980*. Miami: Ediciones Universal, 1995.

Dudley, William. *The Sixties—Opposing Viewpoints*. San Diego, Cal.: Greenhaven Press, 1997.

Encinosa, Enrique. *Cuba: The Unfinished Revolution*. Austin, Tex.: Eakin Press, 1988.

———. *Cuba en Guerra: Historia de la Oposición Anti-Castrista 1959–1993*. Miami: The Cuban American National Foundation.

Ferrer, Edward B. *Operation Puma—The Air Battle of the Bay of Pigs*. Miami: International Aviation Consultants, 1975.

Franqui, Carlos. *Diary of the Cuban Revolution*. New York: Viking Press, 1980.

Fursenko, Aleksandr, and Timothy Naftali. *One Hell of a Gamble—Khrushchev, Castro & Kennedy 1958–1964*. New York: W. W. Norton, 1997.

Garcia, Chris. *Latinos and the Political System*. Notre Dame, Ill.: University of Notre Dame Press, 1988.

Gage, Nicholas. *Eleni*. New York: Ballantine Books, 1983.

Grau, Mongo. *Cuba desde 1930*. Madrid: Agualarga Editores, 1997.

Grupo Areíto. *Contra Viento y Marea. Jovenes Cubanos hablan contra Viento y Marea desde su exilio en Estados Unidos*. Mexico: Siglo Veintiuno, 1978.

Katz, Robert. *Naked by the Window: The Fatal Marriage of Carl Andre and Ana Mendieta*. New York: The Atlantic Monthly Press, 1990.

Klarsfeld, Serge. *French Children of the Holocaust—A Memorial.* New York: New York University Press, 1996.

Kozol, Jonathan. *Children of the Revolution.* New York: Dell, 1980.

Khrushchev, Nikita. *Khrushchev Remembers.* Boston: Little, Brown, 1970.

Krieg, Joann P. *Dwight D. Eisenhower: Soldier, President, Statesman.* Westport, Conn.: Greenwood Publishing Group, 1987.

Legarreta, Dorothy. *The Guernica Generation—Basque Refugee Children of the Spanish Civil War.* Reno: University of Nevada Press, 1984.

Matthews, Herbert L. *Revolution in Cuba.* New York: Scribner's, 1975.

Milanich, Jerald T. *Florida Indians and the Invasion from Europe.* Gainsville: University Press of Florida, 1995.

Oppenheimer, Andres. *Castro's Final Hour.* New York: Simon and Schuster, 1992.

Phillips, R. Hart. *Cuba—Island of Paradox.* New York: McDowell, Obolensky, 1960.

Phillips, R. Hart. *The Cuban Dilemma.* New York: Ivan Obolensky, Inc., 1962.

Quirk, Robert E. *Fidel Castro.* New York: W. W. Norton, 1993.

Rodríguez, Felix, and John Weisman. *Shadow Warrior.* New York: Pocket Books, 1990.

Rodríguez-Nogues, Lourdes. *Psychological Effects of Premature Separation from Parents in Cuban Refugee Girls: A Retrospective Study.* Ed.D. diss., Department of Psychology, Boston University, 1983.

Rosenblatt, Roger. *Children of War.* Garden City, NY: Anchor Press/Doubleday, 1983.

Ruíz, Leovigildo. *Diario de Una Traición 1960.* Miami: The Indian Printing, 1970.

———. *Diario de Una Traición 1961.* Miami: Lorie Book Stores, 1972.

Thomas, Hugh. *Cuba.* New York: Harper and Row, 1971.

Townsend, Peter. *The Smallest Pawns in the Game.* Boston: Little, Brown, 1980.

Wilson, Edmond. *The Sixties.* New York: Farrar, Straus, Giroux, 1993.

Wong, Francisco R. *The Political Behavior of Cuban Americans.* Ph.D. diss., University of Michigan, 1974.

Wyden, Peter. *Bay of Pigs—The Untold Story.* New York: Simon and Schuster, 1979.

Zmora, Nurith. *Orphanages Reconsidered.* Philadelphia: Temple University, 1994.

Index

Printed in the USA
CPSIA information can be obtained
at www.ICGtesting.com
CBHW021724051224
18468CB00004B/54

9 781683 403883